AF631247

A RECONSTRUCTION
OF THE
THIRD SCHOOL OF PŪRVAMĪMĀṂSĀ

SRI GARIB DASS ORIENTAL SERIES NO.—90

A Reconstruction of the Third School of Pūrvamīmāṃsā

UJJWALA PANSE

SRI SATGURU PUBLICATIONS
A Division of :
INDIAN BOOKS CENTRE
DELHI—INDIA

Published by :
©SRI SATGURU PUBLICATIONS
Indological and Oriental Publishers
a division of
INDIAN BOOKS CENTRE,
40/5, Shakti Nagar,
Delhi—110007
INDIA

All rights are reserved. No part of this work covered by the Copyright hereon may be reproduced or copied in any form or by any means—Graphics, Electronics or the Mechanical including photocopying, microfiche reading without written permission from the publishers.

First Edition Delhi 1990

ISBN—81-7030-209-9

Printed in India at :
Kiran Mudran Kendra,
A-38/2, Maya Puri, Phase-I,
New Delhi-110064

Dedicated to
My Teacher,
Dr. V.N. Jha,
Prof. & Director,
Centre of Advanced Study in Sanskrit,
University of Poona,

Acknowledgement

I express my indebtedness to my teacher, Prof. V.N. Jha, Director, Centre of Advanced Study in Sanskrit, for giving me his valuable guidance. He taught me the fundamentals of *Mīmāṁsā and Nyāya*, and gave proper direction to my studies in these fields.

I am grateful to Prof. S.D. Joshi, Ex-director, C.A.S.S. for providing me with all the facilities for research in the C.A.S.S. I am obliged to Prof. M.P. Rege, Ex-Director, Indian Institute of Education, Pune, who encouraged me to complete my work by providing me with the much needed help.

I acknowledge sincerely, the help and facilities provided to me by ths C.A.S.S. staff.

I would love to remain indebted to my parents and my siblings whose love and affection have always encouraged me in my studies, I consider myself very fortunate to the same.

Finally, I thank the publishers for their help and co-operation in bringing out this volume.

Ujjwala Panse

Foreword

Pūrvamīmaṁsā is called the *Vākyaśāstra* or the science of interpreting a sentence. Any philosophical analysis requires the tool of sentence-interpretation, more so if such an analysis is based on sentences. As it is well-known, almost all system of Indian Philosophy require, for some reason or the other, quotation from the Vedas as authority to substantiate their view-point. Therefore, it is but natural that all the system have freely made use of the Pūrvamīmāṁsā—principles of sentence-analysis,

Although Jaimini and Śabara gave us a consolidated single system of philosophical Analysis, the interpretation of Śabara's text resulted into so much variations that led to the formation of different schools of thought. In the beginning there were two great philosopher-interpreters such as Kumārila Bhaṭṭa and Prabhākara Miśra. Because of their basic difference of opinions regarding Philosophical, metaphysical and ontological issues, their interpretations differred very much; so much so that the interpretations of the same text of Śabara assumed the form of basic text books on two distinct schools of *Pūrvamīmāṁsā*. A third school of Pūrvamīmāṁsā came into existence due to another attempt to interpret Jaimini by a very distinguished thinker of the 12th century A.D. He was Murāri Miśra. He seems to have commented upon the entire *Jaimini-sūtras*. Unfortunately, very few fragments have been discovered so far under his name. Murāri held a distinct view regarding various philosophical issues—distinct from both the Bhāṭṭas and the Prābhākaras —which earned him the saying *Murāres tṛtiyaḥ panthāḥ*. It seems that he did not have followers. Not only that his views became object of criticism. But the very fact that almost all prominent philosophers have taken note of Murāri's views—be it for criticism—implies that Murāri must have had a very prominent place among academic circles and that he was not an insignificant entity who would be easily ignored.

It is indeed a very said state of affairs that we do not have today the entire work of Murāri with us. What we are left with are merely references to the views of Murāri Miśra here and there scattered in various philosophical and logical texts. Therefore, to reconstruct the whole school on the basis of a few fragments of Murāri and the references to Murāri's views scattered in the various philosophical Sanskrit texts was not an easy task. This needed profound maturity on the part of the researcher and I am very glad to state that Dr. Ujjwala Panse has shown the courage and that kind of maturity in handling this topic. After a very long time i.e. after eighty years I find such a serious study in the field of Pūrvamīmāṁsā. When very few texts in *Pūrvamīmāṁsā* were available in Print, MM Gaṅgānātha Jha used to work on the *MSS* and his first work on the *Prābhākara School of Pūrvamīmāṁsā* is a testimony of this hard-labour. Dr. Panse too has taken very hard-labour in identifying the views of Murāri from a very wide range of scientific literature and then in analysing them to show their distinction from the other two schools of Kumārila and Prabhākara and her hard labour is reflected in each and every line of this work. This is only work of its kind that gives us a clear picture of the philosophical, epistemological and ontological stand of Murāri at one place in a single Volume.

I am confident that the world of scientific and philosophical Sanskrit literature and particularly the students and scholars of *Pūrvamīmāṁsā* literature will welcome this volume. I am also confident that many more serious students will come forward to take up such ventures to undertake the study of *Pūrvamīmāṁsā* the most neglected branch of Sanskrit research, which has, as a matter of fact, a very high digree of research potentiality.

I am hopeful that Dr. Panse continues her work in this field and makes available the remaining fragments of Mūrāri to all of us with English translation and notes like the present *Arthar vādādhikaraṇa.* I wish her all success in such endeavour.

V.N. Jha
Director,
Centre of Advanced Study in Sanskrit
University of Poona, India

List of Abbreviations

ABORI	:	Annals of the Bhandarkar Oriental Research Institute.
BORI	:	Bhandarkar Oriental Research Institute.
Comm.	:	Commentary.
Ed., ed.	:	Edition or edited by.
ibid.	:	*ibidem*, at the same place.
JORM	:	Journal of the Oriental Research, Madras.
JS	:	*Jaiminisūtra* (s)
p.	:	page.
Pp	:	**Pages**
Pp	:	Pūrvapakṣa.
PM	:	Purvamīmāṃsā.
ŚBh	:	*Śābarabhāṣya.*
Tr.	:	Translation.
T.S.	:	*Taittiriyasaṁhitā.*
TC	:	*Tattvacintāmaṇi.*

Contents

PART I

1

General Background

The system of Pūrvamīmāṁsā can be called the science of interpreting sentences (*vākyārthaśāstra*). There are two prominent schools of Pūrvamīmāṁsā (*PM*), namely, (i) the Bhāṭṭa School and (ii) the Prābhākara School. In addition to these two we also say that there is a third school of *PM*. namely, the School of Mūrāri Miśra, very little about which is known to us.

Now, how did these schools come into existence ? As we already know, the very fundamental text of *PM* is the Sūtras of Jaimini, (*JS*) which consist of twelve chapters[1]. In it Jaimini offered a systematic presentation of logic, epistemology, and philosophy of *PM*, Śabarasvāmin wrote an elaborate commentary popularly known as *Śābarabhāṣya* (*ŚBh*) on the *JS* which is available to us completely. The *JS* are interpreted in detail and logically analysed by Śabarasvāmin in his *ŚBh*. This gave a logical foundation to the philosophy of *PM*. This is the reason why the *ŚBh* became the most authoritative and basic text of *PM*. This *ŚBh* was commented upon further by Kumārila Bhaṭṭa and Prabhākara Miśra, the two great exponents of the first two schools of PM, mentioned above, respectively. Both of them offered two different and independent interpretations of the *ŚBh*. This is, in fact, the reason that gave birth to these two independent schools of *PM*. The interpretations of Kumārila Bhaṭṭa represented what is known as the Bhāṭṭa School and those who followed this line of thought of Kumārila Bhaṭṭa are called Bhāṭṭas or the followers of the Bhāṭṭa school. Likewise, the interpretations of Prabhākara Miśra represented what is known as the Prābhākara School and those who followed Prabhākara Miśra's doctrine are called Prābhākaras or the followers of the Prabhākara school.

The commentary on *ŚBh* written by Kumārila Bhaṭṭa goes by names of *Ślokavārtika*, *Tantravārtika* and *Ṭupṭīka*. The *Ślokavārtika* is a commentary on the *Tarkapāda* of *ŚBh* (on *JS* 1.1), the *Tantravārtika* is a commentary on the *ŚBh* on JS 1.2—3.8, and the *Ṭupṭīka* is a commentary on the remaining portion of the *ŚBh* (on *JS* 4.1—12.4). Fortunately the entire commentary of Kumārila is available to us today.

Prabhākara Miśra wrote, it is believed, two commentaries on *ŚBh*, namely, *Laghvī* also known as *Vivaraṇa*, which is not available at all, and *Bṛhatī* also referred to as *Nibandhana* which is available only upto the 2nd *pāda* of the 6th chapter of *ŚBh*. *Laghvī* might have been a small version of the *Bṛhatī*. Through these two commentaries of Kumārila and Prabhākara the two schools of *PM* came into existence.

Although both these schools have a long tradition, still the Bhāṭṭa school enjoys better tradition comparatively. Even upto 16—17th century scholars have contributed to the Bhāṭṭa School. But we do not find many texts to represent the Prābhākara tradition. While we find scholars like Vācaspati Miśra, Pārthasārathi Miśra and a chain of scholars upto Khaṇḍadeva[2] and Gāgābhaṭṭa[3] to take forward the Bhāṭṭa school, there are not so many to plead the doctrine of Prabhākara. Śālikanātha Miśra wrote, *Ṛjuvimala* on the *Bṛhatī* of Prabhākara. Though the entire *Bṛhatī* on all the twelve *adhyāyas* of *ŚBh* is not available, the *Ṛjuvimalā* is fortunately, available beyond 6.2 of *JS* upto which the *Bṛhati* is available. Śālikanātha Miśra[4] also wrote an independent manual (*Prakaraṇagrantha*) called *Prakaraṇapañcikā* on the Prābhākara school of *PM*. Bhavanātha's *Nayaviveka* is another work belonging to the school of Prabhākara. It is a treatise on Mīmāṁsā. There is another manual on the Prābhākara school called *Tantrarahasya* by *Rāmānujācārya*.

But such is not the picture with regard to the third school of *PM*. We have no knowledge of any tradition of this school. It is indeed very much disappointing that neither any complete work of the founder of this school, nor any work of his follower representative of the doctrine of Murāri Miśra has been handed down to us. But that there was some Murāri who held views different from both the schools of Kumārila and Prabhākara is quite definite. Because, over and above the popular saying, *Murāres tṛtiyaḥ panthāḥ* in many philosophical texts like the *Tattvacintāmaṇi*[5] of Gaṅgeśopādhyāya, the *Kusumāñjaliprakāśa*[6] of Gaṅgeśa's son Vardhamāna, the *Siddhāntamuktāvalī*[7] of Viśvanātha and so on, Murāri's doctrine is referred to either by name or by quoting the content of his doctrine on some philosophical issue. This further points out to the fact that the doctrine of Murāri had such an impact over the philosophers of his days that they had to take into cognition his doctrine before propounding their own doctrine, on various topics. In other words we found Murāri appearing here and there as a *pūrvapakṣin* in various philosophico-logical texts of Indian Philosophy, until 1928. Thanks to the untiring efforts of some scholars ! In 1928 one fragment of Murāri's work was published in the Journal of Oriental Research, Madras (JORM). This text was the *Arthavādādhikaraṇam*[8] which forms a part of the *Tripādīnītinayanam* (i.e. the *Arthavādādhikaraṇa*, the *Mantrādhikaraṇa* and the *Smṛtyadhikaraṇa*) of Murāri, edited by S.K. Ramanatha Sastri of the University of Madras. The text discussed three topics, mentioned above, occurring in the 2nd and the 3rd *pāda* of the Ist chapter of the JS. In the following year another *adhikaraṇa* i.e. the *Ekādaśādyādhikaraṇa*[9] appeared in the Annals of the Bhandarkar Oriental Research Institute, Poona (ABORI). This text dealt with the topic occurring in the first *Adhikaraṇa* of the 11th chapter of the *JS*. This was edited by Umeśa Miśra of Allahabad University.

In 1930 Umeśa Miśra wrote a paper on Murāri and his distinct views on various philosophical topics, which appeared in the proceedings of the All-India Oriental Conference, Lahore, in the year 1930. This article opened a new field for studies on Murāri in particular and *PM* in general.

In 1931 again JORM published two remaining *adhikaraṇas* of the *Tripādīnitinayana*, mentioned above, namely, the *Mantrādhikaraṇa*[10] and the *Smṛtyadhikaraṇa*[11]. These two *adhikaraṇas* were also edited by Ramanath Sastri of Madras University. Such was the state of affairs till 1931: Some texts under the name of Murāri did appear. But it is very likely that Murāri must have commented upon the entire *JS* though we are left with only four *Adhikaraṇas* today. Let us hope that some day the remaining commentary of Murāri will be discovered.

1.1 *Necessity and Scope of the Work*

Under these circumstances one could hope that we could know something definite about Murāri and his views. Umeśa Miśra's article mentioned above was aimed at mere introducing Murāri and his thought, and so no attempt was made by him to interpret and thoroughly analyse Murāri's fragments. Needless to say that no description of any view is possible without thorough understanding and analysis of the text where that view occurs are attempted. Even after Umeśa Miśra no serious attempt was undertaken by any scholar in this regard. It remained a desideratum for more than 50 years. This state of affairs made me interested in the study of Murāri. I observed that now some positive data are at our disposal : Murari's own discussions on at least four *Adhikaraṇas* and his views on various subjects quoted in various philosophico-logical texts of Indian Philosophy. I, therefore decided to attempt a reconstruction of Murāri's doctrine i.e. the doctrine of the third school of *PM.*

This was a long felt desideratum because still we are in the dark about the doctrine of the third school of *PM.* The scholars who took cognisance of Murāri after 1931 have done nothing more than either referring to Umeśa Miśra or adding some passing general remarks on Murāri. No one seems to have paid serious attention and have gone deep into the task of presenting a clear picture, as far as possible, of the third school of *PM.* which still remains in the dark and which is necessary to be brought to light for encouraging further research on Murāri. Hence the necessity of undertaking this topic.

1.2. The Plan of the Work

As stated before, no conclusion could be drawn about the view of a person unless his statements are thoroughly understood and analysed. Accordingly, I chalked out a plan to prepare an English translation of Murāri's remnants with detailed notes and analyse them first and then present the results of this analysis in the form of an Introduction.

Accordingly, the present work is divided into two parts : Part I which is an Introduction and Part II which will consist of English Translation with notes of Murāri's text. Although, in the original plan I had decided to include the English Translation of all the four fragments of Murāri, but looking at the volume of the translation of even one *Adhikaraṇa* I dropped the original idea and finally decided to incorporate only one *Adhikaraṇa* here for the time being. Accordingly, the second part will consist of the English exposition of Murāri's *Arthavādādhikarana* only. Nevertheless, while presenting the results of the IInd Part in the Introduction, the other three remnants of Murāri are also consulted, in order to draw facts and to arrive at a conclusion.

While presenting the results the basic approach would be to point out how a particular view is neither held by the Bhāṭṭa school nor by the Prābhākara school and hence that is held by the third school.

It has been further kept in mind that as far as possible the source of Murāri's statement should be noted. Accordingly, a comparison is also attempted between the *Arthavādādhikaraṇa* of Murāri and that of the *Nayaviveka* of Bhavanātha, which exhibit a very close similarity in approach and language.

In this way, an attempt is made to present the *Prameyas* and the *prāmaṇas* of the Third school in this part of the work.

The Second Part consists of the English Translation of the *Arthavādādhikaraṇa* with elaborate notes. As stated above, I had proposed to translate all the four available *Adhikaraṇas*. But considering the size of the translation of even the *Arthavādādhikaraṇa*, I changed the original plan and decided to present only the translation of the *Arthavādādhikaraṇa* with notes. However, I wish to continue my studies in this direction in future and I hope to present the translation of the remaining *Adhikaraṇas* also separately.

The Sanskrit text is split into several paragraphs in the form of objection and Reply so that a reader looks at it as a dialogue. Each paragraph is translated into English. The translation is a free translation and it has been purposely made free because it will be readable and not awful as it sometimes appears if a literal translation of a śāstric text is attempted. In the notes the intention of the objector and the replier is made clear.

2

Murāri Miśra and His Works

At the very out-set I would like to mention that for all bibliographical informations regarding Murāri i.e. his identity, his date, his works etc. my sole-source has been Umeśa Miśra[11]. Because, as far as my knowledge goes, Umśea Miśra's article[12] is the only authoritative information on Murāri. I have not gone independently in search of these informations because that is not the aim of this work. I have treated Umeśa Miśra's findings as valid unless mentioned otherwise. Umeśa Miśra, in his paper[13] on *Murāreḥ trtīyaḥ panthāḥ* says that there were at least five authors Murāri by name in Sanskrit literature, who wrote in all 15 books in various fields like literature, *Mīmāṁsā*, *Ś*rauta and so on. But, most probably there are only two works out of these fifteen works which are of our Mīmāṁsaka Murāri Miśra, the exponent of the Third school of *PM*. Those two works are, *Tripādīnītinayanam* and *Ekādaśādyādhikaraṇam*.

The fifteen books ascribed to the name of Murāri Miśra are : (1) *Anargharāghava*, (2) *Śubhakarmanirṇaya*, (3) *Śuddhinibandha*, (4) *Iṣṭikālanirṇava*, (5) *Parvanirṇava*, (6) *Pitṛbhaktivyākhyā*, (7) *Śrāddhakalpaṭīkā*, (8) *Tripādīnītinayanam*, (9) *Ekādaśādyādhikaraṇam*, (10) *Aṅgatvanirukti*, (11) *Murāreriyam*, (12) *Prāyaścittamanohara*, (13) *Saptaśatīṭīkā*, (14) *Śabdārthamañjūṣāprakāśa* and (15) *Pāraskaragṛhyasūtrabhāṣya*.

The *Anargharāghava*, of these fifteen, is a drama by some author called Murāri who was the son of Bhaṭṭa Śrīvardhamāna[14]. From the language and the content of the drama though it appears that this Murāri must have a thorough knowledge of Mīmāṁsā, Nyāya and also of Dharmaśāstra still he cannot be held as the founder of the Third school of *PM*. This Murāri seems to have flourished in or before the 9th Century A.D., because he is known to be referred to by a Kashmirian poet by name of Ratnākara who flourished in the 9th Century A.D.[15]

The writer of *Śuddhinibandha* was another Murāri, who was the son of Rudra Śarman. This Rudraśarmā and his forefathers were the judges at the Court of the Kings of Mithilā, namely, Devasiṁha and Bhavasiṁha. These Kings ruled Mithilā during 1359-1402.[16] Thus, this Murāri must have lived in the fifteenth Century A.D. He was also not the exponent of the Third school of *PM*., as it will be clear from the following pages.

Then, *Śubhakarmanirṇava*, *Iṣṭikālanirṇava*, *Parvanirṇava*, *Pitṛbhaktivyākyā* on the *Pitṛbhakti* of Śrīdatta and *Śrāddhakalpaṭīkā* on Śrīdatta's *Śrāddhakalpa* must have been written by one and the same Murāri. Because, the same verse occurs in the beginning of all these five books.[17] In that introductory verse he mentions that he was the pupil of Keśavamiśra whose date is believed to be 15th Century A.D. since he was in the Court of the kings of Mithilā during 1450-1490 A.D. And Śrīdatta whose works Murāri commented upon flourished in the 14th Century A.D.[18], it seems from this that this Murāri must have flourished in the latter half of the 15th Century A.D.

Umeśa Miśra, somehow, wants to identify this Murāri with the author of *Śuddhinibandha* mentioned above[19].

We need not go deep into this dispute because even if they are two different Murāris none of them could be the exponent of the Third school of *PM*.

Now, in the *Śubhakarmanirṇaya* the writer of it, called Murāri refers to Vardhamāna's *Kusumāñjaliprakāśa*, whereas Vardhamāna himself quotes the view of some Murāri in his *Kusumāñialiprakāśa*. This clearly directs to the fact that Murāri referred to in *Prakāśa* and Murāri, the author of *Śubhakarmanirṇava* cannot be identical[20].

Here, I would like to emphasize one point that even if the two Murāris mentioned above, i.e. the author of *Śuddhinibandha* and the author of the five works, namely, *Śubhakarmanirṇaya* etc, are not same there is no possibility whatsoever, of their being identical with our Murāri. For, these two Murāris flourished in the 15th Century

A.D. and the Mīmāṁsaka Murāri's doctrine is referred to by Gaṅgeśa, who wrote his *Tattvacintāmaṇi* in the 13th Century A.D. So Mīmāṁsaka Murāri must have lived earlier than him.

Another observation in this connection one can make is that the view of Umeśa Miśra regarding the identity of the two Murāris mentioned above, requires to be reconsidered. Because two more points come to our mind of which one goes in favour of Umeśa Miśra and the other may go against him. First point is that the *Śuddhinibandha* and the other five works are all on Dharmaśāstra and hence the author of the 5 works on Dharmaśāstra could have written the sixth one also. So far the second point is concerned, the main proof for the authorship of these five works is an introductory verse which occurs in the same form in all the five works. Since this verse does not occur in the *Śuddhinibandha* it creates a doubt whether the author of the *Śuddhinibandha* is the same author who wrote those five texts, as Miśra thinks. Of course, further attempt is required to gather more internal proof to ascertain the exact position.

We do not go into the details on this subject since that is not the aim of our work.

There is another work called *Aṅgatvanirukti*[21] by an author named Murāri Miśra. This work is on *PM* and it attempts to define and analyse the concept of *Aṅgatva* as it is clear from the very name of this work. Now since *Aṅgatvanirukti* is a work on Mīmāṁsā and since it is by Murāri Miśra, it is very likely that people may think that this Murāri is the exponent of the Third school of *PM*. But looking at the content of this text this doubt disappears. It is a text on the Bhāṭṭa school of *PM*, and at the very beginning of the text the author says that he is writing it as per the doctrine of the Bhāṭṭa school[22].

Even from the point of view of the time of the author of *Aṅgatvanirukti*, one cannot hold that this Murāri is the founder of the Third school of *PM*. In this text Murāri refers to the *Vidhirasāyana* of Appayadīkṣita and the *Bhāṭṭadīpikā* of Khaṇḍadeva. Now both these Mīmāṁsā scholars flourished in 16th-17th Century A.D. Thus, Murāri, the author of *Aṅgatvanirukti* must be later than 16th-17th Century while our Murāri, the exponent of the Third School of *PM* must be earlier than Gaṅgeśa.

There is another work named *Prāyaścittamanohara* which is ascribed to one Murāri Miśra. Not much can be said about this Murāri excepting that all the MSs of his text are in the Oriya Script and that the study of the text reveals that the author of this text is neither a Mīmāṁsaka nor a Naiyāyika. According to Umeśa Miśra this Murāri must be placed later than 13th Century A.D.[23]

There are two more works ascribed to the name of Murāri, namely, (1) the commentary on Saptaśatī and (2) *Murārereiyam.*

There was one more book i.e. a *Bhāṣya* on *Pāraskaragṛhyasūtra* by Murāri Miśra, the son of Veda Miśra and grandson of Viśvarūpa Dīkṣita. There is nothing we can say about the time or place of these authors.

There are two more works associated with the name of Murāri Miśra. They are, (1) *Tripādīnītinayanam* and (2) *Ekādaśādyādhi-karaṇam.* Both these works are independent commentaries on the two *adhikaraṇas* of the *JS.* 1.2, one *adhikaraṇa* of the *JS* 1.3 and one *adhikaraṇa* of *JS* 11.1. All these four *adhikaraṇas* are respectively known as (1) *Arthavādādhikaraṇa*, (2) *Mantrādhikaraṇa*, (3) *Smṛtya-dhikaraṇa* and (4) *Ekādaśādyādhikaraṇa.*[24]

Umeśa Miśra's description of these texts of Murāri that "it (the *Tripādinītinayana*) is a work on Mīmāṁsā, being an independent treatise on the *adhikaraṇas* of the Jaimini-Sūtras, Adhyāya I, *pādas* 2 to 4"[25] is partially true. The *Tripādīnītinayanam* deals with the two *adhi-karaṇas* namely, *Arthavādādhikaraṇa* and *Mantrādhikaraṇa* from the second *pāda* of the 1st *Adhyaya* of *JS* and the 1st *Adhikaraṇa* of the 3rd *pāda* of the 1st *Adhyāya* of *JS.* May be, the very name *Tripādīnīti-nayanam* has led both, Umeśa Miśra and Ganganath Jha[26] to describe it as the work dealing with the topics occurring in the three *pādas* of the 1st chapter of *JS*, which is not a fact.

Furthermore, it is very likely that Murāri must have written on the topic or topics of the three *pādas*, the third being either the 1st *pāda* or the 4th *pāda* of the first chapter under the title *Tripādi-nītinayanam*, which is unfortunately not handed down to us today.

The *Ekādasādyādhikaraṇam* deals with *Tantra* and *Āvāpa* which are discussed in the first *Adhikaraṇa* of the 11th chapter of the *JS* as it is clear from the very name of the text and not of the 1st chapter as Umeśa Miśra informs us.[27]

Now, let us see whether the two works namely, the *Tripādīnītinayanam* and the *Ekādaśādyādhikaraṇam* are by one and the same author.

On comparison of these two works we observe the following points :

(1) The Colophon of the *Ekādaśādyādhikaraṇa* reads *Mahāmahopādhyāya* Murāri Miśra as its author.

(2) The style of writing is the same in both, i.e. both the texts are written in the *Adhikaraṇa* style.

(3) Both these works are written on the *JS* directly. It should be noted that there is a striking similarity in the forms of the composition of the *Adhikaraṇas*. In all the *Adhikaraṇas* the beginning of the *Adhikaraṇa* has been shown by mentioning the first *sūtra* of the respective *Adhikaraṇa*, no other *sūtra* is mentioned from the same *Adhikaraṇa* of *JS*.

(4) Both show the same type of language.

These facts hint to the common authorship of these texts.

That this Murāri is the exponent of the Third School of *PM*, can be argued on the following grounds :

(1) He presents an independent exposition of the *JS*. It is not a commentary on any other commentary on *JS*.

(2) He has the title of *Mahāmahopādhyāya* which is expressive of his great scholarship.

(3) The most valid ground is this that, it is observed from the study of these works that the views held on certain topics by Murāri are quite different from those held by the other two schools namely, the Bhāṭṭa school and the school of Prabhākara. This point will be made clear when we shall discuss about his uniqueness in comparison to these two schools.

On these grounds one can say that this Murāri is the founder of the Third school of *PM*.

Let us hopefully wait for the day, to discover the other works of this Murāri, which will enable us to strengthen our deductions.

2.1 *Date of Murāri*

Turning to the date of Murāri, though it is difficult to fix his exact date, the fixing of his relative date can be attempted on the basis of :

(1) Internal sources, and

(2) External sources.

By the term 'internal sources' I mean the references of authors or the works referred to by Murāri in his two works mentioned above. And by the term 'external sources' I mean the references to Murāri made by other authors on Indian Philosophy.

Accordingly, if the author of the *Tripādīnītinayanam* and the *Ekādaśādyādhikaraṇam* is the founder of the Third school of *PM*, as we hold, then we can consider the following facts :

Murāri refers to a work of Prabhākara (600-650 A.D.) the founder of the Second school of *PM*, called *Vivaraṇa*.[28] The *Vivaraṇa* or *Laghvī* was a commentary on *ŚBh* by Prabhākara, which is not available now.

Along with *Vivaraṇa* there are references to the work like *Pañjikā*[29] or *Pañcikā*, which is nothing but the *Ṛjuvimalāpañcikā* of Śālikanātha Miśra (before 9th Century A.D.). There are also references to the *Nayaviveka*[30] of Bhavanātha (before 11th Century A.D.) a follower of the Prābhākara school. We are going to show how Murāri has been influenced by this *Nayaviveka*. At times he verbally follows the style of Bhavanātha's argument.

Murāri also refers to some authors by name. For instance, he mentions Candra[31] (before 11th Century A.D.) and Nandana.[32] It should be noted in this connection that Umeśa Miśra says that Murāri refers to some other names like Śrīkara, Vindhyavāsin etc., which I have not been able to attest in the works of Murāri.

From the above-mentioned references it is clear that the latest authors Murāri has referred to are, (1) Bhavanātha, the author of the *Nayaviveka*, and (2) Candra, the author of *Amṛtabindu*[33] and *Nyāyaratnākara*.[33] The time of Bhavanātha and Candra has been fixed in the 11th Century A.D. So, it is obvious that Murāri was either contemporary of Bhavanātha and Candra or he lived later than the author of *Nayaviveka* and Candra.

So let us treat the 11th Century as the upper limit for Murāri's date.

Turning to the external sources, we find that Murāri is referred to by many authors of Indian Philosophy either by name or by his doctrine. Some of the names who refer to him are, Gaṅgeśa[34] (13th Century A.D.), Vardhamāna[35] (13th Century A.D.), Rucidatta[36] (1275), Jagadīśa[37] (1625), Gadādhara[38] (1650), Annambhaṭṭa[39] (1623), Viśvanātha[40] (1634), Rāmarudra Bhaṭṭācārya[41] (1700), Gāgābhaṭṭa[42] (17th Century) and Rāmakṛṣṇādhvarin[43] (17th Century).[44]

Obviously, of these, Gaṅgeśa is the oldest and so our Murāri must be either contemporary to Gaṅeśa if not a remote predecessor. Thus, the 13th Century A.D. should be the lower limit of our Murāri.

Thus, we conclude that our Murāri must have flourished between the 11th and the 13th Century A.D.

3

A Brief Outline of Murāri's Texts

3.1 : *Arthavādādhikaraṇa*

The aim of the *Arthavādādhikaraṇa* is to establish the validity of the *arthavādas* which form one part of the Vedas. Murāri in the very beginning states the *pūrvapakṣa* of Prabhākara as attested in the *Bṛhatī* of Prabhākara. Prabhākara's *Pp.* is; Since it was decided that only that portion of the veda is valid which enjoins some activity to be performed (*Kārya*) and since the *arthavādas* neither convey any *kārya* nor can they form a sentence-unity with the injunctions they cannot be authoritative.

Murāri, not agreeing with this *Pp* of Prabhākara, states the *siddhānta* or conclusion of Prabhākara which is as follows : Since the *adhyayanavidhi* enjoins the study of the whole Veda, in order to maintain the authority of this *vidhi* the *arthavādas* have to be authoritative. And for that, the *arthavādas* must form sentence-unity with the injunctions even by changing their forms. Another point is that the *vidhis* also require the praise in order to induce a person to take up an activity.

Murāri, after stating these two points, rejects both the *Pp*, and the *siddhānta* of *Prabhākara.* The reason to reject this is this that the *Pp.* formed by Prabhākars fails to establish the consistency and relation with the first *pāda* of *JS.*

Then Murāri suggests a new *Pp.* He says, it is necessary to form a *Pp.* on the basis of sentence-unity. Why ? Because if the *Pp.* is formed in that manner, then alone, the consistency in the argument can be shown by objecting to the authoriry of the injunctions which have formed sentence-unity with non-authoritative *arthavādas.*

Then, in the stream of arguments Murāri has discussed various logico-philosophical concepts such as the concepts of *ekavākyatā*, *viseṣaṇa* and *upalakṣaṇa* etc. which will be discussed in details later on. Advancing his arguments and considering many important points arising from the context Murāri ultimately offers a solution to the problem of the sentence-unity between the *vidhis* and the *arthavādas*. There is no question that the *arthavādas* serve the purpose of either praise or censure. But Murāri discusses clearly how the *arthavādas* get related to the *vidhis* through the praise or censure. He says, in case of the *nindānuvādas* (i.e. the *arthavādas* condemning some particular action), firstly, the knowledge of word-meanings takes place, and then, by illusion the understanding of the sentences meaning arises. The form of that understanding happens to be as follows : (in case of, say, *Barhiṣi rajatam na deyem——Rudraḥ kila ruroda*) 'Since the silver is produced from the weeping of Agni (i.e. Rudra) its offering will cause weeping'.

After this understanding which has taken place by illusion, one realises that giving silver in the Barhis sacrifice is not good. In other words, not offering it, in that sacrifice is what is to be achieved. And, ultimately, the injunctive sentence of that sacrifice produces the understanding of its own meaning along with this above-mentioned meaning of the *arthavāda*.

Similarly, the case of the *praśamsārthavādas* (i.e. the *arthavādas* praising some particular action), by *lakṣaṇā* the praise is understood first. Here *lakṣaṇā* arising through illusory cognition has been accepted.

Another point which Murāri makes and which is worth-noting in this connection is that it is not necessary that one must praise something by something really existent. The act of praising involves qualities of the object of praise. It is not necessary that all the qualities highlighted by the act of praise must be existent in the object of praise. This is corroborated by our ordinary experience of day-to-day behaviour also.

This is, we can say, the conclusion of Murāri's *Arthavādādhikaraṇa*. After stating this he summarises the statement of Prabhākara from his *Vivaraṇa*.

3.2 *Mantrādhikaraṇa*

The *Mantrādhikaraṇa* discusses the authoritativeness of *mantra*-portion of the Vedas. The main doubt raised is whether the *mantras* help the sacrifice only by their recitation or through expressing their meanings.

The stand of *pūrvapakṣin* is that they do not express their meaning but they help the performance of the *yāga* merely by their recitation. This is refuted by the *siddhāntin* and it is established ultimately that the *mantras* help the sacrifice through expressing their meaning. As usual Murāri has stated the first *sūtra* of the *adhikaraṇa* namely, *Tadarthaśāstārt* (*JS*. 1.2.31) and begins his discussion on the line of the *ŚBh.*

In this *adhikaraṇa* Murāri has recorded the views of *Candra* and *Nandana* as well as of Śālikānātha Miśra and Bhavanātha.

In conclusion Murāri has taken up the problem of the employment of the *Mantras*.

Murāri points out that it is not the case that all *mantras* are enjoined by *vidhis*. It is also not the case that all *mantras* are enjoined by *liṅga pramāṇa.* Because in some cases the meaning of a *mantra* is something else and it is employed by an injunction to a rite which has no relation with that meaning. Such injunctions are called *Anyārthaśāstras*.[45] Again there are some *mantras* which are employed by *vidhi* in a specific sense since on the basis of the general meaning of the *mantras* there is likelihood of their being employed in an unwanted case. Thus, the purpose of the *vidhi* is to specify the employment of the mantra. Again there is another set of *mantras* which are enjoined by some *vidhi*. the meaning of which does not differ from that of the *mantra*. These *vidhis* are called the *Tadarthaśāstras*.[46] In such cases it is accepted in the *siddhānta* that the injunctions simply repeat the meaning of the *mantra*.

Thus, from all these a general rule can be evolved that unless otherwise specified, a *mantra* will be employed, taking into account its meaning. Murāri says the general rule as follows; *Yo yat prakāśakaḥ tat tena prakāśayet*.[47]

Finally, Murāri states the *Pp*. of the *Vivaraṇa* and says the *siddhānta* is same as that of the *Nibandhana* (*Bṛhatī*), the commentary of Prabhākara.

3.3 *Smṛtyadhikaraṇa*

The *Tarkapāda* of *JS* discussed the validity of the injunctive sentences (*vidhis*), the *arthavādādhikaraṇa* established the authoritativeness of the *arthavāda*-portion of the Vedas and the *mantrādhikaraṇā* established the vaiidity of the *mantras*. In the *Smṛtyadhikarāṇa*, now, the authoritativeness of the *smṛti*-literature is being established.

There are certain acts like the *aṣṭakākārya*, the digging of a well, preparing a shade and making an arrangment for distribution of water, and the like which are part of the Vedic culture and which are performed to earn *Dharma*, by way of service to the departed soul or people at large.

The question is, on what authority these acts are performed. Obviously there is no *vidhi* in the Vedic lore, to enjoin these acts. Nevertheless these acts are part and parcel of the Vedic culture and these are performed on the authority of the *smṛti*-literature. Naturally, the question arises whether *smṛtis* have authoritativeness with regard to these rites which are aimed at producing unseen results and hence are *Dharma*. In other words, whether the source of the *smṛtis* on the basis of which these rites are performed is illusion or the Veda itself.

The *Pp* denies its authority on the ground that they are based on illusive cognition. And since the *smṛtis* are non-authoritative, the Vedic *mantras* which are united with them are also non-authoritative and since the *mantras* are the Veda the entire Veda becomes non-authoritative. Now, since the main proposition is challenged in this way, there is relevance to discuss here in this *adhikaraṇa* the autoritativeness of the *smṛtis*.

In the *Aṣṭakā-śrāddha* which is enjoined by the *smṛti*-sentence '*Aṣṭakāḥ kartavyāḥ*', the following *mantra* is employed :

Yām janāḥ pratinandanti
Rātrim, dhenumiva āyatīm
Saṁvatsarasya yā patnī
Sā no astu sumaṅqalīsvāhā.[48]

Here, the *mantra* which is authoritative is associated with an unauthoritative *smṛti*-injunction. And hence it becomes non-valid;

and thereby the entire Veda becomes unauthoritative. Therefore there is propriety of beginning of this *adhikaraṇa*.

After stating, thus, the relevance of the *adhikaraṇa* Murāri states various opinions of Bhavanātha, Candra and Nandana on this issue.

Thereafter Murāri presents the *Pp.* view on the authoritativeness of the *smṛtis*.

The *Pp.* holds that the *smṛtis* are not authoritative because they are not based on the Veda since no corresponding Vedic injunctive sentences are attested at present. One cannot argue that the particular Vedic injunction on which the *smṛti*-rites depend is not available now because the branch of the Veda to which that sentence belonged is lost. Because, if this argument is allowed there should have been no branch left now which is not a fact. This argument is discussed in detail and finally it is maintained by the *Pp.* that the *smṛtis* are not authoritative.

Then Murāri presents the *siddhāntin's* view. According to the *siddhāntin*, although, it is a fact that we do not find today the Vedic injunctions corresponding to the *smṛti*-rites; still we can infer those injunctions. Now the question remains, on what ground we can infer those injunctions ? Murāri turns down the possibility of employing *smṛtitva*, 'being a *smṛti*' or *Manvādi-smṛtitva*, 'being a *smṛti* of Manu etc.,' as the ground or probans for such an inference, and finally suggests that one can infer those Vedic injunctions by *pariśeṣānumāna*.[49]

3.4 *Ekādaśādyādhikaraṇa*

Murāri as usual quotes the beginning *sūtra* of the 11th chapter of *JS.* i.e. *Prayojanābhisaṃbandhāt pṛthak satāṃ tataḥ syādaikakarmyam ekaśabdābhisaṁyogāt*, while starting this *adhikaraṇa*. And then he takes up the discussion on *Tantra*. Before we discuss what Murāri has to say about it, let us see what actually *tantra* is.

The context of the *Ś Bh* where *tantra* is discussed is as follows: The *Darśapūrṇamāsa* sacrifice is enjoined by the *vidhi Darśapūrṇamāsābhyāṁ svargakāmo yajeta*' Now, this sacrifice namely the *Darśapūrṇamāsa* consists of six main *yāgas*, namely, *Āgneya*[50] etc. Now here a doubt is raised whether result of this sacrifice, namely the heaven, is associated separately with the six *yāgas*, or it is associated with the collection of the six *yāgas*,

Here, Śabara introduces the concept of *tantra* and says the result i.e. heaven is associated with the collection of the *Darśa-pūrṇa-māsa* sacrifices by *tantra*. He defines *tantra as* : *Yat sakṛtkṛtam bahūnām upakaroti tattantram ity ucyate*[51] i.e. that which helps many things being performed only once is called *tantra*. For instance, a lamp lit once illumines many brahmins at a time.[52] As the lamp reveals many things simultaneously, in the same way the single result namely the heaven is associated with all the six sacrifices of *Darśapūrṇamāsa*.

With this background of *ŚBh* let us turn to the *Ekādaśādyādhikaraṇa* of Murāri. Murāri too attempts to reach a clear definition of *tantra* and accordingly, he discusses many possible definitions of tantra. The definitions discussed are :

(1) *Sakṛttvam eva tantratvam*, 'that which is one is *tantra*'.

(2) *Anekopakārakatve sati ekatvam*, that which is one and at the same time helps many is *tantra*'.

(3) *Anekaśeṣatve sati ekam anekopakārakam*, 'that which is one and which helps many and which is auxiliary to many is *tantra*'.

(4) *Anekoddeśenānuṣṭhānasakṛttvam*,

'A single performance aimed at many is *tantra*.'

(5) *Āvṛttyabhāvaḥ tantratvam*

'The absence of repetition (*āvṛtti*) is *tantra*.

Disagreeing with all these definitions of *tantra*, Murāri gives his own definition as follows : *Ekasyānuṣṭhānasya sarvārthatvam*, i.e. 'A *Tantra* is that single performance which is meant for all.' He explains this definition further and says that since there is no purpose in performing the same act again and again, it is not performed. But that itself is not *tantra*, i.e. not performing the rite again is not called the state of being *tantra*. In other words, *tantra* is not a negative concept but it is a positive one. *Tantra* is actually a single performance that is meant for many.[53]

In this context incidentally Murāri talks about *āvāpa* also and defines it as : *Anekārthasyānekam anuṣṭhānam āvāpaḥ*. That is many performances, performed many times for many purposes is what is called *āvāpa*.

While concluding the discussion on *tantra* Murāri refers to the definition of *tantra* as given in the *ŚBh* namely, *Yat sakṛtkṛtam bahunām upakaroti*, and states the interpretation of this definition by some *Tīkākṛt*,[54] according to whom, since this definition of *ŚBh* is over-applicable to *prasaṅga* it should be interpreted as, *tantram nāma bhedena prāptau satyām sakṛd anuṣṭhānenārthasiddhiḥ*. '*Tantra* means the achieving of the purpose by single performance, when there is an occassion for separate performances.'

Murāri points out how this explanation of the *Tīkākṛt* is in consonance with the *ŚBh*, and concludes his discussion on *tantra* by explaining the view of the *Tīkākṛt*.

Thereafter the definition of *āvāpa* is taken up for consideration. At the very out-set he states the definition of *āvāpa*. It runs as follows : *Āvāpastu yathāprāptibhedenānuṣṭhānam iti suvyaktam eva*. i.e. *āvāpa* means different performances of a rite as and when it is due. And then he further adds that the discussion on *āvāpa* is not as a matter of fact the purpose of this *adhyāya*. But to discuss the nature of *tantra* is the purpose of this chapter. Because, Murāri says that there is no doubt about the nature of *āvāpa* since it is an obvious fact that *āvāpa* refers to different performances as per different injunctions. Having stated this he again turns to the discussion of *tantra*.

In the end as per his framework and style he refers to the opinion of the *Vivaraṇa* on *tantra*.

This is in short the content of *Ekādaśādyadhikaraṇa*.[55]

4

Sources of Murāri Miśra

Here we would like to discuss the sources of Murāri. By 'Sources of Murāri' we mean the texts from which Murāri has drawn in order to compose his own texts. So let us see what works does Murāri accept as his base. These sources of Murāri are arranged chronologically here.

In his *Ekādaśādyādhikaraṇa* Murāri has referred, at least thrice,[56] to the *ŚBh*. Once he has quoted a line i.e. the definition of *tantra* from *ŚBh*. In his *Smṛtyadhikaraṇa* also he refers to the *ŚBh* once.[57]

In the *Arthavādādhikaraṇa* though Murāri has not referred to the *Bhāṣya* directly, he has argued on the line of the *Bhāṣya*. He has freely drawn from the *Bhāṣya*. For instance, he utilises the examples of *ŚBh* like, '*Malinaḥ snāyāt*', '*Iyam qauḥ krayyā stryapatyā*' etc. and explains them in his own way to suit his context.

Next to the *ŚBh* is the *Vivaraṇa* of Prabhākara which Murāri has mentioned so frequently. It seems to be the style of Murāri that he normally mentions *Vivaraṇa* at the concluding part of his discussion.[58] After the discussion is over, he presents the view of the *Vivaraṇa* by saying, '*Vivaraṇe tu*'[59] Murāri also refers to *Nibandhana* (the *Bṛhatī*) of Prabhākara in the *Mantrādhikaraṇa*.

Murāri has referred, once, to *Pañjikā*[60] which is a commentary on *Bṛhatī* of Prabhākara by Śālikanātha Miśra.

In addition to these, Murāri has referred to two authors, namely, Candra[61] and Nandana.[61] We have already seen that

Candra is the author of *Amṛtabindu* and *Nyāyaratnākara*. But we know nothing, yet, about Nandana.

Finally, we find that Murāri refers to the *Nayaviveka* of Bhavanātha once in the *Mantrādhikaraṇa* and twice in the *Smṛiyadhikaraṇa*.

It is interesting to note here that excepting this Nandana about whom we do not know anything yet and the *ŚBh*, all the authors or the works Murāri has referred to are of the Prābhākara school of *PM*. Not a single reference to any author or work of the Bhāṭṭa school of *PM* is found in Murāri's texts.

While studying the *Arthavādādhikaraṇa* of Murāri and comparing it with that of *Bhavanātha*[62] I find that there is a striking similarity in the argument of both these texts. Even a cursory look at these two texts leaves an impression in our mind that Murāri has taken Bhavanātha as his base for composing his own text. From (4.1) one can see to what extent Murāri has drawn from the *Nayaviveka* of Bhavanātha.

4.1 *The Arthavādādhikaraṇa of the Tripādīnītinayana and that of the Nayaviveka.*

I have hinted above, there is a striking resemblance in the frame-work and approach between the *Arthavādādhikaraṇa* of Murāri and that of Bhavanātha. Now let us compare and contrast the two texts and examine the validity of the above statement of ours.

The following table will make the picture clear :

	Arthavādādhikaraṇa of Tripādīnītinayana		*Arthavādādhikaraṇa of Nayaviveka*
(1)	*Uktam kāryam artham pratipādayato vedasya prāmāṇyam. Na Cārthavāḍānām kāryārthatā, vidhinā saha ekavākyatve pramāṇābhāvāt. Tasmādaprāmāṇyam iti pareṣām pūrvapakṣaḥ.*	(1)	*Uktam kāryam artham pratipādayato vadasya prāmāṇyam Parapūrvapakṣaḥ—kāryasya hi kārye vākyārthe 'nvaya karaṇetikartavyatayoḥ svarūpatassādhyayor eva sādhanatayānvayaḥ-Arthavādānām tu asādhyārthānām nānvayaḥ atas teṣāmaprāmāṇyam iti.*

(2) *Na ca—prathame eva pāde prāmāṇyam vyutpādyam, dvitīye vidhyanuvādamantrāṇām upayogakathanam, tṛtīye tu smṛtiprāmāṇyam, caturthe nāmadheyopayoga iti. Tataścaudumbaramantrānuvādādyādhikaraṇānām nāsaṅgatiḥ iti vācyam Tathā sati ekādhyāyārthatvānupapatteḥ.*	(2) *Athedam paramatam--vidhyupayogo vidhivannigadādhikaraṇe, vidhau hi bhāvyatā paśvādeḥ tadabhāve ceti. Arthavādānām pravṛttau rucyutpādaḥ mantrāṇām anuṣṭheyasmṛtiriti. Evam upayogakathaiva tripādyām iti. Tanna, Evam hi dvividho 'dhyāvārtha ityadhyāyabheda eva syāt.*
(3) *sāmānyato jñātam viśeṣajñānārtham kāmyeta kāvyālaṅkārārthavad iti cet.*	(3) *Yadapi paroktam sāmānyato jñānavato viśeṣajijñāsā kāvyālaṅkārādiṣv iveti.*
(4) *Na, sāmānyato vedārthasva nityaniyogarūpasya vedam antareṇābhyūdayakāritayā puṁvākyamātrāt pramāṇāntare virodheṇa pratyetum aśakteḥ.*	(4) *Tannirastam. Na hi kaścidartho 'sti ityetāvataiva mahāprayāse pravṛttyupayogini viśeṣajñāne kāmanā.*
(5) *Niyamārtho vidhiriti cet. Na, laukike arthajñāne niyamābhāvāt.*	(5) *Na niyamārthatā, Svādhyāyād anyato vedārthajñānāsambhavāt, puṁvākyebhyo 'pi vedam evānumāya tata evārthaniścayāt.*
(6) *Siddhārthasādhyārtha yorapyākhyātayoḥ ekavākyatvam vyutpannam. Hetuhetumadbhāvena cānvayaḥ. Yathā malinam te vapuḥ vartate, snāyāḥ, iti. Malinaḥ snāyād iti tu nodāharaṇam, tatra malinasya kartṛtvenādhikāritvena vānvitasya sādhyakoṭitvāt hetutvena anvayābhāvāt. Ekākhyātatvācca.*	(6) *Siddhasya ca sādhye hetutayānvayadarśanāt. Bhūtam bhavyāya iti nyāyāt bhavyotpatyarthatā eva bhavyotpatyarthatā ca 'malinaḥ snāyāt ityādau dṛṣṭeti Rudrarodanādihetvanvitam sannihitam sat kāryam codanārthaḥ.*

(7) *Katham tarhi sauryam carum nirvaped iti nirvapatiḥ anuvādaḥ iti cet. Na, tasyāpi stāvakatvat. avidheyānvavitavā tu anuvādoktiḥ.*	(7) *Nanu ekavākyatve 'pi anuvādaḥ padārthamātrasyāstī. Satyam. Stutipara evāsau nānuvādamātram. Anuvādoktistu avidheyārthatāmātrāt gauṇī.*
(8) *Na ca vidhyuddeśe anākāṅkṣitatvāt prāśastyasya nānvaya iti vācyam raktapaṭavad ākāṅkṣā upasthāpanasaṃbhavāt.*	(8) *Stutipadeṣu satsu na tair vināvagatiḥ sambhūya padānām avagatyupāyatāvyutpatteḥ. Raktaḥ paṭaḥ bhavatītivat. Nānupāyata stutipadānām.*
(9) *Vivaraṇe tu—Bāhyahetūtthamaprāmāṇyam prathamapāde nirastam. Idānīm tu vedavākyottham evāprāmāṇyam nirṇīyate iti pādabhedaḥ pādāvāntarasaṅgatiśca pūrvapakṣaṇ—Hetusāpakṣakāryapratipādakatvat liṅas tādṛśasvābhāvāvadhāraṇāt. Yatrāpi heturnāsti, tatrāpi sāpekṣam eva kāryam pratipādyam iti sakalavedaprāmāṇyākṣepaḥ. Na ca stāvakatvena anvayaḥ, tathāpi hetutvāparityāgāt yasmāt praśastaḥ ayam tasmāt kartavyaḥ iti tadā api anvayaḥ.*	(9) *Vivaraṇoktam adhikam ucyate vedānugatam bāhyasamuttham sāpekṣatvam nirastam. Adhunā vedavākya ikadeśotthā śaṅkā nirasyate. Anena pādāntaratām gatapādānantaratām cāha Hetutāyārthavādānvayāt, hetusāpekṣamānāntaragamyam kāryam liṅādivācyam iti niścayādanarthavādako 'pi liṅādiḥ tadartha eveti kṛtsnavedaprāmāṇyākṣepaḥ... Rāddhānte tu stutipūrvakatā neṣṭā yato hitāhitalābhahānahetutayā śreyānayam ataḥ kāryam iti nāmāntareṇa hetvanvaya eva uktaḥ.*

Thus, it is quite evident from the above table that Murāri has been very much influenced by Bhavanātha.

4.2 *References to Murāri Miśra*

In the earlier section we have identified the sources from which Murāri has drawn his materials. In this section we would identify the passages which refer to Murāri's doctrine.

As we have already said we would like to reconstruct the doctrine of Murāri Miśra on the basis of his own works and the references to his doctrine in the logical and philosophical texts on Indian philosophy. It is interesting to note that we find a considerable amount of such references in many Nyāya texts and also in the texts of some later Mīmāṁsakas.

While discussing the date of Murāri, we have already hinted at some of these references. But the specific passages of those were not given there. So here we would like to record and identify some important references to Murāri, and his doctrine. We shall arrange these references chronologically.

As we have already stated the earliest reference to Murāri is made by Gaṅgeśa (13th Century). The following are the passages from the *Tattvacintāmaṇi* (*TC*).

(a) *Jñānaprāmāṇyam tadaprāmāṇyāgrāhakayāvajjñānagrāhakasāmagrīgrāhyam na vā.*[63] (*Prāmāṇyavāda*)

Tr. :

'Whether the validity of knowledge is known by all those factors that reveal the knowledge and that do not reveal the invalidity of that knowledge ?

While commenting on this line Rucidatta (13th Century) says :

(a-1) *Mīmāṁsaka-tritaya-sādhāraṇim vādāṅgasaṁśayabījabhūtām vipratipattim darśayati jñānaprāmāṇyam iti*[64] (*Prakāśa*)

Tr. :

'(Gaṅgeśa) points out the controversial issue common to all the three schools of *PM* and which is required for the dialogue to settle the problem'.

While explaining the above comment of Rucidatta, Rāmakṛṣṇādhvarin (17th Century) identifies the three schools of *PM* as the schools of Bhaṭṭa, Guru,and Murāri. He says :

(a-1.1) :

Mīmāṁsaketi. Tathā ca Bhaṭṭa-guru-Murāri-sammata-jñātatāliṅgaka-anumiti-vyavasāya-anuvyavasāyānām jñānagrāhakatvena[63] . . . (*Nyāyaśikhamaṇi*).

'*Mīmāṁsaka.* Thus, since according to Bhaṭṭa, Guru (Prabhākara) and Murāri, knowledge is known by the inference having *jñātatā* for its probans, determinate cognition (*vyavasāya*) and awareness of that *vyavasāya* respectively. . . . .'

(b) *Svāśrayagrāhakeṇa gṛhyata eva na vā* (*prāmāṇyavāda*)[66].

Tr. :

'whether (the validity of knowledge) is known by the revealer of its own locus'.[67]

According to Mathurānātha Tarkavāgīśa, the author of the commentary (called *Rahasya*) on *TC*, this *vipratipatti* refers to the view of Murāri alone. He observes :

(b-1) :

Tṛtīyā (*viprattipattiḥ*) *Miśra-matamātra—sādhāraṇī.*[68]

Tr. :

'The third *vipratipatti* refers to the opinion of (Murāri) Miśra alone'.

Rucidatta, however, thinks that this *vipratipatti* is common to all the three schools of *PM*. While commenting on the above passage of the *TC* he says :

(b-2) :

Tritayasādhāraṇam vipratipatty-antaram āha svāśraya-grāhakeneti.[69] (*Prakāśa*)

Tr. :

(Gaṅgeśa) gives another form of *vipratipatti* which is common to all the three schools (of *PM*).

The *Nyāyaśikhāmaṇi* observes while commenting on the above *Prakāśa* that Rucidatta is explaining this *vipratipatti* keeping in mind the view of Upādhyāya (Yajñapati Upādhyāya) He says :

Etadvipratipatteḥ Bhaṭṭa-Murāri-sādhāraṇyam eva iti upādhyāyamatam.[70] (*Nyayaśikhāmaṇi*).

Tr. :

According to Upādhyāya, this *vipratipatti* is common to Bhaṭṭa and Murāri.

(c) *Nanu pramāṇādīnām tattvam pratipādayat śāstram paramparayā niḥśreyasena sambadhyate iti na yuktam pramāṇatattvāvadhāraṇasya aśakyatvāt. Taddhi pramātattvāvadhāraṇāhdīnam, tacca svataḥ parato vā na sambhavati, vakṣyamāṇa—dūṣaṇagrāsāt.*[71] (*Prāmāṇyavāda*).

Tr. :

Well, Gautama's statement that the science of logic which explains the true nature of sixteen *padārthas* namely, *pramāṇa* etc. is indirectly associated with the highest goal of life, is not correct. Because, it is impossible to decide the true nature of *pramāṇa*, because, the knowledge of the true nature of *pramāṇa* depends upon the knowledge of the true nature of correct knowledge (*pramā*). And that can never be known either intrinsically or extreneously, because it is affected by the defects being described later.

While commenting on the word *parataḥ* in the above passage, Mathurānātha writes in his *Rahasya* :

(c-1) :

Parataḥ tadanyasāmagrītaḥ. Etacca
Miśramata—Bhaṭṭamata—Nyāyamateṣu[72]

Tr. :

The word *parataḥ* means (known) from the factors other than *vyavasāya*. This view is held by Miśra, Bhaṭṭa and Naiyāyikas.

(d) :

Yattu abhāvo na kāraṇam, kintu daṇḍatvādivat kāraṇatāvaccedakatvena sāmagrībhedopalakṣaka iti, tanna[73] (*Prāmāṇyavāde utpattivādaḥ*).

Tr. :

The view that the absence of *doṣa* is not the cause (of *pramā*) but like the stickness (*daṇḍatva*) it is the indicator of the difference of causal factors as the delimitor of *Kāraṇatā*, is not proper. While commenting on this passage, Rucidatta in his *Prakāśa* identifies the opinion contained in this passage as that of Murāri. He says :

(d-1) *Murārimatam āśaṅkya nirākaroti yattviti*[74]

Tr. :

By *Yattu* etc. (Gaṅgeśa) refutes the view of Murāri after presenting it.

The *Nyāyaśikhāmaṇi* while elaborating this comment of *Prakāśa* writes :

(d-1.1)

Nanu yattvityāśaṅkā na Naiyāyikasya tena abhāva-kāraṇatvābhyupagamāt. Nāpi Mīmāṁsakasya tasya svatastvavāditvena paratastvasādhye arthāntaranirākaraṇāyogāt ityata āha Murārīti. Murārimatam avaṣṭabhya yā Naiyāyikasyāśaṅkā tām niṣedhati ityarthaḥ[75] (*Nyāyaśikhāmaṇi*)

Tr. :

The view presented by *yattu* etc. in the *TC* cannot be of the Naiyāyika because he accepts *abhāva* as the cause (of an effect), nor can it be of the Mīmāṁsaka because he is the holder of the view that knowledge is self-valid. And so when the view that the knowledge is valid extreneously is to be established there is no point in refuting something else. Hence, Rucidatta says Murāri etc. which means, (Gaṅgeśa) refutes the view raised by the Naiyāyika on the basis of the doctrine of Murāri.

Mathurānātha, while commenting on the above line, identifies the view as that of Murāri Miśra. He says :

(d-2) *Abhāvaḥ kāraṇatāvacchedakaḥ na kāraṇam iti Miśramatam utthāpayati yattviti.*[76] (*Rahasya*)

Tr. :

The absence (of *doṣa*) is the delimitor of *kāraṇatā* and not a cause, (Gaṅgeśa) presents this view of Murāri Miśra by saying *yattu* etc.

That such a view was held by Murāri Miśra is also clear from the observation made by Vardhamānopādhyāya, the son of Gaṅgeśopādhyāya, while commenting on the *Nyāyakusumāñjali* of Udayanācārya. He writes :

(e) *Murāri Miśrāstu na pratibandhakābhāvaḥ kāraṇam no vā śaktiḥ, kintu tattatkālīnadāhaviśeṣam prati tattatkālapratibaddhetaravahneḥ kāraṇatvam iti pratibandhakābhāvaḥ kāraṇatāvacchedako daṇḍatvavat, na kāraṇam. Ākāśādau tu ekavyaktike kvacitprati-*

bandhe 'pi anyatra śabdotpatteḥ atathātve 'pi bheryāder eva tathātvena kāraṇatvam ityāhuḥ[77]. (*Prakāśa* on *Nyāyakusumāñjali*)

Tr. :

Murāri Miśra holds the following view : The absence of obstructing factor is neither a cause (of an effect) nor the potentiality (*śakti*) but with reference to a particular burning at a particular time, the fire other than the fire obstructed at that particular time is the cause and so, the absence of obstructing factor is the delimitor of *Kāraṇata* like the stick-ness (*daṇḍatva*) and not cause. In case of the sky, however, which is a single entity, even if there is obstruction some times (for the arising of sound) still since sound is produced elsewhere, and so although (the sky) cannot be that type of cause the drums etc. can be the cause of that type.

(f) *Jñānasya mānasatve ca prāmāṇyajñānavat tatsāmagrī api saṁśayapratibandhikā, tanniścāyakatvāt*[78]. (*Prāmāṇyavāda-siddhānta*).

Tr. :

If knowledge is mentally perceived as in the case of knowledge of the validity of knowledge, the factors of that knowledge will be the obstructor of doubt because that is the determiner.

On this line Rucidatta and Mathurānātha comment as follows :

(f-1) *Miśramate doṣamāha jñānasya mānasatve ca iti*[79].

Tr. :

(Gaṅgeśa) points out the defect in the doctrine of Murāri by saying *jñānasya* etc.

The *Nyāyaśikhāmaṇi* has the following to comment on the above line of *Prakāśa*.

(f.1.1) *Nanu jñānasya mānasatva ity etat jñānātīndriyatvavādimate na yuktam ityāśaṅkya dvitīyapakṣanirākaraṇaparam etat, ityāha Miśreti*[80].

Tr. :

The view expressed by *jñānasya mānasatve* etc. cannot be held by the holder of the view that knowledge is beyond the reach of sense-organs (Bhaṭṭa) and so having stated this view (Gaṅgeśa) refutes the second alternative and this is what Rucidatta says by Miśra etc.

(g) *Siddhāntastu satyasthale, pravṛttimātram prati iṣṭapurovartijñāne hetutayā vyavasthite atiprasaṅgavāraṇārtham viṣayatāyā vaiśiṣṭyam eva kāraṇatāvacchedakatayā kalpyate lāghavāt*[81]. (*Anyathākhyātivāda*).

Tr. :

'The conclusion is, in case of a cognition which refers to the fact, once it is decided that for inducement in general the knowledge of the desired object present before us is the cause, the *vaiśiṣṭya* (relation) itself is postulated as the delimitor of the *kāraṇatā* being an object (of knowledge), because of parsimony in order to avoid the over-application of the definition of the true knowledge'.

Mathurānātha while commenting on the above passage says :

(g. 1) *Miśrānuyāyinastu satyasthala iti saṁvādipravṛttau ityarthaḥ*[82]. (*Rahasya*)

Tr. :

The followers of the Miśra school interpret the word *Satyasthala* with reference to the inducement by a knowledge which corresponds to the fact.

(h) *Yadi pramā apramātvasamānādhikaraṇarūpanirūpita-kāryatvapratiyogika-kāraṇajanyā na syāt apramā syāt*[83]. (*Prāmāṇyotpattivāda*).

Tr. :

If a true knowledge were not produced by a cause the counterpositive of which is the effectness (*Kāryatva*) described by the form of locus, which is not the locus of *apramātva* (the state of not being correct knowledge), then it would be an incorrect knowledge.

Mathurānātha comments on this as follows :

(h-1) *Miśrāstu 'apramā syāt', apramāvijātīyakāryam na syāt ityarthaḥ*[84]. (*Rahasya*)

Tr. :

'According to Miśra *apramā syāt* means the effect belonging to a class other than the class of incorrect knowledge will not arise'.

(i) *Paraprakāśe liṅgena manasā vā jāyamānam na bhramavyāvṛttam prāmāṇyam gṛhṇīyāt vyabhicārāt*[85]. (*Prāmāṇyavāda*)

Tr. :

'In the view that the validity of knowledge is known extreneously, the knowledge arising either from probans or by mind will not reveal the validity of knowledge excluding doubtful knowledge, because there will arise inconsistency'.

While commenting on the words *paraprakāśe* in the above passage, Mathurānātha says :

(i-1) *Gurumatam dūṣayitvā Bhaṭṭa-Miśra-matam dūṣayati paraprakāśa iti. Paraprakāśe, paraprakāśamate Bhaṭṭa Miśra-mate iti yāvat*[36]. (*Rahasya*).

Tr. :

'After having criticised the view of Prabhākara, (Gaṅgeśa) criticises the view of Bhaṭṭa and Murāri Miśra by *paraprakāśa* etc. The word *paraprakāśe* stands for 'according to the view that the validity of knowledge is known extreneously' i.e. according to the view of Bhaṭṭa and Murāri Miśra.

Now, we give below some important references from various texts on Nyāya and Mīmāṃsā :

(1) *Manasaiva jñānasvarūpavat tatprāmāṇyagrahaḥ iti Murāri Miśrāḥ*[87].

Tr. :

'According to Murāri Miśra, the validity of knowledge is known by mind itself as the knowledge.

From the *Rahasya* on *Pratyaksakhaṇḍa* of *TC* we cite the following passages :

(1) *Evam Miśramate jñānatvāvatityādiprāmāṇye-pakṣīkṛte-bābhāpatteḥ. Jñānam aham jānāmi iti anuvyavasāyasya jñānaviṣayakajñānajanyatvaniyamāt.*[88]

Tr.

In this way in the doctrine of Murāri Miśra if the validity of knowledge namely the state of having knowledge-ness as its qualifier etc. is taken as the subject (*pakṣa*), there will arise the contingency of fallacy of *bādhā* because, the awareness that I know the knowledge is invariably produced by the knowledge which has knowledge as its object.

(2) *Vyavasāyavyavahitottarotpannameva jñānam Miśramate prāmāṇyagrāhakam.*[89]

Tr. :

'According to Murāri Miśra, the knowledge which arises immediately after *vyayasāya* is the revealer of the validity of knowledge'.

(3) *Miśrāstu anuvyavasāya ityasya idamviśeṣyaka-rajatatvaprakārakadhījanakatayā iti śeṣah. Rajatatvāvacchinnatveneti yadviśeṣyakayatprakārakadhījanyam yatpratyakṣam bādhakam vinā tadviśesyakatatprakārakam iti niyamāt iti bhāvaḥ.*[90]

Tr. :

'Since the *anuvyayasāya* is produced by knowledge the qualifier of which is silverness and the qualificand of which is this (in the case of "*idam rajatam*") The object present before appears in the knowledge possessed of silverness because, there is a rule that a perception, if it is produced by a knowledge in which 'X' is the qualifier and 'Y' is the qualificand, then the 'X' and 'Y' will be the qualifier and the qualificand in the perception also.

(4) *Miśramate cānuvyayasāvasāmagryā prāmāṇyagrahaḥ.*[91]

Tr. :

'According to Murāri Miśra, the validity of knowledge is known by the factor namely *anuvyavasāya*.

(5) *Jñānam-dvividham-vidyā ca avidyā ca iti prathamam vibhāgāt. Ayam ca vibhāgaḥ Bhaṭṭasya Miśrasya vā grāhyaḥ.*[92]

Tr. :

'Knowledge is of two types : correct knowledge and incorreet knowledge. This division is according to Miśra and Bhaṭṭa.[93]

In *Nyāyasiddhāntamañjari* Jānakinātha Bhattācārya refers to Murāri as follows ;

(6) *Murāri Miśrāstu, tadviśeṣyakatve sati tatprakārakatvam prāmāṇyam tacca prathamānuvyavasāyenaiva gṛhyate.*[94]

Tr. :

'According to Murāri Miśra a true knowledge is that which has 'X' as a qualifier and 'Y' as a qualificand (both 'X' and 'Y' being factually related) and that truthfulness of knowledge is known by the subsequent awareness of that knowledge.

In his *Nyāyasiddhāntamuktāvali* Viśvanātha Pañcānana says :

(7) *Murāri Miśrāṇām mate anuvyayasāvena jñanam gṛhyate.*[95]

Tr. :

'According to Murāri Miśra the knowledge is known by *anuvyavasāya*' (i.e. awareness of *vyavasāya*).

Raya Narasiṁha elaborates the position of Murāri in his commentary *Prabhā* while commenting on *Siddhāntamuktāvali* as follows :

7.1) *Tathā ca svāśrayaviṣayaka pratyakṣajanaka-sāmagrītvavyāpaka-svagrāhakasāmagrītyakatvam tādṛśa-pratyakṣatva-vyāpaka-viṣayatānirūpakatvam vā Miśramatasiddha-nirgalitasvatastvam iti hṛdayam.*[96]

Tr.:

'The essence of his theory is that the real concept of self-validity of knowledge according to Murāri Miśra is the property which describes the *viṣayatā* which pervades the state of being a perceptual cognition or it is the state of having the factors which reveal the *vyavasāya* that pervades the state of being the factors which generate the perception of the knowledge, which is the locus of validity.

Jagadīśa Tarkālaṅkāra mentions Murāri and his doctrine on the validity of knowledge in his *Tarkāmṛta* as follows :

(8) *Murāri Miśramate ayam ghaṭaḥ iti jñānānantaram ghaṭam aham jānāmi iti anuvyayasāvaḥ, tenaiva prāmāṇyagrahāḥ.*[97]

Tr. :

'According to Murāri's doctrine, after the knowledge' this is a a pot' the awareness namely, 'I know the pot' arises and by that awareness alone the validity of that knowledge is known.

Annambhaṭṭa in his *Tarkadīpikā*[98] introduces the discussion on validity of knowledge by stating the first *vipratipatti* of *TC*. (*Prāmāṇyavāda.*) He writes :

(9) *Jñānāñam tadvati tatprakārakatvam svatogrāhyam parato vā iti vicāryate. Tatra vipratipattiḥ jñanaprāmāṇyam tadaprāmāṇyā-grāhaka yāvajjñanagrāhakasāmagrīgrāhyam na vā iti.*

Tr. :

'Whether the validity of the knowledges is known intrinsically or extreneously is being discussed now. On this issue the controversy is, whether the validity of knowledge is known by all those factors that reveal the knowledge and that do not reveal the invalidity of that knowledge'.

Rāmarudra Bhaṭṭācharya while commenting on the above passage writes :

(9.1) *Atra Guru-Miśra-Bhaṭṭāḥ Mīmāṃsakāḥ trayaḥ . . . . . Miśramate tu anuvyavasāyagrāhyaḥ vyavasāyaḥ. Anuvyavasāyaśca vyavasāya-pratyakṣam. Tajjanikā sāmagrī manassāṁyukta-samavāyādi-ghaṭitā. Tadgrāhyam eva vyavasāyaniṣṭham prāmāṇyam iti Miśrāḥ*[99].

Tr. :

'There are three schools of Mīmāṃsakas, namely that of Prabhākara, Murāri Miśra and of Kumārila Bhaṭṭa. . . . . According to Murāri Miśra the *vyavasāya* is known by *anuvyavasāva*, *Anuvyayasāya* is the perception of *vyavasāya*. The factors which produce that *anuvyavasāya* consist of the inherence associated with that (soul) to which mind is connected. The validity existing in *vyavasāya* is known by that only. This is the opinion of Murāri Miśra.

Nīlakaṇṭhaśāstri in his *Nīlakaṇṭhaprakāśikā* on *Tarkasaṅgraha-dīpikā* writes,

(9.2) *Murāri Miśramate anuvyavasāyaḥ (tādṛśagrahaḥ) . . . . Miśramate ayam ghaṭaḥ ityākārakajñānānantaram ghaṭatvena ghaṭam aham jānāmi iti jñānaviṣayakam laukikamānasam utpadyate, tena prāmāṇyasya grahaṇam*[100].

Tr. :

'According to the doctrine of Murāri Miśra *anuvyavasāya* is the revealer of the validity. . . . . . . According to Miśra, after the knowledge 'this is a pot', there arises a mental perception of the knowledge, namely, 'I know the pot as pot' and by this mental perception the validity is known.

It is surprising to note that very few Mīmāṃsakas have taken note of Murāri's views in their texts. Quite a good number of Mīmāṃsā texts has been written after 13th Century but very rarely we find any reference to Murāri's doctrine. It is Gāgābhaṭṭa of 17th Century who has mentioned Murāri's view in his *Bhāṭṭacintāmaṇi* while discussing the validity of knowledge. He writes ;

(10) *Murāri Miśrāstu ghaṭādijñānottaram ghaṭam jānāmi ityādi anuvyavasāyo jāyate. Tena ghaṭatvavad-viśeṣyakatve sati ghaṭatvaprakārakatvarūpa-prāmāṇyagrahaḥ ityāhuḥ*[101]

Tr. :

Murāri Miśra holds the view that after the knowledge of 'this is a pot', an *anuvyavasāya* namely, 'I know the pot' takes place. By that (knowledge) the validity namely, 'it is a knowledge in which a pot possessed of potness is the qualificand and the potness is the qualifier' is known.

5

Doctrine of Murāri

5.1 *Background*

Needless to say that to attempt to reconstruct the doctrine of Murāri on the basis of the available materials namely, the two remnants of Murāri's work and the various references to his doctrine in various philosophical texts is indeed an interesting endeavour. Nevertheless, it is not so easy to do. It is interesting because, Murāri must have been a great original thinker who has left behind his own mark in his field and if we succeed in reconstructing his doctrine we would have an access to another store of knowledge in Indian Philosophy. But it is not easy and hence a challenging task because the material on Murāri at our disposal is very scanty.

Under these circumstances, it would be fair to define and demarket the scope of this section. In other words, it is necessary to to spell out the limitation of this section and also the line of thinking and investigation which we are going to follow. Firstly, we should be clear, what we mean when we say that Murāri was the founder of the third school of *PM*. Do we intend to show that Murāri held independent views quite different from the other two schools of *PM* on each and every topic of *PM* or Indian Philosophy? Obviously not. That will be an absurdity. No two schools of thought differ on each and every point. It is not true that even Kumārila Bhaṭṭa and Prabhākara Miśra held different views on one and all points of Mīmāṃsa philosophy. But the fact is that these two schools have independent views on certain issues only and on the rest of the issues they share identical opinions. Similarly, Murāri need not differ on each and every philosophical, logical and ritual point, from the other two schools, in order to establish a third school of *PM*. Nevertheless, it is but necessary that he holds distinct views on certain issues, relevant to the school of *PM* in particular and Indian Philosophy in general, which would allow him to claim a new school of thought quite distinct from the other two schools of *PM*.

Thus, our aim in this section would be to point out only a few issues where Murāri maintains altogether different views in comparison to the views of Bhaṭṭa and Prabhākara.

Another guiding principle adopted by us in this is, not to do anything more than to infer Murāri's opinions on various issues of Indian Philosophy from the arguments Murāri himself has presented in his available works and from the references to his doctrine by other scholars as collected in the section (4.2). We have to resort to inferences and implications because we do not have to-day any access to Murāri's complete works, which might have presented a clear picture of his own distinct views.

Another guiding line of thought followed by us is an already accepted stand that if certain view is presented by some scholar and if it is not refuted by him in any form then it implies that he shares that view. Thus, if Murāi employs certain tools for his analysis and if he does not show any adverse opinion towards them, it has been believed in this section, that Murāri agrees to those tools. This approach of philosophical enquiry would be quite in keeping with Vātsyāyana, the composer of *Nyāvabhāṣya* on the *Gautamasūtras* who says : *paramatam apratiṣiddham anumatam iti hi tantrayuktiḥ.*[102]

The main structure of this section will be to state first the views of the Bhāṭṭa school and those of the Prābhākara school on a particular topic and then try to see, compare and contrast with these two schools the views of Murāri on the same topic, if available. If, in case, there is none, corresponding to the two schools in either Murāri's texts or in the references to him in the other texts, we will clearly state so and would go to the next issue.

With this background let us now proceed to search out Murāri's ideas pertaining to philosophy, logic and ritual. To begin with his philosopical ideas, let us see what his attitude is towards this world of ours. In other words, let us see whether he is a realist like the Naiyāyikas or an idealist like the Vedāntins and the Buddhists.

In the *Anyathākhyāivāda* of the *TC* Gaṅgeśa begins his conclusive discussion as follows : '*Satyasthale pravṛttimātram prati* . . . .'[103] etc. While commenting upon this line, Mathuranatha, in his *Rahasya* has recorded an interpretation of the word '*Satyasthale*' by Murāri's followers. He writes :

Miśrānuyāyinastu, satyasthale iti saṁvādipravṛttau ityarthaḥ'[104].

Thus, '*Satyasthala*' is paraphrased as '*Saṁvādipravṛtti*' which means the inducement towards fact or reality.

This implies that Murāri agrees to the dichotomy ; *Saṁvādi-pravṛtti* Vs *Visaṁvādipravṛtti*, i.e. a fruitful endeavour Vs frastrated endeavour.

Again, in the *Arthavādādhikaraṇa* Murāri says, '*Yatra viśiṣṭo' rthaḥ satya eva tatra bhramatvam na bhavati*,'[105]. That is, where the qualified meaning corresponds to the fact, there is no illusion there. Here also the contrast between a true knowledge and a false knowledge or illusion is brought about very clearly.

From these two statements, we can definitely draw some conclusions. There is in them a clear reflexion of Murāri's view on the reality of the world. Fruitful endeavour (*saṁvādipravṛtti*) presupposes existence of entities with which human being behaves—and frastrated endeavour (*visaṁvādipravṛtti*) presupposes the illusive existence, of entities. Now, since both the types of behaviour are prompted by knowledge, ultimately we will have to have two categories of knowledge—one that leads to fruitful behaviour or endeavour, and the other that leads to frastrated behaviour or endeavour. In other words, it is clear from this that Murāri agrees that there are true knowledges and illusions or false knowledges. Once this is accepted we can easily deduce that the objects of true knowledge are real and those of false knowledge are unreal.

At the level of our ordinary behaviour the above concept of reality works quite well. But we have no means to ascertain whether Murāri also accepted any ultimate reality over and above the objects of true knowledge. Umeśa Miśra quotes a line from *Nyāyamata*, which runs as follows : '*Brahmaike, vyavahāre tu dharmidharmādhāra-pradeśaviśeṣāḥ pañceti padārthāḥ vedāntāḥ Murāri Miśrāśca*'[106]

If this statement really belongs to our Murāri then we will have to accept that Murāri accepted relative reality of this world and the ultimate reality is the Brahman only.

In that case Murāri will not only differ from the Prābhākara school which does not accept illusion, but he will no longer remain a Mīmāṃsaka since according to both the schools of *PM* the realities are many and not one like the Advaitins. But it seems very unlikely considering the influence of the Prābhākara school and that of the *Naiyāyikas* on our Murāri.

Following this line of approach we will try to construct the views of Murāri on various issues.

5.2 GENERAL CONCEPT OF PRAMĀṆA

Before we give an account of the specific *pramāṇas* accepted by Murāri let us have a survey of the concept of *Pramāṇa* according to the other two schools of *PM*.

The Bhāṭṭa School

Though the Bhāṭṭa School will define *pramāṇa* as '*pramākaraṇa*', 'an instrument of valid knowledge', still the word *pramā* here stands for '*ajñātatattvārthajñāna*' i.e. 'a valid knowledge of an entity which was not known before' according to them. Thus, their definition of *pramāṇa* becomes, '*ajñātatattvārthajñānasādhanam pramāṇam*'[107] which means, an instrument of the valid knowledge of real object, that was not known before.

By the adjective *ajñāta* 'unknown' in this definition, remembrance and restatement are excluded from becoming *pramāṇa* and by the word *tattvārthajñâna*, doubt and illusion are excluded from being valid cognitions.

The Prābhākara School

The Prābhākaras define *pramāṇa* as *anubhūtiḥ pramāṇam*[108], i.e. an experience is *pramāṇa*. According to them there is nothing called a false knowledge or illusion. While distinguishing *pramāṇa* from *phala*, they say that if the word *pramāṇa* stands for the valid cognition then the *phala* will be either *hāna* or *upādāna* and if the word *pramāṇa* stands for the instrument by which the valid knowledge is generated then the *phala* will be the valid cognition itself. Thus, when the word *pramāṇa* stands for cognition it would be derived as, *pramīyate yat* and when it stands for the instrument of knowledge its etymology would be, *pramīyate anena*.

Schaol of Murāri

Turning to Murāri we find that there is no specific statement attested which can be said to be the definition of *pramāṇa*. Nevertheless, we can guess in a very general way from some of his statements what Murāri had in his mind regarding the general concept of *pramāṇa*. Let us have a look at the following statement of Murāri in his *Arthavādādhikaraṇa* :

> *Codanāsūtre ko dharmaḥ ityetasmin praśne na pratyakṣādigamyaḥ, kintu codanāgamyaḥ*[109]

Here, the word *pratyaksādigamyaḥ*, can be dissolved as *pratyakṣādinā gamyaḥ* and the word *codanāgamyaḥ* as *codanayā gamyaḥ*. Thus, when Murāri says that the knowledge of *dharma* is generated by an injunctive sentence (*codanā*) and not by perception it is clear that, he conceives *pratyakṣa* and *codanā* as the instruments of valid knowledge.

Similarly, Murāri has also used such expressions as, *pramāṇāntarasiddha*[110], 'known by another *pramāṇa*', *kāryam artham pratipādayataḥ vedasya prāmāṇyam*[111], 'veda i.e. an injunctive sentence which generates the knowledge of *kārya* is *pramāṇa*' and the like.

All these point out to the fact that Murāri looks at *pramāṇa* as an instrument of valid knowledge.

Now observe the following statement of Murāri from his *Mantrādhikaraṇa*.

> *Na hi tatkālīnam mantroccāraṇam rāddhānte 'pi pramāṇam, tasya prameyatvāt. Tatkālinasya ca prakāśanasya smaraṇarūpasyāpramāṇatvena akiñcitkrīyārūpatvāț'*[112].

Tr. :

'Neither the utterance of the *mantra* at the time of sacrifice is authoritative even in the conclusion, because it is *prameya* (that is, to be known). And since the understanding of the meaning from the *mantra* at the time of sacrifice is remembrance, it is not authoritative and hence it does not serve any purpose.'

Here the expression '*smaraṇasya apramāṇarūpatvāt*' is to be noted. Murāri clearly says that remembrance is not *pramāṇa*. From this we can easily infer that Murāri also must have contributed to the view that a knowledge of an object which was not known before is *pramāṇā*.

Although we don't find any clear-cut definition of *pramāṇa*, from all these discussed above we can conclude that Murāri too like the Bhāṭṭas will define a *pramāṇa* as that which reveals an object which was not revealed before.

5.3 : *PRAMĀṆA*

Let us now take up the *pramāṇas* one by one and see what Murāri has to say about them. However, we shall first see how the Bhāṭṭas and the Prābhākaras have defined them.

PRATYAKṢA

The Bhāṭṭa School

The *pratyakṣa-pramāṇa* is defined by the Bhāṭṭa School as, *indriyārthasannikarṣajam pramāṇam pratyakṣam,*[113] i.e. the true knowledge produced by the sense-object-contact is called *pratyakṣa*. The Bhāṭṭas accept six senses namely, *cakṣu* (eyes), *rasanā* (tongue) *ghrāṇa* (nose), *sparśana* (skin) *ś*rotra (ears) and *manas* (mind)[114]. The *sannikarṣa* i.e, contact according to them is of two types (1) *saṁyoga* and (2) *saṃyukta-tādātmya*[115].

The Prābhākara School :

Prabhākara has defined perception as '*sākṣāt pratītiḥ*'[116] i.e. direct apprehention. This direct apprehention consists of three things-namely, the object of the knowledge, the knowledge itself and the knower.[117] For instance, if 'X' knows a pot by perception then the knowledge of 'X' will reveal three things, namely, the pot, the knowledge of the pot and the knower. The form of the knowledge of 'X' will be, *ayam ghaṭaḥ ghaṭam aham jānāmi*. This peculiar theory of perception, by Prabhākara, is known by the name, *tripuṭi-pratyakṣavāda*[118].

The School of Murāri. :

Turning to Murāri, we again find that although there is mention of the word *pratyakṣa*[119] in his works, still we do not find any clear cut description of the process of perceptual cognition. Neither there is any direct description nor is there any clue to infer such a process. The only statement we can make with certainty is that Murāri accepted *Pratyakṣa* as one of the means of valid knowledge.

ANUMĀNA

The Bhāṭṭa School :

The Bhāṭṭas define inference as follows :

'*Vyāpyadarśanādasannikṛṣṭārthajñānam anumānam*',[120] 'An *anumāna* is that knowledge of the object which was not known before, on perceiving the pervaded (*hetu* or probans).

The Bhāṭṭas maintain their stand that inference also like any other valid cognition apprehends something that was not known previously. So far the *parārthānumāna* is concerned he accepts only three members[121] and not five members, as the Naiyāyikas propose.

The Prābhākara School :

The definition of *anumāna pramāṇa* given by the Prābhākaras is as follows :

The cognition of the invariable relation between two things 'X' and 'Y' helps the cogniser to know 'Y' when 'X' is seen, through the remembrance of the invariable relation between 'X' and 'Y'.

Like the Bhāṭṭas the Prābhākaras also accept only three *avayavaṣ* in the *parārthānumāna.*[122]

The School of Murāri :

Before making any statement about Murāri's concept of Inference, let us first have a look at the following statements of Murāri which will give us clues to come to a conclusion.

(1) *Anumānaikadeśābhūta hi pratijñā tatsādhakena hetuna sambadhyate.*[123]

Here he clearly states that *pratijñā* is a member of an inference or syllogism. This inference is certainly the *parārthānumāna.* Obviously, he has also accepted that another member of the Inference is the probans (*hetu*) on the basis of which what is to be established is established.

Let us see the following now :

(2) *Na hi anumānavākyāni hetusvarūpatatpratibandhādipratipādakatvena vyutpannāni; kintu pramāṇāntarasiddhahetusvarūpatatpratibandhādismaraṇadvārā anumānajñānotpādakāṇi. Ataḥ śābda eva anumānavākyasya nāsti, śabdabhāvena prāmāṇye pratijñāmātreṇa sādhyapratītau, hetvādiprayogavaiyarthyāt.*[124]

Here, there is a clear mention of *parārthānumāna* (*anumānavākyāni*). It consists of sentences. Some sentence states the proposition (*pratijña*) some other probans (*hetu*) and still other the relationship between the *hetu* and *sādhya* (*pratibandha* or *vyāpti*).

Not only this, Murāri also states the process by which an inferential cognition is generated. Thus, Murāri says that the sentences in the syllogism do not stop only by telling the nature of *hetu* and the relation between a *hetu* and a *sādhya*. But the function of these syllogistic sentences terminates only after the inferential cognition is produced through the remembrance of the invariable relation (*vyāpti*) between the *sādhya* and the *hetu* which is already known by other *pramāṇa* like perception etc.

Naturally, what we find here is that Murāri has presented a clear account of the epistemology of inferential cognition. We understand that according to Murāri, a *hetu* is already known by other *pramāṇa* along with its invariable relationship with the *sādhya*. This is the reason that he says that the inferential cognition is generated by the remembrance of *vyāpti*. But it is not clear, whether Murāri accepted a three-member-syllogism like the other two schools of *PM* or he accepted five-member-syllogism like the Naiyāyikas.

In this connection Murāri has made a valuable observation. He says that to generate a verbal understanding is not the sole purpose of the members of the syllogism. Because, if it were so, the understanding arising from those sentences would not, in any way, be different from the verbal understanding. Therefore Murāri emphatically says that the understanding arising from a member of the syllogism is not a verbal understanding. And if it is accepted that, that knowledge is a verbal knowledge then the mention of the members other than the *pratjiñā* would become redundant. Because the *pratijñā*-sentence itself will cause the knowledge of the *sādhya*.

This comment of Murāri is very fundamental because he clearly points out the distinction between the *parārthānumāna* and the *śabda-pramāṇa*.

Similarly, in the *Ekādaśādyādhikarāṇa* we find the reference to the well-known example of *anumāna* namely *parvato vahnimān-dhūmāt*. This has come in the context of *Tantra*. Murāri says. '*yathā hi dhūmasyoparibhāgasthitasyāpi parvatasyaikatvānnāpakṣa-dharmatā tathā ca vikṛtāviva tantratvavyutpādanam prakṛtau phalataḥ sidhyati ityeke tadvat*'.[125]

Here, Murāri has given the similie of the well-known example of the inference to explain the nature of *tantra*.

He says that as in case of *dhūma* and *parvata, dhūma* is not present all over the mountain, but as it is present on the top of the mountain, still, since the mountain is only one, there is no difficulty in explaining the *pakṣadharmatā* in the smoke.

ŚABDA

The Bhāṭṭa School :

Mānameyodaya defines *śabda-pramāṇa* as
Atra tāvatpadairjñātaiḥ
padārthasmaraṇe kṛte
Asannikṛṣṭavākyārtha—
jñānam śābdam itīryate[126]

First, the words are known, then the meanings of the words are known and then by *lakṣaṇā* these word-meanings convey the meaning of the sentence not known before.

The Bhāṭṭas like the Naiyāyikas and the Prābhākaras accept *ākāṅkṣā, yogyatā* and *sannidhi* as the causes of verbal understanding.

There are two types of *śabda* namely, *pauruṣeya* and *apauru-ṣeya*[127]. *Pauruṣeya śabda* is the sentence of a reliable person, and *apauruṣeya śabda* is the vedic sentence.

The Prābhākara School

Śabda pramāṇa is defined as a cognition of something not present before the eyes, and which is produced by the knowledge of words. Obviously, the verbal cognition is also the cognition of the things which were not known by any other means of knowledge before.[123]

According to Prabhākara words express their meanings together with their relations with other meanings. Thus. the sentence-meaning is expressed by the words. This theory of the Prābhākaras is known as the *Anvitābhidhānavāda.*[129]

According to the Prābhākaras, the verbal cognition arising from the vedic words or sentences alone is valid.[130] Since the sentences other than the vedic ones are not capable of expressing the meaning not known by the other means, before.

The School of Murāri

Before we reconstruct Murāri's concept of *śabda-pramāṇa* let us consider the following statements of Murāri.

(1) ...... *Ataḥ śābda evānumānavākvasya nāsti, śabdabhāvena prāmāṇve pratijñāmātreṇa sādhyapratītau hetvādiprayogavaiyarthyāt.*[131]

We have discussed this passage in connection with *Anumāna,* and have pointed out how Murāri has distinguished *Anumāna* from *Śabda.* Thus *śabda* is a distinct *pramāṇa* which causes a verbal understanding quite distinct from other varieties of cognitions.

Now consider the following sentences :

(2) *Pratyekam padārthāḥ smaryante teṣām ca bhedāgrahād viśiṣṭaikārthavyavahārakāritvam bhramatayā avabhāti.*[132]

This has been said while explaining how verbal understanding arises from the *arthavāda*-sentences. He spells out the sequence or process of verbal understanding here. First, the knowledge of a word reminds one of its meaning and then the meanings of the constituents of a sentence form a sentence meaning.

Murāri says the following at another place :

(3) *Krameṇānvitābhidhāne ekasmin api vākye prāptyanuvādayoḥ sambhavāt*[133].

Here also it is stated clearly that the verbal understanding arises in a sequence. He very often uses the word *anvitābhidhāna* in the sense of verbal understanding. It should be noted that Gaṅgeśa also uses sometimes the same word for verbal understanding.

About *yogyatā* Murāri says :

(4) *Tasmādanvitābhidhāne eva yogyatā kāraṇam na tu ekavākyatāvadhāraṇe.*[134]

Here, the role of *yogyatā* is clearly stated. *Yogyatā* is the required condition for verbal understanding. It is very likely that Murāri would agree to all the three factors for verbal undertsanding namely, *ākāṅkṣā*, *yogyatā* and *sannidhi.*

All these statements of Murāri clearly demonstrate the epistemology or the process of verbal understanding intended by Murāri. He seems to be the upholder of the theory of *Abhihitānvayavāda* since he does not say that a word expresses its meaning along with its relation with other meaning. On the other hand he says that each word expresses its own meaning and then the verbal understanding arises.

UPAMĀNA

The Bhāṭṭa School

The *Upamāna* is defined as follows :
Dṛṣyamānārthasādṛśyāt smaryamāṇārthagocaram.
Asannikṛṣṭasādṛśyajñānam hyupamitirmatā.[135]

Having seen the similarity in the object present before one's eyes, one acquires the knowledge of similarity with the remembered object. This is analogy.

The Prābhākara School

There is no difference of opinion on this point between the Bhāṭṭa school and the Prābhākara school—excepting the fact that the Prābhākaras accept similarity as an independent category of entities.

The School of Murāri

Nothing could be said about Murāri's concept of *upamāna-pramāṇa* since no statement regarding it is attested either in his texts or in the references to Murāri.

ARTHĀPATTI

The Bhāṭṭa Sehool

The *arthāpatti* is defined as :
Anyathānupapattyā yadupapādakakalpanam
Tadarthāpattirityevam lakṣaṇam bhāṣyabhāṣitam.

i,e. 'when something cannot be explained otherwise, that presumption which makes it explicable is called *arthāpatti.*'

For instance, suppose, Devadatta is alive and he is not in the house then his absence in the house cannot be explained unless it is presumed that Dcvadatta exists somewhere else.

According to the Bhāṭṭas, the difference between *arthāpatti* and inference is this irreconcilability of two well ascertained facts. This is not the required condition of *anumāna.*[137]

The Prābhākara School

According to Prābhākaras, in a case, where the well-ascertained perception of a thing or things remains unexplained unless another thing is presumed, then this presumption of the another thing is *arthāpatti.*

The Prābhākaras explain the difference between *arthāpatti and anumāna* in a different way. They say, the basis of the difference is the doubt. The perception of one thing remains unexplained in the absence of something and therefore it becomes doubtful. And to remove this doubt the help of the presumption is taken. Such is not the case in Inference, the *hetu* i.e. the basis of *anumāna* is well-established and not at all an object of doubt. Had it been an object of doubt there could have been no inferential cognition from such a *hetu* at all.[138]

The School of Murāri

There is no definition as such of the *arthāpattipramāṇa* in any of the Murāri's texts. But there are expressions which can give us clue to infer Murāri's position. Consider the following sentences of Murāri from his *Arthavādādhikaraṇa* :

(i) ......*arthājjātasyārthajñānasya*[139]

(ii) *Sahetukam kāryam pratipannam sahetukatvāya pratibandham ākṣipati*[140]......

(iii) *Na, pratibandhasya pratītihetutvāt tadākṣepam antareṇa pratīterevāsiddhatvāt. Na tu sarvatra ākṣepaḥ sambhavati Rudra-rodanādihetusvarūpe nityānityasaṁyogavirodhāt.*[141]

Similarly the following from the *Ekādaśādyādhikaraṇa* :

(iv) *Niyojyastu niyoge pratīte caramam ākṣepaṇīyo viṣayavat pratīti-aghaṭakatvāt.*[142]

In these expressions Murāri has used the words, *arthāt, ākṣipati*, and *ākṣepa*. *Arthāt* means by implication, *ākṣipati* will stand for 'implies' and *ākṣepa* will mean implication. These words are very often used in the context of *arthāpattipramāṇa*

Thus, it is almost certain that Murāri too approves of the *arthāpattipramāṇa* and the nature of this *pramāṇa* is also the same as that of the other two schools of *PM*.

One point could not be ascertained, is that whether Murāri accepted *śrutārthāpatti* or not. The Prābhākaras did not accept *śrutārthāpatti* as we all know.[143]

ANUPALABDHI

The Bhāṭṭa School

The *Bhāṭṭas* define *anupalabdhi* or *abhāvapramāṇa* as :
Athopalambhayogyatve satyapyānupalambhanam
Abhāvākhyam pramāṇam syād abhāvasyāvabodhakam.[144]

If something is not perceived even when there is a capacity of its being perceived, then, that which reveals the absence of that thing, is called *anupalabdhipramāṇa* or *abhāvapramāṇa*.

The Prābhākara School.

The Prābhākaras do not require to accept the *anupalabdhi pramāṇa* because they do not accept absence as a separate entity.[145].

The School of Murāri.

Only once Murāri has used a typical and important term connected with the *abhāva pramāṇa*. That term is *yogyānupalabdhi*. He says in the *Smṛtyadhikaraṇa*, *yadyapi pratyakṣo vedo yogyānupalabdhyā nirākṛtaḥ, tathāpi nityānumeyo vedo mūlam bhaviṣyati.*[146]

While establishing the authoritativeness of the *smṛtis* Murāri says, even if the vedic injunctions cannot be found which are the basis of the *smṛti*-rites, because there is *yogyānupalabahi*, still those rites could be said to be based on the inferred vedic injunctions.

The term *yogyānupalabdhi* ends in the instrumental case-ending which indicates that *yogyānupalabdhi* is a *kāraṇa* and hence a *pramāṇa*. It cannot be ascertained whether Murāri treated *anupalabdhi* as a *sahakāri-kāraṇa* with reference to the perception of absence like the Naiyāyikas. Most probably it is not the case and he accepts the *anupalabdhi* or *abhāva-pramāṇa*.

By saying *yogyānupalabdhi* Murāri clearly accepts that we can talk of an absence of only that entity which is fit to be known by some *pramāṇa* like *pratyakṣa* etc. This condition is acceptable to the Bhāṭṭas as well as the Naiyāyikas too.

5.4 : THE PRAMEYAS

In this section we would like to discuss the *prameyas* accepted by the third school of *PM*. While doing so, as in the section on *Pramāṇa*, we would state in brief the position of the Bhāṭṭa and Prābhākara Schools first and then in that background we would see what Murāri has to say on the *prameyas*.

THE BHĀṬṬA SCHOOL

This school has accepted five *prameyas* namely, *dravya*, *guṇa*, *karma*, *Sāmānya* and *abhāva*.

Dravya[147] is defined as the locus of the quality namely size. There are eleven *dravyas* accepted by the Bhāṭṭas. They are, *pṛthivī*, *ap*, *tejas*, *vāyu*, *ākāśa*, *kāla*, *dik*, *ātman*, *manas*, *śabda* and *tamas*.

Guṇa[148] is defined as that which is different from action, which possesses *aparajāti* and which is free from being a meterial cause.

The Bhāṭṭas define *jāti*, in the following way : *Jāti* or genus exists in an individual, it is eternal, it is the object of perception and it is different at the same time identical with the individual.

Karman[149] or action is that which resides in the *dravyas* other than the *vibhu* (omnipresent) *dravyas*, it is perceived, and it is the cause of conjunction and disjunction according to the Bhāṭṭas. It is of five types, such as *utkṣepaṇa*, *apakṣepaṇa*, *ākuñcana*, *prasāraṇa* and *gamana*.

Abhāva[150] is defined as, the entity which is known by the sixth means of valid cognition. It is of four types, namely, *prāgabhāva*, *pradhvaṃsābhāva*, *atyantābhāva* and *anyonyābhava*[151].

THE PRĀBHĀKARA SCHOOL

According to the Prābhākaras the categories are eight in number. They are *dravya*, *guṇa*, *karma*, *sāmānya*, *samavāya*, *saṅkhyā*, *śakti* and *sādṛśya*[152].

Substances are nine[153] according to him, such as *pṛthivi*, *ap*, *tejas*, *vāyu*, *ākāśa*, *kāla*, *dik*, *ātman*, *manas*. *Guṇas* are 22. They are *rūpa*, *rasa*, *gandha*, *sparśa*, *parimāṇa*, *pṛthaktva*, *saṁyoga*, *vibhāga*, *paratvāparatva*, *gurutva*, *dravatva*, *sneha*, *saṃskāra* *śabda*, *buddhi*, *sukha*, *dukkha*, *icchā*, *dveṣa*, *prayatna* and *dharma*.[154]

Karman[155] is not a perceptible category. It is inferred from the conjunction or disjunction of a thing.

Jāti[156] is real, distinct from its locus i.e. an individual and is perceptible by senses.

Samavāya[157] is a relation according to prabhākara but it is not *nitya* or eternal. Because it is produced in an individual of the same class and character and is destroyed along with the individual.

Saṅkhyā[158], a number is a distinct category according to the Prābhākaras, unlike the Bhāṭṭas. According to the Bhāṭṭas it is a quality.

Śakti[159] or potentiality is also a distinct category according to this school. For the Bhāṭṭas, it is a quality.

Sādṛśva[160] is similarity. It is not accepted by the Bhāṭṭas as a distinct category. The Prābhākaras, however, argue that, it cannot be Substance, nor Quality, nor Generality nor Inherence. It is entirely different from these. Moreover, it is known by us, exactly in the same way we know any other category, and our consciousness being the sole criterion to decide a category, we say that *Sādṛśya* or similarity is a separate category.

With this brief accounts of the *Prameyas* of the two schools, let us now turn to Murāri.

The School of Murāri

Murāri has used the following terms in various contexts in his texts : *dravya, guṇa, karman, jāti* and *abhāva*. Let us have a cursory look at the expressions or passages, one by one, where Murāri has used these terms :

Dravya

In the *Ekādaśādyādhikaraṇa* Murāri presents a view of kecit and says the following :

Sa ca upakāraḥ ātmāśraya eva utpadyate.
Na tūtpattyapūrvāśritaḥ-Dravyasyaiva
samavāyikāraṇatvāditi kecit.

Tr.

The *upakāra* (help) is produced in the soul and not in the *utpottyapūrva*.. Because a substance alone can be the material cause.

This has been refuted by others (*anye tu*) by saying that this view favours the doctrine of the Nyāya-vaiśeṣikes and hence it should be rejected. As a matter of fact this *upakāra* is a *śakti* and it ean exist in the *utpattyapūrva*.

Neither of these views has been refuted by Murāri. In any case, we find here the use of the term *dravya* which is a categorical term and hence it requires to be noted. Needless to say that we do not find any definition of *drvvya* here. But most probably, it is conceived as the locus of quality by Murāri, but not as a locus of *parimāṇa* as the Bhāṭṭas have defined it.

Guṇa

In the *Arthavādādhikaraṇa* Murāri makes a comment, saying.

Yathā hi paṭasya rakto guṇah tathā
prāśastyam api vāyvādīnām[161]

Obviously, here *dravya* is conceived as the locus of quality and the quality as the *ādheya* of *drava.*

Jāti

Now, see the following statement of Murāri in his *Ekādaśādhi-kkaraṇa.*

Sa tvaneka (eka ?) eva
jātivadanekāśrita iti kecit.

Tr. :

That (*Upakāra*) is to be postulated as one and it can reside in many as a universal (*jāli*) is accepted as one and it resides in many individuals of the same class.

This statement demonstrates Murāri's acquaintance with the concept of *jāti* a universal, namely, it is one and resides in many.

Karman.

Although Murāri has used *Karman* quite often, still we do not find this word used in the categorical sense. It is used in the sense of vedic rite or sacrifice. For instance, Murāri says,

(1) *Jivanasya karmavyāpyatvam avagamyate.*
(*Ekādaśādyādhikaraṇa*).

As per the injunction, *yāvat jīvām Agnihotram juhoti,* an *Agnihotrin* is required to perform the *Agnihotra* as long as he lives. Thus, the performance of the sacrifice is the parvader of his life.

(2) *Śrāddhan ca smārte karmaṇi bahūnām*
mantrāṇām eva smṛtyā viniyogāt.
(*Smṛtyadhikaraṇa*)

Here the word *karman* stands for rites.

(3) *Kānicit karmāṇi smārtāṇi kānicit Śrautāni.*

Here too the term *karman* does not stand for the category but only for rites.

But in any case, a rite is an act and therefore *karman*. So, it is very probable that Murāri accepts a category called *karman* though we do not find any definite statement in this regard.

Abhāva.

We have already seen in the previous section on *Pramāṇa* that Murāri accepts *Anupalabdhipramāṇa* to ascertain the absence of any vedic injunction. Thus, absence is conceived by Murāri as an object of *Anupalabdhipramāṇa.*

Similarly, we have also recorded Murāri's views in the section 'Reference to Murāri' before, what Gaṅgeśa and Vardhamāna had recorded in the *TC*[162] and in *Kusumāñjaliprakāśa*[163] respectively, regarding the role of absence of *pratibandhaka* in defining a cause. Murāri is of the opinion that *pratibandhakābhava* should not be treated as a cause but it should be treated as a delimitor of the state of being a cause.

Both of these statements clearly show that Murāri accepted absence as an entity. However, we do not come across any mention of the varieties of absence accepted by Murāri.

5.5 *THEORY OF KNOWLEDGE*

Here, We would like to discuss the following issues and would like to search the views of Murāri on that :

(1) Nature of knowledge,

(2) Whether a knowledge can be true and false or not, and

(3) whether a knowledge can be an object of another knowledge or not.

with regard to (1), all Indian philosophers agree that knowledge reveals an object, and hence *prakāśakatva* is the nature of knowledge. Murāri too does not differ on this issue.

So far the issue (2) is concerned all do not see eye to eye. The Prābhākaras are on one side and the Bhāṭṭas and the Naiyāyikas on the other. The Prābhākaras hold that a knowledge can never be false. It is only the *vyavahāra* that can be false and never the knowledge. The Prābhākaras are afraid of the fact if knowledge is accepted as false also, since knowledgeness is present in all knowledges, true or false, there can be no confident (*niṣkampa*) behaviour possible, because always there will be doubt in the mind of the knower. But this stand of the Prābhākaras has been challenged by the Bhāṭṭas and the Naiyāyikas, Both these schools accept false knowledge.

Murāri too, accepts the dichotomy of true knowledge and false knowledge. A knowledge, the object of which corresponds to the fact is a true knowledge, and the knowledge, the object of which betrays the fact is a false knowledge, Murāri holds. He has used several times the words like *yathārtha*, *bhrama*, *bhrānti* and *viparyaya* in the context of knowledge.

With regard to issue (3), we can say that, while the Prābhākaras hold that the knowledge is self illuminating, the Bhāṭṭas think that knowledge cannot be an object of preception. They say that knowledge cannot be known directly, but it can only be inferred. When some object is known by someone there arises known-ness in that object and on the basis of that known-ness the revealer knowledge is inferred. Thus, one knows, his own knowledge by inference.

The Prābhākaras on the other hand hold that knowledge is revealed by itself. It is *sva-prakāśa* or self-illumined. It does not require another knowledge for its illumination. To make it clear the Prabhākāras give a similie of a lamp. As the lamp does not need another lamp to reveal itself and as it reveals itself at the same time it reveals its objects, in the same way, knowledge reveals itself and at the same time it also reveals its objects.

Murāri :

Turning to Murāri we find that he holds, unlike the other two schools of *PM*, an altogether new doctrine and says that a knowledge is perceptive. A determinate knowledge (*vyavasāya*) becomes the object of *anuvyavasāya* according to him. This view of Murāri has already been recorded in many passages, collected in the section '*References to Murāri*'. While discussing the validity of knowledge we shall be discussing about it in detail.

In this matter Murāri seems to have been influenced by the Naiyāyika's theory of knowledge. The Naiyāyikas too accept that knowledge is perceptible. and accordingly *vyavasāya* is known by *anuvyavasāva.*

This is how Murāri shows his distinctness with reference to the theory of knowledge from the other two schools of *PM*[164].

5.6 *VALIDITY OF KNOWLEDGE*

The problem of the validity of knowledge is much debated a topic in Indian Philosophy. All Indian philosophers do not see eye to eye on this problem. If we classify their opinions they will fall under following groups :

(i) Both validity and invalidity of knowledge are known internally—a view held by the *Sāṅkhyas.*[165]

(ii) Both the validity and invalidity are known externally—an opinion of the Naiyāyikas.[166]

(iii) Invalidity is internally known and validity is known externally—a Buddhist view.[167]

(iv) Validity is known internally whereas invalidity is externally known - the view of the Mīmāṃsakas.[168]

We are mainly concerned, here, with the *Mīmāṃsā* view on the validity of knowledge only. Though; This is a fact that all the three schools of *Pūrvamīmāṁsā* unequivocally hold that knowledge is self-valid, still they differ in their explanation of this self-validity.

Before we take up the main issues for discussion, let us first make it clear what self-validity of knowledge means. Self-validity is the property of the knowledge that is self-valid. It is formally defined as the state of being an object of a cognition which is produced by the factors which reveal the cognition.[169] What does it mean ? Let us try to understand this with an example.

Suppose : 'X' has perceptual knowledge of pot. Then 'X' will express this knowledge as, 'This is a pot'. In other words this will be the verbalisation of the perceptual knowledge of pot, which is technically known as *vyavasāya* i.e. direct knowledge of a pot. This knowledge is revealed by another knowledge called *anuvya-*

vasāya which is expressed, as, 'I know a pot'. Since this *anuvyavasāya* makes 'X' aware of his knowledge of pot i.e. *vyavasāya*, this *anuvyavasāya* is called *vyavasāyagrāhaka*, the reavealer of *vyavasāya* i.e *jñānagrāhakasāmagrī* which means the factors which reveal the *vyavasāya*. In other words, this second knowledge i.e. *anuvyavasāya* has an object in the form of the first knowledge i.e. *vyavasāya*.

Thus the factors that reveal the *vyavasāya* i.e. *jñānagrāhakasāmagrī* is *anuvyavasāya* and the object of knowledge produced by such factors (*tajjanyagrahaviṣaya*) is *vyavasāya*. Therefore, 'the state of being an object of a cognition which is produced by the factors which reveal the cognition' (*jñānagrāhakasāmagrījanyagrahaviṣayatva*) exists in *vyavasāya* which amounts to saying that self-validity (*svatogrāhyatva*) exists in *vyavasāya*. Therefore *vyavasāya* is self-valid.

Now, let us analyse step by step how all the three schools of Mīmāṁsā differ in their views while explaining this *jñānagrāhakasāmagrī* in the above-mentioned definition of self-validity.

Let us first examine the view of Prābhākaras. For Prābhākaras knowledge is self-illumined.[170] So they do not require another knowledge to reveal one knowledge. The same knowledge reveals object as well as itself, just like a lamp reveals all the things in a room as well as it reveals itself.[171] This also explains why *vyavasāya* itself, for the Prābhākaras, is expressed as 'I know a pot', and not as, 'This is a pot',[172] This means that *vyavasāya* has revealed not only its object i.e. *ghaṭa* but also the *vyavasāya* as well. Thus *jñānagrāhakasāmagrī* for the Prabhakaras is *vyavasāya* itself, and the same *vyavasāya* i,e. *jñānagrāhakasāmagrī* produces the knowledge of validity existing in *vyavasāya*.

Bhāṭṭa School of Mīmāṁsā on the other hand holds that knowledge is supersensuous. It cannot be an object of perception. According to them knowledge is inferred on the basis of some probans (*liṅga*) which is produced in an object by knowledge. Now, what can be the probans for such inference ? They say, when an object is known by perception some property called known-ness (*jñātata*) is produced in the same object by knowledge and on the basis of this 'known-ness' the knowledge is inferred. The following is the form (*prayoga*) of the inference in case of the direct knowledge of a pot : The pot is the object of knowledge which possesses the potness as its qualifier and that possessed of potness as its qualificand, because it possesses known-ness qualified by potness.[173] On the basis of this inference of knowledge based on 'known-ness', the validity existing tn the same knowledge is known.

Thus, according to the Bhāṭṭas this inferential knowledge reveals the validity existing in the *vyavasāya*, therefore this inference is the *sāmagri* which reveals the knowledge i.e. *vyavasāya* and the knowledge produced by such inference i,e. inferential knowledge only—produces the knowledge of validity existing in *vyavasāya*.

In this way, *vyavasāya* is self-valid for the Bhāṭṭas.[174]

Now we proceed to the Third School of *Pūrvamīṃāṃsā* i.e. the School of Murāri Miśra. According to Murāri Miśra, however, *anuvyavasāya* reveals the validity of *vyavasāya*. For him also, the form of *vyavasāya* in case of the direct knowledge of a pot is, 'this is a pot'. And the second knowledge i.e. the awareness about the first knowledge i.e. *anuvyavasāya* is, 'I know a pot'.

As this *anuvyavasaya* reveals *vyavasāya* it also reveals the validity existing in *vyavasāya*, Murāri holds. Thus, *anuvyavasāya* is the revealer of the *vyavasāya*, and the same reveals the validity in *vyavasāya*, therefore, the knowledge i.e. *vyavasāya* is self-valid.[175]

Thus, as far as the self-validity of knowledge i.e. the state of being an object of a cognition which is produced by the factors which reveal the cognition, is concerned all the three schools of Mīmāṁsā agree to it but they differ in stating what the *sāmagrī* is.

As we have seen above, according to the Prābhākaras this *sāmagrī* is *vyavasāya* itself, according to the Bhāṭṭas this *sāmagrī* is *anumiti* and according to the school of Murāri Miśra this *sāmagrī* is—*anuvyavasāya*.

Now let us turn to the *Prāmāṇyavāda* of *TC* where Gaṅgeśopādhyāya has discussed five forms of the self-validity of knowledge. We have chosen here, only the first form for discussion out of the five.

The first form runs as follows: '*jñānaprāmāṇyam tadaprāmāṇyāgrāhaka-yāvajjñānagrāhakasāmagrīgrāhyam na vā*.[176]

Let us look into the meaning of this form first and then we shall discuss the propriety of each and every expression in the form, one by one. The meaning—whether or not; the validity of knowledge is the state of being an object of all those cognitions which are produced by the factors which reveal the cognition and which do not reveal the invalidity of the same cognition. The question is answered in affirmative by the Mīmāṁsakas and in negative by the Naiyāyikas. In other words, affirmative answer to this question leads to the theory of self-validity of knowledge and vis-a-vis.

We have just seen the meaning of the expression *jñānagrāhaka-sāmagrī*. We have also observed that there are three qualifiers to this *sāmagrī* in the above-mentioned first form of self-validity of knowledge discussed by Gaṅeśopādhyāya. Let us now discuss the propriety and purpose of adding these qualifiers.

First of all we shall discuss the necessity of adding *yāvat* as an adjective to *sāṁagrī*. *Yāvat* means as many, so many i.e. all. Although it appears—apparently to be an adjective of *sāmagrī*, as it is impossible because the diverse factors cannot produce a single knowledge.[177] it requires to be interpreted as a qualifier of *graha* (knowledge) because otherwise there will arise the contingency of having no contradiction with the theory of Naiyāyikas. No such contingency will arise however, if it qualifies the knowledge. How ? Let us discuss in detail, in order to catch the point.

According to the Naiyāyikas the validity of knowledge is known by an inference like, 'This knowledge is valid, since it has produced fruitful inducement.[178]

Now, if the word *yāvat* is totally dropped, the definition will get applied to any knowledge which includes even inferential knowledge as well, and in that case there will arise a contingency called *siddhasādhanatva*.[179] If the Mīmāṁsakas also accept that inferential cognition reveals the validity of knowledge then there is no need of raising such a question as, whether a knowledge is self-valid. Thus, to avoid all this the word *yāvat* is added.

With this addition the form under discussion will mean : Whether or not, the validity of knowledge is known by all possible and accepted knowledges namely, *vyavasāya*. *anuvyavasāya* etc. produced by the factors that reveal the knowledge but do not reveal the—non-validity of the knowledge. Thus, by adding *yāvat* the cognitions like *vyavasāya* etc. are included, with which the Naiyāyikas will not agree. Because, the Naiyāyikas accept that *anumiti* alone reveals the validity of knowledge and never a *vyavasāya* or an *anuvyavasāya*.[180] In this way, the word *yāvat* establishes the contradiction.

Now, let us examine the propriety of the qualifier *aprāmāṇyāgrāhaka* i.e. that which does not reveal the invalidity. Suppose, this adjective of *sāmagrī* is absent then what would be the result ? Obviously, there will arise a contingency that an invalid knowledge also will be called self-valid. What does it mean ? Let us consider one case where such a contingency may arise : Let us take up the case of a knowledge. 'This knowledge is false'. That this knowledge is false is a fact. Now, if the condition *aprāmaṇyāgrāhaka* is not laid down, the invalidity existing in the above knowledge will not be revealed and as a consequence of this, the above-mentioned knowledge will have to be treated as valid. Thus in order to exclude such an incorrect knowledge from the expression this adjective is added.

Moreover, only that which does not reveal the invalidity is not a sufficient condition but one should add which does not reveal the invalidity of the same knowledge, i.e. *vyavasāya*. Why ? In the abovesaid example, i.e. 'This knowledge is false', the *anuvyavasāya* of it is a valid cognition, but nevertheless it reveals the invalidity of *vyavasāya*. Here *vyavasāya* will become self-valid, which in fact is invalid unless we specify the locus of the validity to be revealed, and that of the invalidity not to be revealed. This is achieved by adding the adjective '*tad-aprāmāṇyāgrāhaka*' in this statement.

Thus, the self-validity means not requiring any factor, other than those required for the revelation of the knowledge and the validity existing therein. Having understood, in this way, the exact implication of the theory of self-validity let us now reconstruct the theories of self-velidity relating to all the three schools of Mīmāṁsā, and then let us attempt to show how the same statement is true and uniformly applicable to all these three schools.

Self-validity accordingly to the Prābhākara school : Let us take one example, in order to construct the whole theory of this school. Suppose 'X' has a direct knowledge of a pot. This knowledge is produced, say, by the contact of the sense-organs and the object. Since, according to the school of Prabhākara, knowledge is self-illumined, the form of the *vyavasāya* will be, 'I know the pot'. Now, as 'X' has the knowledge of a pot, as per the statement of self-validity the knowledge is revealed by the same knowledge and the factors which revealed the knowledge also revealed the validity of that knowledge. Now, what are the factors here which revealed the knowledge? Naturally, according to Prabhākara it is *vyavasāya* only.[181]

Thus, the validity existing in *vyavasāya* is known by the factors which revealed *vyavasāya* namely the *vyavasāya* itself. So the knowledge i.e. *vyavasāya* is self-valid. Again since the same *vyavasāya* did not reveal the invalidity existing in itself it is self- valid according to the definition of self-validity.

For the Bhāṭṭa school of Mīmāṁsā the process is not so simple, because as we know, knowledge is inferred according to them and not perceived as knowledge is beyond the reach of any sense-organ (*atīndriya*). So when 'X' has a knowledge of an object say, pot, that is when the *vyavasāya* is there as, 'This is a pot', some property called knowness (*jñātatā*) is produced in the pot and on the basis of this know-ness as probans the knowledge is inferred. The following is the form and process of the inference: The pot forms the object of the knowledge which has the pot as its qualificand and the potness as its qualifier. Because it possesses the property called knownness qualified by potness.[132] On the basis of such inference the knowledge is inferred.

Here, the factors which produced this inferential cognition are *parāmarśa* etc.[183] As they produce this inferential cognition which reveals the knowledge of the validity of the knowledge i.e. of *vyavasāya*. Thus, as per the generalisation expressed in the statement *vyavasāya* is self-valid for the Bhāṭṭas also.

Murāri Miśra holds that *anuvyavasāya* reveals the validity existing in *vyavasāya*. Thus for this school, the form of the *vyavasāya* is 'this is a pot' and the form of the *anuvyavasāya* is, 'I know a pot', and the same i e. *anuvyavasāya* reveals the validity of *vyavasāya*.

According to Murāri the fact is as follows: The second knowledge is the direct knowledge or after knowledge of the first knowledge. In other words, an *anuvyavasāya* has *vyavasāya* as its object, and *vyavasāya* is produced by the contact of sense-organ and an object. An *anuvyavasāya* is produced by mind. Nevertheless it is a perceptual knowledge. The following is the process of its production: By definition any perceptual knowledge has to be produced by sense-organ-and-object contact.[184] What could be the contact here ? The object here is the knowledge (*vyavasāya*), which is the quality of the soul. Since the object is internal no external sense-organ can come in contact with this knowledge which is internal. Naturally, the senseorgan will be the mind itself. What is the contact ? The contact is obviously *saṁyukta-samavāya*, because the mind is connected with the soul by the relation of contact. In the soul the knowledge is present by the relation of inherence. Thus, the contact between the mind and the object namely the *vyavasāya* will be the *saṁyukta-samavāya.*

This contact is one of the factors which produce the direct knowledge of *vyavasāya* i.e. *anuvyavasāya.*[185] And this *anuvyavasāya* reveals the validity of the *vyavasāya.* In this way, *vyavasāya* is self-valid for the Miśra School.

The above description of the theories of self-validity also clearly demonstrates how the statement of self-validity is uniformly applicable, to all the three schools of *Pūrvamīmāṁsā.* This could be possible because of the word *yāvat* introduced in the statement which incorporates all possible opinions of the Mīmāṁsakas. Thus *vyavasāya, anumiti* and *anuvyavasāya* are included as the revealers of this validity with which the Naiyāyikas disagree.

Now let us turn to the third *vipratipatti* of the *Prāmāṇyavāda* of *TC.*[186] This *vipratipatti* is identified as referring exclusively to the doctrine of Murāri on the validity of knowledge by Mathuranatha in his gloss called *Rahasya.*[186] According to this third *vipratipatti* the validity of *vyavasāya* is known by the revealer of this *vyavasāya* i.e. the *anuvyavasāya.* We have already discussed before how *anuvyavasāya* reveals the validity of the *vyavasāya.*

This distinct view of Murāri was noted by many scholars, after Gaṅgeśa also. Gaṅgeśa's son Vardhamāna, Rucidatta Miśra, Jagadīśa, Viśvanātha, Rāmarudra Bhaṭṭācārya and Gāgā Bhaṭta are a few among them. It is interesting to note that all of them have uniformly stated Murari's view on this issue.

By the by some remarks on the stand of Murāri Miśra regarding the theory of self-validity are in order.

(1) The above discussion has amply demonstrated the fact that it is this view of Murāri on the validity of knowledge which has

been continuously quoted since the time of Gaṅgeśa, upto recent commentators. Thus, it is not unlikely that Murāri was recognised as the holder of a new school of thought because of his this very doctrine. His other views might have been treated as marginal ones.

(2) It seems that Murāri is very much influenced by the Nyāya School in this context. Though he maintains that knowledge is self-valid like the other two schools of Mīmāṁsā, he accepts many concepts of the Naiyāyikas. For example ; He accepts that the object of *anuvyavasāya* is *vyavasāya*. By accepting this he distinguishes his doctrīne from that of Prābhākaras and Bhāṭṭas. Nevertheless he accepts that '*anuvyavasāya* is *vyavasāyapratyakṣa*' which amounts to saying that knowledge is known by perception, which is a Nyāya view.

(3) He accepts *manas* as an internal sense-organ for the perception of internal objects.[187] This is also basically a Nyāya concept.

5.7 *CONCEPT OF QUALIFIER AND INDICATOR*

In the preceding section we have seen the stand of Murāri on 'Validity of Knowledge'. In this section I propose to discuss the concepts of *viśeṣaṇa* and *upalakṣaṇa* as per the definitions given by Murāri Miśra in one of his works namely, '*Tripāditinitinyanam*'.[188] Before we take up the definitions given by Murāri for discussion, let us see how the other systems of Indian philosophy conceive these two terms namely, *viśeṣaṇa* and *upalakṣaṇa*. Accordingly this section is divided into four parts.

I Mīmāṁsakas' Opinion.

II Naiyāyikas' Standpoint.

III Murāri's Conception.

IV Conclusion.

Although, we are mainly concerned here in this section to discuss, compare and contrast the concepts of *viśeṣaṇa* and *upalakṣaṇa* of Murāri, in the background of Bhāṭṭa School of Mīmāṁsā, Prābhākara school of Mīmāṁsā and Nyāya system of Indian philosophy, still a line or two about the position of these concepts in Pāṇini, Kātyāyana and Patañjali will not be out of the place.

Pāṇini uses the word *viśeṣaṇa* in the rules 2.1.57 i.e. *viśeṣaṇam viśeṣyeṇa bahulam* and in 1.2.52 i.e. *viśeṣaṇānām cājāteḥ*, and the word *lakṣaṇa* in the rule 2,3.21 i.e. *itthambhūtalakṣaṇe*. Naturally in the rule 2.1.57 he states a pair of concepts.[189] The word *viśeṣaṇa* is paraphrased as *viśeṣaka* by *Kātyāyana* and as *bhedaka* by *Kāśikākāra*. Kāśikākara also paraphrases *viśeṣya* as *bhedya*. Thus what distinguishes is a *viśesaṇa*. Udyota makes it further specific by rendering the pair as *vyāvartya* and *vyāvartaka*. Needless to say that this paraphrasing of Udyota is based on later development in systems like Mīmāṁsā and Nyāya.

I *MĪMĀṀSAKAS' OPINION*

Although any elaborate discussion on the conceptual analysis is not found in any Mīmāṁsā texts, still from the use of these terms in those texts and from the contexts in which these are used, we can form some idea about Mīmāṁsakas' concepts of *viśeṣaṇa* and *upalakṣaṇa*.

While pleading for his own doctrine of *ākṛti* as the expressed sense of a word, Śabara states that if a *viśeṣaṇa* is not known to a person, he cannot have *viśiṣṭajñāna*.[190] Thus, since it is observed that after hearing the word *go* one gets the knowledge of *gotva-viśiṣṭa-go* which is a *viśiṣta-jñāṇa*, it is necessary that one must have the knowledge of *gotva*, prior to the knowledge of *gotva-viśiṣṭa-go*.

Naturally, if the word *go* is to generate a *viśiṣṭajñāna*, *gotva* must be known from the word itself. Therefore, it is argued that the word *go* expresses *gotva* i.e. *ākṛti* and the individual i.e. *gotva-viśiṣṭa-go* is understood by implication.

The opponent holds that an individual indicated by an *ākṛti* is the expressed sense of a word. To refute this position of the opponent, Śabara argues, let us compare two words, namely *daṇḍin* and *go*. Both these words generate *viśiṣṭajñāna*. We have already noted that the word *go* generates the knowledge of *gotva-viśiṣṭa-go*. Similarly, the word *daṇḍin* also generates the knowledge of 'a man with a stick' which also is a *viśiṣṭa-jñāna*. But in the knowledge of a man with a stick we can account for the knowledge of stick from the part of the same word i.e. from *daṇḍa* and man from the suffix *in*, whereas there is no part in the word *go* which can be taken to express *gotva*. Naturally, as the *viśeṣaṇa* cannot be understood from any part of this word and since without the knowledge of it, the qualified knowledge is impossible to occur, it should be accepted that the word *go* itself expresses *gotva*.[191]

Śabara does not use the word *upalakssaṇa* but he uses two words, namely, *lakṣaṇa* and *cihna* in the sense of *Upalakṣaṇa*. It is also very clear from this discussion that Śabara talks of these two terms i.e. *viśeṣaṇa* and *upalakṣaṇa* in the context of a qualified knowledge. Naturally, according to him, both these terms are expressive of *prakāra* or qualifier in a qualified cognition.

Kumārila expresses his views on this issue in his *Tantravārttika* which are in full agreement with Śabara's *Bhāṣya*. While commenting on Śabara, Kumārila clearly states that *viśeṣaṇa* as well as *upalakṣaṇa* are the distinguishers or qualifiers.[192]

While explaining the comparison between the two words i.e. *daṇḍin* and *go*, offered by Śabara, Kumārila adds one more example of *upalakṣaṇa*. He says that, it is not improper to hold that the *viśeṣya* is conveyed by a word like *daṇḍin* or *devadattagṛha*, because the *viśeṣaṇa* i.e. *prakāra* namely, the *daṇḍa* and *kākanilayana* can be known by word and by perception respectively in the case of *daṇḍī puruṣaḥ* and *kākavad devadatta-gṛham*. But such is not the case with the word *go*. Because there is no part in it which can generate the cognition of *gotva*.[193] And unless *gotva* i.e. *viśeṣaṇa* is known there cannot arise a qualified knowledge from the word *go*. Thus, kumārila says that since *viśiṣṭa-jñāna* occurs when we hear the word *go*, it means that *viśeṣaṇa* is known, and since it is not known from any other means as mentioned above, *gotva* itself is to be treated as the *vācya* i.e. expressed meaning of the word *go* and the individual is understood by implication.

It is interesting to note that Kumārila replaced the word *lakṣaṇa*, used by Śabara, by *upalakṣaṇa*, in the same sense of *cihna* as used by Śabara. Nevertheless it is different from *viśeṣaṇa*.

Now let us turn to the Prābhākara school of *Pūrvamīmāṁsā*. In the *Bṛhatī* of Prabhākara Miśra we get still better picture because he discusses the issue a bit more elaborately, in the same context i.e. *ākṛti* is the expressed meaning of a word.

Prabhākara in a way tries to define *upalakṣaṇa* which was not done either by Śabara or by Kumārila. He states : '*upalakṣaṇam hi nāma nātmākāratayā upalakṣyam upalakṣyayati*'[194] and gives an example : '*Yathā yatra ayam kākaḥ ado devadattasya gṛham iti na kākākāram gṛham avasīyate.*[195] That is, *upalakṣaṇa* say 'X' is that which does not indicate something say 'Y' in the form of 'X'. For instance, the house of Devadatta is not presented in the knowledge as identical with the crow by the expression, '*Yatra ayam kākah ado devadattasya gṛham*'. In other words, crow does not generate an understanding of the house as crow, but as distinct from crow.

Prabhākara makes his idea of *upalakṣaṇa* further clear by giving another example. The example is of *pañjarastha siṁha,*[196] i.e. a lion in a cage and it is explained by Śālikanātha in *Ṛjuvimalā* as, suppose, one has seen a lion always in a cage, it is but natural that whenever he hears the word *siṁha* he understands a *pañjara* as well. Similarly, when *vyakti* is understood from the word *go*, *gotva* is regularly understood along with it, because of the regular association.[197] Thus, individual can be the expressed meaning of a word and the *ākṛti* could be understood by indication. This is the stand of the opponent which is answered by Prabhākara in the following way : He says that, it is true that such a person understands the cage also, whenever he hears the word lion, but he understands it as being different from the lion. That is to say, he does not understand the cage in the form of lion but as distinct from the lion. It is not true in the case of *go* and *gotva.* That is, the cowness in not understood as different from cow. Thus, the example given by the opponent does not prove the contrary.[198]

Needless to say that we are not concerned with the argument about the meaning of the word here, but nevertheless this discussion helps us to form the idea of *upalakṣaṇa* in the mind of Prabhākara.

The concept of *upalakṣaṇa* is further elaborated by Prabhākara as follows : *yatra ākārāntaravivekaḥ tatra ākārāntaram upalakṣaṇam. Yathā daṇḍī ityeva daṇḍī-veśeṣāvagatau na ānayane daṇḍasya anvayaḥ. Yatra punaḥ daṇḍītayā eva avagamyate na viśeṣataḥ tatra tathābhūtasyaiva anvayaḥ śakyate vaktum.*[199]

That is, when something, say 'X' is known distinct from something say 'Y', 'X' is called *upalakṣaṇa.* For instance, when the very word *daṇḍin* is expressed to indicate some particular person, the stick is nothing but a mark which indicates that person. And in that case in the expression '*daṇḍinam ānaya*' the stick need not be connected with the act of bringing. But when some particular person is not conveyed by the word *daṇḍin* but a person with a stick, then naturally the stick is a *viśeṣaṇa* and it is not an *upalakṣaṇa* or indicator any more, and in such a case, the stick is connected with *kārya* i.e. an action, say, bringing. This clearly reveals the view of Prabhākara that *upalakṣaṇa* is not connected with action. Moreover, he has expressed this view himself when he says '*upalakṣaṇatve na aṅgam bhavati*.[200]

It can be observed from this that Prabhākara also does not talk of *viśeṣaṇa* so elaborately. He only states keeping in line with the *ŚBh* that the knowledge of *viśeṣaṇa* before *viśiṣṭa-jñāna* is essential.[201] Nevertheless it is clear that it is Prabhākara who attempted to define the concept of *upalakṣaṇa*, for the first time. In other words, he provided a criterion to decide whether 'X' is *upalakṣaṇa* or not, over and above that 'X' is a mark.

Bhavanātha, a follower of Prabhākara puts the same concept in his *Mīmāṁsānayaviveka*[202] as '*pṛthag bhūte hi dharmiṇy upalakṣaṇam*.[203]

That is, when something known is different from that on the basis of which it is known then that on the basis of which it is known is called *upalakṣaṇa*. This is how this definition is explained by the commentator Varadarāja : To be more precise, when something, say, 'X' is known as differenciated on account of something, say 'Y' then 'Y' is called *upalakṣaṇa*.[204] Thus the house of Devadatta is known as differenciated on account of *kāka* but of course, as a house of Devadatta only then *kāka* is an *upalakṣaṇa*. But this is not the case with *viśeṣaṇa* obviously because, it is not the case that cow, possessed of cowness is known on account of some property other than cowness. Naturally, cowness is a *viśeṣaṇa* and so the expressed meaning of the word *go* has to be *gotva*. Bhavanātha establishes this point with the same example given by Prabhākara.[205]

From the above discussions by both the schools of Mīmāṁsā we observe that there is full agreement with the fact that cowness, in the knowledge of 'cow with cowness', arising from the word *go* is a qualifier and cannot be treated as an indicator, whereas the crow, in the knowledge of Devadatta's house arising on account of crow, is nothing but an indicater. The only contribution if claimed by Prabhākara is a positive attempt to define the concept of *upalakṣaṇa*.

Although they have not talked much about *viśeṣaṇa* excepting the *Bhāṣya* statement that, that which is dīrectly connected is *viśeṣaṇa* and that which is distantly connected cannot produce a qualified knowledge, still by implication, we understand that they treat *viśeṣaṇa* as something which is diretly connected to the *viśeṣya* in the knowledge.

II *NAIYĀYIKAS STANDPOINT*

Let us now turn to the Naiyāyikas. Unlike the Bhāṭṭas they concentrated on defining these two concepts right from the beginning. It was Udayana among the old Naiyāyikas, who in his *Kiraṇāvalī*, initiated a semantic definition of these terms.[206] The discussion occurs in the context of a qualified knowledge, '*dve dravye*' i.e. 'there are two substances'. In this cognition number two, i.e. *dvitva* is *viśeṣaṇa* and the substances are the *viśeṣya*. But the problem is according to the metaphisical and ontological stand of the Nyāya-vaiśeṣika system, number two onwards all higher numbers are produced by a knowledge called *apekṣā-buddhi* and since knowledge is not a permanent entity, after disappearance of the *apekṣā-buddhi* number two is bound to disappear. In the process of cognition, by the time one gets the qualified cognition, there are two substances, number two has already disappeared.[207]

Naturally, the question arises : how can this knowledge take place when, *dvitva* i.e. *viśeṣaṇa* is not present at the time of its production ? In answer to this question, Udayana argues that although *viśeṣaṇa* or qualifier is the cause of the *viśiṣṭa-jñāna* or qualified knowledge, it need not be an object of the same knowledge.[208] Therefore, though *dvitva* i.e. number two is not present at the time of the *viśiṣṭa-jñāna*, the knowledge of it can be the cause of the qualified knowledge '*dve dravye*', and thereby its state of being a *viśeṣaṇa* remains intact.[209] The only condition for being *viśeṣaṇa* is that, it must exist in the same *viśeṣya* which is the *viśeṣya* of the qualified knowledge.

Udayana defines *Viśeṣaṇa* as, "*samānādhikaraṇam avacchedakam Viśeṣaṇam*.[210] i.e. A *viśeṣaṇa* is that, which distinguishes its locus being existent in the same locus. He also illustrates the case with the example of *nīlam utpalam*.[211] Here, the blue colour, being present in it distinguishes the locus of the blue colour, from the loci i.e. lotuses of red, white etc. Therefore, blue colour is a qualifier.

He defines *upalakṣaṇa* as '*avacchedakatva aviśeṣe' pi vyadhikaraṇam upalakṣaṇam.*[212] It means : An *upalakṣaṇa* is that which distinguishes a locus which is not its locus. No example of *upalakṣaṇa* is given by Udayana. But it is quite obvious from the definition that when the *kāka* is not connected with the house of Devadatta, at the same time it distinguishes the house, it is *upalakṣaṇa.*

It is quite apparent from the definitions offered by Udayana, that both the *viśeṣaṇa* and *upalakṣaṇa* share the nature of differenciating something from the other, which is in quite accordance with Kumārila. In addition, Udayana has also provided the criterion to distinguish *viśeṣaṇa* from *upalakṣaṇa* namely, *samānādhi-karaṇatva* and *vyadhikaraṇatva.*

In his *Saptapadārthī*, Śivāditya Miśra reproduces Udayana's definitions of *viśeṣaṇa* and *upalakṣaṇa* by simply replacing the word *avacchedaka* by *vyāvartaka.* Thus, the respective definitions are : *Samānādhikaraṇam vyāvartakam viśeṣaṇam and vyadhikaraṇam sad vyāvartakam upalakṣaṇam.*[213]

It is worth noticing that he gives his own interpretation of the word *Sāmānādhikaraṇya* and *vaiyadhikaraṇya*[214] He interprets *Sāmānādhikaraṇya* as *ekavibhaktyantapadavācyatvam*[215] and *vaiyadhikaraṇya* as *bhinnavibhaktyantapadavācyatvam.*[216]

Thus Śivāditya tries to define these concepts formally. If there is a formal agreement of adjectival and substantive forms, it is *viśeṣaṇa* whereas, if there is no such agreement, it is a case of *upalakṣaṇa.* Naturally, in *rūpavān ghaṭah, rūpa* is *viśeṣaṇa*, whereas in the case of *jaṭābhīḥ tāpasaḥ, jaṭā* is *upalakṣaṇa.*[217]

When we come to Gaṅgeśa, we find that an elaborate discussion (*vāda*) on these concepts is added by him in his *TC* where he has taken into account various previous definitions given by his predecessors.

While refuting Śivāditya's interpretation of *sāmānādhikaraṇya* Gaṅgésa argues that if *veśeṣaṇa* is *defined as* '*viśeṣyasamānavibhaktikatvam*' the definition will over apply to the case of *kākavaddevadattagṛham*, where *kāka*, in fact is *upalakṣaṇa* and not *viśeṣaṇa.*[218]

The commentator Rucidatta adds that it will not only apply to the crow but also to the string of the expression *ghaṭaḥ paṭaḥ* etc., because here too both *ghaṭa* and *paṭa* show one and the same nominative ending.[219]

In this way, having refuted some other views Gaṅgeśa gives his own view. He explains the point as follows: After the qualified knowledge namely, *daṇḍī puruṣaḥ* i.e. a person with a stick, has occurred, it is understood that the person with a stick is different from those who do not have sticks. Although there are two properties in the person namely, *daṇḍa* and *puruṣatva*, the locusness of difference in the person with the stick is delimited by the stick and not by *puruṣatva* (personness), because in that case *puruṣatva* cannot differenciate this person from other persons who do not have sticks simply because in them too *puruṣatva* exists. Not only that, even at the time when the stick is not with that person there is no difference of that person from other persons (who do not have sticks) and as such no difference exists in that person and so no knowledge of difference is possible. Therefore, *daṇḍa* alone is the delimitor of the locusness of difference in the person with the stick.[220]

In case of *kākavad-devadatta-gṛham*, of course, the difference from all those houses that are not of Devadatta is understood in the house of Devadatta but the delimitor of this locusness of the difference cannot be *kāka* since even in the absence of *kāka* namely when *kāka* is moving in circle over the house of Devadatta or when it was associated with the house in the past, the difference is known alike.[221]

The following is the main difference between these two concepts according to Gaṅgeśa :

The knowledge of difference in the qualified object cannot occur in the absence of *viśeṣaṇa*, whereas, even if the *upalakṣaṇa* is absent it can cause the knowledge of difference through its own knowledge.

Accordingly, Gaṅgeśa defines *viśeṣaṇa* and *upalakṣaṇa* as follows :

That which distinguishes something from other being a delimitor of the locusness of the difference to be known is a *viśeṣaṇa* and any other distinguisher different from it is called *upalakṣaṇa*.[222]

Gadādhara while explaining the rule of Pāṇini '*Iitthambhūta-lakṣaṇe*' (P. 2.3.21), looks at this problem in a bit different way.[223]

He has tried to establish that *viśeṣana* is understood from a possessive suffix, whereas, *upalakṣaṇa* is known by an Instrumental suffix.[224] For example, *daṇḍī puruṣaḥ* and *jaṭābhiḥ tāpasaḥ*. Here, *daṇḍa* is *viśeṣana* because it is understood from a word ending in the possessive suffix-*in*, where as, *jaṭā* is upalakṣaṇa because it is understood from a word ending in *Instrumental*.[225]

If this view is accepted then both *kāka* and *jaṭā* will have to be treated as *viśeṣaṇa* in the expressions, *kākavad-devadatta-gṛham* and *jaṭāvan tāpasāḥ*, which is contrary to the fact as it is shown by Gaṅgeśa.

No doubt, it would have been ideal position to corelate one particular concept with one particular expression, but it cannot be maintained since in the expression, *kākavad devadattasya gṛham kāka* is treated by all as *upalakṣaṇa*.

Śaṅkara Miśra, on the other hand, makes a very bold statement in his *Upaskāra* as follows :

Yadā Devadattagṛhe kākavattā tadā kākaḥ viśeṣaṇam eva,

Yadā tu upari bhraman asan kākaḥ tadā upalakṣaṇam.[226]

Thus according to this view, when crow sits on the house of Devadatta it is *viśeṣaṇa* and the same crow if it is not connected with the house but if on the basis of its knowledge Devadatta's house is located it can be called *upalakṣaṇa.*

What is deduced from Śaṅkara Miśra is, when a person observes the crow sitting on the house, the crow must be treated as *viśeṣaṇa* because in that knowledge the crow itself appears as a qualifier of the house, but when the crow is not there and still one gets the knowledge of the house on account of the previous existence of the crow on the house, the crow does not appear as the qualifier of the house, but merely the structure of the house indicated by the knowledge of the crow appears as the qualifier of the house and so crow is called *upalakṣaṇa.*

This is how the Naiyāyikas have contributed to these notions by way of defining these concepts as comprehensively as possible in order to include all cases, discussed above.

III. *MURĀRI's VIEW*

Coming to Murāri we find that in his *Arthavādādhikaraṇa* of *Tripādīnītinayana* he has offered a different set of the definitions of *viśeṣaṇa* and *upalakṣaṇa.* The context in which Murāri defines these two terms is the question of establishing a connection between the *arthavāda* sentences and the *vidhi* sentences i.e. between the *prāśastya* and the *vidheya* i.e. *yāga.* Murāri holds that *prāśastya* (praise of deity, the constituent of the sacrifice) is an *upalakṣaṇa* to *yāga* i.e. sacrifice[227] and then defines the two terms i.e. *viśeṣaṇa* and *upalakṣaṇa* as intended by him.

When he starts defining, the beginning remark itself is surprising. He says : *Na vyāvartakam upalaṣaṇam viśeṣaṇam vā*[228]. Neither *upalakṣaṇa* nor *viśeṣaṇa* is a distinguisher.

Naturally, by making such a statement he attracts all our attention towards him because it is apparently all contrary to what we have been discussing so far. But we are pacified by his next statement which is in reality definitions of *viśeṣaṇa* and *upalakṣana.* He says : *Kāryāṅgam sat sambaddham viśeṣaṇam, kāryānaṅgam sat sambaddham ca upalakṣaṇam.*[229]

That is, that which is subsidiary to *kārya* and at the same time which is connected with the *viśeṣya* is called *viśeṣaṇa* and that which is not subsidiary to *kārya* and at the same time which is connected with *viśeṣya* is called *upalakṣaṇa.*

Naturally, it is evident from the definitions that *vyāvartakatva* does not constitute the body of the definitions. While explaining the reason for it, he points out that *vyavaccheda* or *vyāvṛtti* or differenciation is the purpose of both *viśeṣaṇa* and *upalakṣaṇa* and as such it need not enter into the text of the definition. Also because *vyāvṛtti* i.e. differenciation is common to both the concepts. Strictly speaking, in a definition, only *asādhāraṇadharma* i.e. unique property is to be stated as per the definition of definition.

Let us now see how the definition of *upalakṣaṇa* given by him applies to *prāśastya.* The sentence, '*vāyavyam śvetam ālabheta bhūtikāmaḥ*' enjoins the *kāmya-paśuyāga.* And this sacrifice has been praised, through praising the deity by the *arthavāda* sentences, '*vāyur vai kṣepiṣṭhā devatā*, etc. Now, how to connect this praise with the *yāga* is a problem. That is solved by Murāri by saying that it is connected to *yāga* being an *upalakṣaṇa*. Let us see how it is connected to *yāga* :

Devatā, which is praised, is directly connected with *yāga*, being the very form of *yāga*. But *prāśastya* being connected with the deity of that sacrifice directly, simply acts as a distinguisher of the *yāga* and is not connected with it directly. And thus becomes an indicator of *yāga*.

Thus, according to Murāri's concept, whether something is *upalakṣāṇa* or *viśesaṇa* can be decided only in the context of an action. Say, for instance, in the expression, '*Kamaṇḍalunā chātram ānaya*' *kamaṇḍalu* is *upalakṣaṇa* because it is not a subsidiary to action of bringing, but it simply points to the student who is to be brought. If the speaker intends that the student should be brought along with the *kamaṇḍalu* the normal expression would be *Kamaṇḍalu-mantam chātram ānaya*' or *Kamaṇḍalunā saha chātram ānaya*' and in that case the *kamaṇḍalu* will be a *viśeṣaṇa*. But if it is simply, '*kamaṇḍalunā chātram ānaya*' then it is not necessary that the student should be brought along with the *kamaṇḍalu* because that is not intended there.

Let us now analyse and examine another statement of Murāri regarding *viśeṣaṇa* and *upalakṣaṇa*. In his *Ekādaśādyādhikaraṇa* he writes :

> '*Dvitīye tu svargakāmanopalakṣitakartṛviśeṣa eva samarpyamānaḥ kim kāmanayā kālaviśeṣayoginyā upalakṣyate gṛham iva kākena, yad idānīm kākavad devadattīyam iti, sadā yogena vā.*

Tr.

In the second chapter of Jaimini it has been discussed whether the desire of heaven associated with a particular time indicates the performer of the sacrifice as the crow indicates the house such as, this house is of Devadatta indicated by the crow present at this moment of time. Or whether the performer is known by his having the desire of heaven always.

Here, an occasional desire of heaven is conceived as an *upalakṣaṇa*. Thus, here, Murāri thinks that, that which being present for a particular time only, distinguishes 'X' from 'Y' is an *upalakṣaṇa*. Where as that which being always present distinguishes 'X' from 'Y' is a *viśeṣaṇa*.

IV *CONCLUSION*

From the above discussion we arrive at the following conclusion regarding *viśeṣaṇa* and *upalakṣaṇa*.

(i) Pāṇini used the terms *viśeṣāṇa* and *Lakṣaṇa*, although the terms *Viśeṣaṇa* continued to be used in that sense, the term *Lakṣaṇa* seems to have been replaced by *upalakṣaṇa*.

(ii) Till Śabara the same term *Lakṣaṇa* is used, in the sense of *cihna* i.e. a mark, but it is replaced by *upkalakṣaṇa* from Kumārila onwards.

(iii) Prabhākara seems to be the first among the Mīmāṁsakas to attempt a definition of the term *upalakṣaṇa*.

(iv) Among the Naiyāyikas, it is Udayana who presented definitions for both *viśeṣaṇa* and *upalakṣaṇa*.

(v) Gaṅgeśa supplied a comprehensive definition of these concepts.

(vi) Murāri defined them with a different parameter, the hint of which he obtained from Prabhākara. To be precise, Murāri's concept of *viśeṣaṇa* and *upalakṣaṇa* is totally different from that of the Bhāṭṭa school of Mīmāṁsā and the Nyāya school but it is closer to that of Prābhākara to the extent that both conceive these concepts in terms of action. Nevertheless, Murāri states them in clear terms with further specification by adding the qualification *sambaddha* to the respective definitions.

(vii) Duration of time is another factor to distinguish *upalakṣaṇa* from *viśeṣaṇa* according to Murāri.

5.8. *THE CONCEPT OF SENTENCE-UNITY*

In this section we are going to discuss what Murāri has to say about the concept of sentence-unity, and how the sentence-unity is achieved. The discussion about sentence unity appears in the context of the establishment of the authoritativeness of the *arthavādas* in Murāri's texts. The *pūrvapakṣin* argues that the *arthavādas* are merely the narrative sentences and they do not convey any action to be undertaken. And therefore, they are not fit to get construed with the *vidhis* i.e. injunctions that express *kārya* or an action to be undertaken. But the fact is this that unless the *arthavādas* are connected with the *vidhis* it cannot be established that they are authoritative. Now the question arises how to connect them. Here comes the discussion on the concept of *ekavākyatā* according to the *PM*.

Now, before we examine what Murāri has to say about this, let us, first, see what Jaimini has to say on this issue. Jaimini has defined a single sentence in the context of fixing the extent of *Yajurmantra* in his *sutra* 2,1.46 which runs as follows : '*Arthaikatvād ekam vākyam sākāṅkṣam ced vibhāge syāt*'.

Tr.

If it were a case that (an expression or expressions) serve a single purpose (or that it expresses a single composite meaning) and if it were a case that on separation of any constituent of the expressions the separated constituents become expectant of each other (i.e. they cannot express one composite meaning any more), then that expression or those expressions can be said to form sentence-unity or a single sentence.

Let us consider the following example, so that the context will become clear : In the context of the *Darśapūrṇamāsa* sacrifices there occur the following expressions : '*Devasya tvā savituḥ prasave-asvinor bāhūbhyām puṣṇo hastābhyāṁ-agnaye juṣṭam nirvapāmi*[230]. Now, here, we can clearly observe that there are four parts of the expressions or *mantras*. As a matter of fact, each part could be taken as a separate sentence or *mantra*. But if we think of the conditions laid down in Jaimini's definition given above regarding the extent of a single sentence, we realise that if we take any of the four parts of the *mantra* mentioned above separately, it will be expectant of something to express its meaning fully. To demonstrate, let us take the first part separately and see. The first part is '*Devasya tvā savituḥ prasave*' Does this part of the sentence express any complete meaning ? The answer is, 'no'. Obviously because, there is no verb in this sentence (if at all we want to call it a sentence) and so, it cannot express any idea by itself. One can easily observe the same position in the case of the other three parts also.

But, on the other hand, if we take all the four parts together, they do express one single idea, namely, 'I measure the grains for Agni by the arms of Aśvins and the hands of Puṣan'.

Thus, the conditions stated in *JS.* 2.1.46 help to decide the extent or unit of a single sentence. And accordingly the *nirvāpa* is performed by reciting the whole *mantra.*

Now let us see some other cases which are different from the above case. In the above-mentioned *mantra* there was only one verb. But, there are some expressions which contain more than one verb. Even then they are not fully independent or inexpectant so far as their meanings or purposes are concerned. Though they have independent verbal forms, they do expect something to make their meanings fully complete.

Let us take an example and see : There is one injunction, '*Agnihotram juhuyāt svargakāmaḥ*' and there is another one, '*Dadhnā juhoti*'. Now, both these sentences have separate verbal forms and they are also capable of expressing some action to be undertaken. Still, they have an expectancy of each other. Because even if the first sentence makes one know about the action to be performed, he does not know after reading this sentence how and with what he should perform the same. On the other hand, when one reads only the second sentence he knows that he has to offer curds in the sacrifice but here, he does not understand what the main sacrifice is for which he has to offer the oblation of curds and for what purpose.

Thus, these two sentences, read separatelv, do not make much sense. But if they are read together as a single expression or sentence they will express a complete meaning. Thus, in this case, these two sentences are required to get connected with each other so that a complete meaning is understood from them.

Now let us see still another case where there are different verbal forms but all of them are not injunctive forms, as in the preceding case. In such cases also it is necessary to unite the two or more sentences as a single sentence for understanding a consistent and complete meaning from them.

There is one group of *arthavāda-sentences*, namely, '*Vāyur vai kṣepiṣthā devatā*. . . etc. And there is another sentence which enjoins a sacrifice, namely, '*Vāyavyam śvetam ālabheta bhūtikāmaḥ*'. The first group of sentences here, contains all narrative sentences and they do not express any *kārya* or action to be performed. These sentences simply praise the deity *Vāyu,* which is the deity of the sacrifice to be undertaken as per the second sentence. Naturally, it has an expectancy towards some sentence that expresses an action which has *Vāyu* as its deity. And, on the other hand, the second sentence, namely, '*Vāyavyam śvetam ālabheta bhūtikāmaḥ*', has an expectancy of some praise that will produce an inclination in the mind of a man to take up the activity enjoined by it.

So, if these two sentences get connected, they will express a complete meaning that can lead to the inducement of a man to the activity enjoined by that injunctive sentence.

Now, here the question arises, how to connect these two sentences, namely, the *vidhi* and the *arthavāda*. This question arises because the *arthavāda*-sentences do not express any *kārya*-sense and because their meanings lose relevance for connection with the sense expressed by the *vidhi*. Naturally, to make the relation possible one has to discard the sentence-meaning of the *arthavāda* and in its place one has to accept some meaning which could be related to the meaning of *vidhi*. Naturally one has to resort to *lakṣaṇā*. But which *lakṣaṇā*, *padalakṣaṇā* or *vākya-lakṣaṇā* ?[231] Obviously, one should accept here *vākyalakṣaṇā* in order to discard the whole meaning of the *arthavāda*-sentences. Thus, by the *vākya-lakṣaṇā* the *arthavāda*-sentence will express *prāśastya* i.e. praise (of the *yāga* or sacrifice) which is just a word-meaning. In this way, the *arthavāda*-sentence is brought to the level of a word and then the *prāśastya* gets connected with the *vidhi*-sentence. And thus, the united sentence expresses the praised *yāga* that is to be performed.

So far we have seen two different cases where two sentences are connected. In one case, two sentences, both expressing *kārya*-sense, formed one single sentence. In the other case one sentence expressing *kārya* formed sentence-unity with the other being a narrative expression. In the first case the two sentences are fit to be related with each other since they are on the same level with reference to the meanings they convey and hence they are connected without any difficulty. This type of sentence-unity is called *vākyaikavākyatā* i.e. the unity of two sentences. In other words, when the expressed meanings of two independent sentences are fit to be united and when consequently get united the entire expressions of the two sentences are said to form one single sentence.

In the second case we saw that one sentence is an injunction whereas the other sentence is a narrative sentence and we also saw that the expressed meaning of the narrative sentence was not relevant to the meaning of the *vidhi* and hence to make it relevant the entire narrative expression was treated to convey 'praise' by *vākyalakṣaṇā* and later it was connected with the meaning of the injunctive sentence. This type of sentence-unity is called *padaika-vākyatā* i.e. unity of a sentence with a *pada.*

Here since the *arthavāda*-sentence conveyed mere 'praise' which is nothing more than a word-meaning it is, as if, the fact that the injunctive sentence is being united with another word (*pada*). Hence *padaikavākyatā.*

Thus, there are two types of sentence-unity accepted by the Mimamsakas, namely, the *vākyaikavākyatā* and the *padaikavākyatā.*

With this background let us now turn to Murāri and see what his concept is about these two types of sentence-unity.

Needless to say that when the verbal understandiug of the sentence—meanings from two sentences have *kārya* as their object and both the meanings are related with each other it is said that there is sentence-unity between the two sentences. Compare the following remarks from the *Arthavādādhikaraṇa*, '*Yatra dvayam evānvitābhidhānam kāryaviṣayam, dvayoś ca vākyārthayoḥ paras-parānvayaḥ, tatraikavākyatā yathā adhikārāṅgavākyayoḥ kāryā-bhidhānena vākyaparyavasānāt.*[232]......

Consider the following statement in the *Arthavādādhikaraṇa* :

Vākyaikavākyatā caivamanuvādavidhyuddeśayoḥ syāt syārtha-bodhe paryavasānāt.[233]

Here it is clearly stated that if the sentence meanings of the sentences which are to be united are significant those sentences can be said to form a single sentence.

Now observe the following statement from the same *Arthav-ādādhikaraṇa* :

Padārthapratītisthānīyatvād atropadeśavākyatā eva.[234]

Since the *prāśastya-jñāna* is nothing more than a knowledge of word-meaning there is sentence-unity called *upadeśavākyatā* or *padaikavākyatā* between the *arthavāda*-sentence and the injunctive sentence.

From these statements it is very clear that Murāri's concept of *vākvaikavākyatā* and *padaikavākyatā* does not differ from that of the established views of the other two schools of *PM*.

Let us see some more cases from the same *adhikaraṇa.* Here, one opponent makes a remark that the sentence-unity is possible only among words expressive of an action and the *kārakas* that help the action come into existence. And this is possible only on the basis of the case-endings that are expressive of the relations between the *kārakas* and the action. But in the present case of the *arthavādas* and the *vidhis*, however, there are two different and independent verbal forms governing two independent sets of *kārakas*, and so, these two cannot form one single sentence but they are explicitly two different sentences.[235]

On this, Murāri says that even if these are two different sentences, one having an injunctive verbal form and the other having a verbal form that expresses an already established thing or past action, they can form one single sentence. Because they can be construed with each other as expressive of *hetu* and *hetumat* i.e. a ground and that which requires that ground.[236]

To explain what he means by that Murāri gives the following example :

'*Malinam te vapuḥ vartate, snāyāḥ*'.[236]

'Your body is dirty, you should take bath'.

These are two different sentences having two different verbal forms. One expresses existence (*vartate*) and the other is an injunctive form of a verb namely (you) should take bath (*snāyāḥ*). Thus, the first sentence namely, 'your body is dirty' is the ground or reason (*hetu*) for the second sentence, 'you should take bath', (*hetumat*). So, according to Murāri any two sentences can form a single sentence provided the meanings of the two sentences are related by the relation of *hetu-hetumadbhāva*.

Thus, the condition laid down to form a single sentence is the causal relationship between the meanings of the two expressions to be united as a single expression.

In another place Murāri says that, *Naikapratīti-kāritvam ekavākyatāvadhāraṇahetuḥ kintu ekārthapratītiparatvam.*[237]

Here, Murāri talks about how the extent or unit of a single sentence is to be known or decided. He says that to decide that a particular expression or expressions constitute one single sentence, it is not necessary that it must cause one single verbal understanding but what is required is that it must stand for an understanding of one single composite meaning. Because, even if the sentence-meaning is not understood from an expression still the expression can be one single sentence. To illustrate Murāri gives an example of the sentences of a cheat (*vipralambhaka*). Now, from the sentence of a cheat one can never have an understanding of something real but still the sentence of a cheat is one single sentence.[238]

Murāri further argues that to determine the *ekavākyatā*, *yogyatā* or compatibility is also not a ground because, again, the sentences of a cheat inspite of their being incompatible, are understood as separate sentences, In other words, in each sentence, *ekavākyatā* is understood.

Thus, according to Murāri, *yogyatā* is a necessary condition with reference to getting the verbal understanding only but it is not so in the case of ascertaining the sentence-unity.

From all these stated and discussed above we conclude that Murāri too held the same notion of *vākyaikavākyatā* and *padaikavākyatā* as held by the other two schools of PM.[239] Nevertheless, Murāri has made better clarification of the idea by pointing out the ways and means by which the sentence-unity is determined. His discussion on the function of *yogyatā* is very much illuminating.

6

Conclusion

In this section we propose a brief survey of the main results of our study. We would like to highlight some of the points, both logical and philosophical, on which Murāri held his own opinion quite distinct from others. Similarly, we would also like to point out those well known philosophical concepts of Indian Philosophy which are known to him.

As we have already stated before, that our study has unavoidable limitations because of insufficient materials available to us. We had at our disposal only four *adhikaraṇas* of Murāri and the references to some of his doctrines made by various philosophico-logical texts. Naturally, the conclusions drawn here are not claimed to be final. There is every scope for revision if we succeed in discovering other works of Murāri. But till the contrary is found our reconstruction should continue to be valid.

Let us now first of all jot down the concepts Murāri either mentions or has made use of, from *PM* and from other systems of Indian Philosophy.

We have seen in the *Pramāṇa* Section (5.2) above that Murāri mentions the following *pramāṇas* :

(1) *Pratyakṣa*, (2) *anumāna*, (3) *śabda*, (4) *arthāpatti* and (5) *abhāva*. No reference is however found to *upamānapramāṇa*. These *pramāṇas* are conceived by him as the instruments of valid cognition. We may further add that Murāri mentions the word *pratyabhijñā* in his *Ekādaśādyādhikaraṇa*. He says :

> *Yadākhyātena kartuḥ saṅkhyā bodhitā tadā saiveyam saṅkhyeti pratyabhijñānāt kartṛparatā.*

Obviously, one can say from this expression that Murāri accepted the category of cognition called *pratyabhijñā* just as the Naiyāyikas accepted it.

So far the *anumāna* is concerned, Murāri uses almost all terms of the *anumānaprāmaṇa* such as, *pakṣa, hetu, sādhya, pratibandha (vyāpti)*, and so on. Murāri has given the full account of the process of the operation of the *parārthanumāna*. As a matter of fact his entire argument has the form of the *parārthānumāna*. He states the *pratijñā* which contains the mention of *pakṣa* and *sādhya* and then he writes the *hetu-vākya*. Then he examines whether the given reason is invariably concomitant with the *sādhya* or not. Eventually he also points out if the given *hetu* is fallacious or not. In this connection he uses the terms like *anaikāntika, vyabhicārin, bādhita* etc.

Murāri has used many technical terms relating to inference. They are, *pratijñā, hetu* etc. Another point worth-noting in this connection is that *parārthānumāna* consists of sentences (*avayavas*); still the knowledge generated by these sentences is not a verbal knowledge but it is an inferential cognition.

It is to be noted that Murāri refers to *pariśeṣānumāna* in his *Smṛtyadhikaraṇa*. He writes :

> *Pariśeṣānumānam idam* .... *Pariśeṣād jñānam avaśiṣṭam.*

It refers to the notion of *pariśeṣa* as given by Vātsyāyana in the *Nyāyasūtrabhāṣya*, namely,

> *Prasaktapratiṣedhe anyatrāprasaṅgāt śiṣyamāṇe sampratyayaḥ.*

Thus, it can be seen that Murāri is fully conversant with the entire technique of inference as proposed by the Naiyāyikas. Though we do not find any specific definitions of the terms it is very likely that Murāri must be using those terms in the sense already being used in.

As Murāri has given a full account of the process by which inferential cognition is generated he has also given the description how verbal understanding is generated. But we cannot reconstruct a fuller description of the epistemology of other types of cognitions.

Out of the *prameyas* Murāri directly mentions *dravya, guṇa, karaman, sāmānya* (*jāti*) and *abhāva* by name. If he accepted these five *prameyas* only then he is in full agreement with the Bhāṭṭas who too accept these five only. But we can say nothing with certainty at present because we have no access yet to the entire work of Murari.

No reference is found to the *premeyas* like *samavāya, śakti, saṅkhyā* or *sādṛśya* which are accepted by the Prābhākaras, or to *viśeṣa* as accepted by the Naiyāyikas. Therefore, for the time-being we can say that Murāri accepted five categories like the Bhāṭṭas.

6.1 : *Murāri's Contribution to Mīmāṁsā System*

The very fact that Murâri created a new school of thought among the Mīmāṁsakas is the greatest contribution to the system. He selected the Jaiminisūtras to discuss the main problems of the Mīmāṁsā system and presented his discussion in the *adhikaraṇa*-style. While composing each *adhikaraṇa* he has taken into account all the existing thoughts on a particular issue. This has enriched not only his discussion but the Mīmāṁsā system as a whole. We find references to even such authors and texts which are not available to-day. For instance he makes mention of the view of some Nandana in his *Mantrādhikaraṇa* and *Smṛtyadhikaraṇa*. But no text is handed down to us under the name of Nandana to-day. Likewise, he presents the interpretation of a l ne from the *ŚBh* by some commentator under the name *Tīkākṛt* in his *Ekādaśādyādhikaraṇa*. Śabara defines *tantra* as '*tantram nāma yat sakṛtkṛtam bahūnām upakaroti*'. Here, the *Tīkākṛt* thinks that this definition will over-apply to *prasaṅga* and hence he interpretes the line as *tantram nāma bhedena prāptau satyām sakṛdanuṣṭhānenārthasiddhiḥ*.

This line could not be traced in any existing literature on Mīmāṁsā. But it is obvious that there must have been some commentator on the *ŚBh*, whom Murāri has referred to here. The source of this information is Murāri only.

While examining the above interpretation of the *Tīkākṛt*, Murāri comments on the expression '*arthasiddhiḥ*' as follows :

> '*Siddhyati anena iti karaṇavyutpattyā kāryasādhanatayā prayājādiḥ uktaḥ. Na tu kāryasiddhir eva tantram iti uktiḥ bhāṣyavirodhāt.*

From this statament one can judge easily that Murāri does not want to go against the *ŚBh*.

As a matter of fact, Murāri wants to explain everything in consonance with the *Bhāṣya* unless it becomes obligatory on his part to go against it, because of some fundemental difference in the philosophical views of Murāri. For instance, in the sentence, *Vaiśvadevena yajeta* the term *vaiśvadeva* is treated as the name of a sacrifice in the *siddhānta*. But according to Murāri this term stands for the deity *Viśvedeva* and not for the sacrifice. This information could be gathered from the following statement of Vardhamāna in his *Prakāśa* on the *Jātiśaktivāda* of the *śabdakhaṇḍa* of the *TC* :

> *Viśvadevatātvāṅgīkartṛ-miśra-matam tu na siddhāntaḥ, uktayukteḥ iti nirgarvaḥ.*[240]

Likewise, Murāri has contributed to Mīmāṁsā by clarifying various Mīmāṁsā concepts namely, *Kiñcitkriyā*, *śruti*, *liṅga*, *pari-saṅkhyā* etc. He has also discussed, at times, the preference of these *aṅgabodhaka-pramāṇas*.

These are a few angles from which we should consider the contribution of Murāri to the Mīmāṁsa system.

6.2 : *Murāri's Contribution to Indian Philosophy*

In the preceding section we evolved our angles to look at the contribution of Murāri to the Mīmāṁsā system in particular. In this section we would try to identify Murāri's contribution to Indian philosophy in general. To achieve this, we would point out Murāri's independent views on philosophical and logical issues. Some of such issues are as follows :

(1) Murāri held quite a different view on the validity of knowledge. We have already seen in the previous section that according to Murāri, the validity of *vyavasāya* is known by *anuvyavasāya*.

(2) Regarding the theory of knowledge Murāri seems to have been influenced by the Naiyāyikas to the extent that a *vyavasāya* can be the object of *anuvyavasāya*. This position is not acceptable to the other two schools of *PM*. For the Prābhākaras *vyavasāya* becomes the object of *vyavasāya* itself and for the Bhāṭṭas *vyavasāya*

can never be an object of perceptual cognition. It is always an object of inference. Though Murāri differed from both the schools, still he maintained that the knowledge is self-valid and he differed from the Naiyāyikas too.

(3) On the concepts of *Viśeṣaṇa* and *Upalakṣaṇa* also we have seen that Murāri differs from all while defining the two concepts. He defines *viśeṣaṇa* as 'that which is connected (to *viśeṣya*) being a susidiary to an action' and *Upalakṣaṇa* as 'that which is connected but which is not subsidiary to an action', He needed such a definition of *upalakṣaṇa* to declare that *prāśastya* is related to the sacrifice as its *upalakṣaṇa*. This was indeed a new approach to the problem of relating the *arthavāda*–sentences with the injunctive sentences in order to achieve the validity of the narrative sentences of the *veda*.

(4) The Naiyāyikas hold that the absence of obstacle or impediment *pratibandhaka*) is a common cause to any effect. On this point too, Murāri maintains his distinct view. According to him, the absence of impediment should not be given the status of a cause when it can be treated as the delimitor of the state of being the cause (*karaṇatāvacchedaka*). And a delimitor of the state of being the cause is never a cause since it is redundant as a cause (*anyathāsiddha*). Hence, Murāri does not accept the absence of impediment as a cause of an effect.

(5) Murāri has contributed to Indian Philosophy in various ways. One such way is to clarify and define various concepts. As he attempted definitions for various concepts of the Mīmāṁsā system like *liṅga*, *kiñcitkriyā*, *tantra* and *āvāpa*, he also offered clearcut definitions of concepts like *kārya* (*sādhya*) and *siddha* which are basic concepts of Indian philosophy. He defines *kārya* as '*kṛtyanurañjanayogyam*', that which is fit to be associated with volition is *kārya* or *sādhya*'. Similarly, he defines *siddha* as 'that which is out side the sphere of that which is fit to be associated with volition'. That which is associated with the volition falls under two groups—(1) the performer of the action and (2) the object of the external activity of the performer. Anything which is neither (1) nor (2) will be treated as *siddha*. This notion of *kārya* and *siddha* of Murāri, should solve the problem of relating an already accomplished entity with a to be accomplished entity in a sentence-meaning.

(6) Another example of Murari's contribution by way of clarification of concepts would be his remarkable observation on the nature and function of the *parārthānumāna* and the *śabdapramāṇa.* Though *parārthānumāna* consists of sentences (*avayayas*), still it is not a *śabda-pramāṇa* as we have already pointed out. The *avayayas* of the *parārthānumāna* form a process by presenting *pakṣa, sādhya, hetu, vyāpti* and so on, the knowledge of the relationship of which ultimately results into an inferential cognition. Hence the *parārthānumāna* represents a process complex through which a particular knowledge comes into existence. Had the *parārthānumāna* not been different from the *śabdapramāṇa* the very *pratijñā-vākya* would have been enough to know the *sādhya,* Thus, the *pratijñāvākya, 'parvato vahnimān'* itself would have generated the inferential knowledge, the mountain has fire. The other sentences (*dhūmāt* etc.) would have become redundant and hence unnecessary. Therefore, Murāri categorically denies that these member-sentences of the *parārthānumāna* do not produce verbal understanding in the sense that the knowledge arising from them is produced by the *śabdapramāṇa.* The function of these sentences is simply to reveal the nature of *hetu, vyāpti* etc. and nothing more nothing less. This is indeed a very valuable comment of Murāri.

(7) If anyone simply reads just the beginning portions of Murāri's four available *adhikaraṇas* one gets an impression that Murāri's composition has a particular logical structure. At the beginning of each *adhikaraṇa* the foremost problem before Murāri is how to show the relevance (*saṅgati*) of the discussion of the subject matter of this *adhikaraṇa* with that of the immediately preceding *adhikaraṇa.* It implies that he wants to follow strictly the structure of an *adhikaraṇa* laid down by the tradition which consists of *viṣaya,* 'subject matter', *viśaya,* 'doubt or various alterative propositions', *pūrvapakṣa,* 'opponents view', *siddhānta,* 'conclusion' and *saṅgati,* 'propriety or relevance of the discussion'.[241]

Murāri has made his contribution on the form of *adhikaraṇa* also by proposing various ways how to achieve *saṅgati.*

These are some of the points which require special mention with regard to Murāri's contribution to Indian Philosophy.

Notes

1. Four more *adhyāyas* of *JS*, by the name *Sāṅkarṣa-Kāṇḍa* were published at Benares, 1894. Vide Pūrvamīmāṁsa in its sources of Ganganatha Jha, Benares Hindu University, 1964 pp. 10-11.
2. Khaṇḍadeva (17th Cen. A.D.) wrote *Bhāṭṭadīpikā, Mīmāṁsā-kaustubha* and *Bhāṭṭarahasya.*
3. Gāgābhaṭṭa (17th Cen. A.D.) wrote *Bhāṭṭacintāmaṇi.*
4. For a full account of the ancient authors and their works on both the schools see the annotated bibliography by Umeśa Miśra in the Pūrvamīmāṁsā in its sources ed—Benaras Hindu University, 1964, Appendix pp. 5.
5. Gaṅgeśa has referred to the view of Murāri on the validity of knowledge in the *Prāmāṇyavāda* of the *TC*. vide *TC* of Gaṅgesa, ed. N.S. Ramanuja Tatacarya, Kendriya Sanskrit Vidyapeeth, Tirupati, 1973, pp. 124.
6. Kusumāñjaliprakāśa of Vardhamāna, Kashi Sanskrit Series-30, Banares, 1957, p. 120.
7. Nyāyasiddhāntamuktāvali of Viśvanātha Pañcānana. The Kasi Sanskrit Series—212, Benares 1972, p. 435.
8. See Journal of Oriental Research, Madras Vol. II part III-IV, 1928 pp. 270-278.
9. See Annals of the Bhandarkar Oriental Research Institute, Pune, Vol. X, Part III-IV, 1929, pp. 238-243.
10. See Journal of Oriental Research, Madras, Vol. V Part III, 1931, pp. 1-8.
11. *Vide Murāreḥ Tṛtīyaḥ Panthāḥ* By Dr. Umeśa Miśra proceedings, Fifth All India Oriental Conference, Vol. II, 1930, Lahore, pp. 967-994.
12. The article referred to in 11.
13. The article referred to in 11.
14. Vide *Anargharāghava* of Mūrari, ed. Pdt. Durgaprasad and K.P. Parab, Nirnayasagar Press, Bombay, 1887, p. 15.
15. Vide Umeśa Miśra's article in the Proceedings, Fifth Indian Oriental Conference, Lahore, Vol II, 1930, p. 968.

16. ibid, p. 969.
17. ibid, p. 969.
18. ibid, p. 970.
19. ibid, p. 970.
20. ibid. p. 971.
21. This work has been published by Ānandāśrama, Pune. Vide : Ānandāśrama Sanskrit Granthḍvaliḥ, Granthāṅka— 137, 1973.
22. *Murārisaṁsevanaśuddhabuddhiḥ Kumārilaproktamatānusārī Murārirangatvaniruktimetam Karoti Saduktigaṇairupetam* *Aṅgatvaṇirukti* of Murāri Miśra. p. 1.
23. Vide Umeśa Miśra, p. 972.
24. We have already seen that these works are published in JORM, 1928, 1931 and ABORI 1929.
25. Vide Umeśa Miśra, p. 978.
26. Vide *Pūrvamīmāṁsā in its sources* of Ganganath Jha, Benares Hindu University, Benares, 1964, p. 20.
27. "This is a small independent work dealing with the *Tantrāvāpa* definition which forms part of the first *Adhyāya* of the Jaimini-Sūtra". Vide Umeśa Miśra, p. 975.
28. Vide *Arthavādādhikaraṇa*, *Mantrādhikaraṇa* and *Ekādaśādyādhikaraṇa* of Murāri Miśra.
29. *See Ekādaśādyādhikaraṇa* of Murāri Miśra.
30. *Vide Mantrādhikaraṇa* as well as *Smṛtyadhikaraṇa* of Murâri Miśra.
31. *See Mantrādhikaraṇa* and also *Smṛtyadhikaraṇa*.
32. ibid.
33. These works are not yet published.
34. In *TC*.
35. In *Nyaya-Kusumāñjaliprakāśa*.
36. In *Tattvacintāmaṇiprakāśa*.
37. In *Tarkāmṛta*.

38. In *Śaktivāda.*
39. In *Tarkasaṃgrahadīpikā.*
40. In *Nyāyasiddhāntamuktāvali*
41. In *Rāmarudrīyam on Tarkasṃgrahadīpikā.*
42. In *Bhāṭṭacintāmaṇi.*
43. In *Nyāyaśikhāmaṇi* on *Prakāśa* of Rucidattamiśra on *TC.*
44. For the relevant passages see the Section (4.2) References to Murāri.
45. To give an example, there is a *mantra*, '*Kadācana starīrasi nendra saścasi dāśuṣe*' which refers to Indra according to its meaning but the injunction, '*Aindryā gārhapatyam upatiṣṭhate*' employs it in the *gārhapatya-upasthāna* (i.e. praise of *Agni*) See *Arthasaṁgraha* p. 47.
46. To give an example, there is a *mantra*, '*uru prathā uru prathasva*' which reveals the same meaning as enjoined by the injunction '*iti puroḍāśam prathayati*' cf. *ŚBh* on *JS* 1.2.35.
47. See the *Mantrādhikaraṇa* of Murāri.
48. *Āpastamba-Mantrapāṭha*-2.20.27.
Pāraskara Gṛhyasūtra-3.2.2.
49. *Śeṣavannāma pariśeṣaḥ. Sa ca prasaktapratiṣedhe 'nyatrā-prasaṅgāt śiṣyamāṇe sampratyayaḥ*
—*Nyāyabhaṣya* on *Gautama-sūtra* 1.1.5.
50. i.e. *Āgneya. Upāmsu* and *Aindrāgna* in *Darśa*—and *Āgneya, Upāmsu* and *Agniṣomiya* in-*Pūrṇamāsa* sacrifice.
51. See *ŚBh* on *JS* 11.1.1.
52. *Yathā bahūnām brāhmaṇānām madhye kṛtaḥ pradīpāḥ. ŚBh* on *JS* 11.1.1.
53. *Tathā ca prayojanābhāvādanuṣṭhānāntaram na bhavati. Na tu saiva tantratā. Yata eva padārthasya ekam anuṣṭhānam anekār-tham tantratā. Ekādaśādyadhikaraṇa* of Murāri.
54. This commentator could not be identified.
55. Though brief summaries of Murāri's texts are added here in the presents work, I have a plan to study in detail all these *adhikaraṇas* separately later.

56. (i) *Atra bhāṣyam—tantram nāma "Yat sakṛtkṛtam bahūnām upakaroti."*
(ii) *Na tu kāryasiddhireva tantram ityuktiḥ bhāṣyavirodhāt*
(iii) *Bhāsye hi upakārakam eva, 'Sādhāraṇam tantram ityuktam', "bahūnām upakaroti" ityabhidhānāt : Ekādaśādyādhikaraṇa* of Murāri.

57. *Tasmādbhāṣyakṛdvacanādaṣṭakāsambandhaḥ api samākhyayā astīti kalpyate. Smṛtyadhikaraṇa of Murāri.*

58. *See Ekādaśādyādhikaraṇa. Arthavādādhikaraṇa* and *Mantrādhikaraṇa* of Murāri.

59. See *Arthavādādhikaraṇa* and *Mantrādhikaraṇa*

60. *Tathā ca prayājāditantratādhyāyānugatyā eva Pañjikāyām uktam. Ekādaśādyādhikaraṇa.*

61. See *Mantrādhikaraṇa* and *Smṛtyadhikaraṇa* from *Tripādinītinayana.*

62. See, *Nayaviveka* (*Arthavādādhikaraṇa*) of Bhavanātha Miśra, ed. S. Subrahmanya Shastri; Rashtriya Sanskrıt Samsthan, New Delhi, 1977, pp. 1-29.

63. *TC* of Gaṅgeśa (*Prāmāṇyavāda*) ed. N.S. Ramanuja Tatacharya, Kendriya Sanskrit Vidyapeeth Series No. 20, Tirupati, 1973 p. 124.

64. ibid, p. 124.

65. *Nyāyaśikhāmaṇi* on *Prakāśa* on *TC*. p. 125.

66. See *TC*. p. 166.

67. *Svāśrayagrāhakena ityādi. Idam tu Miśramate. Rahasya* of Mathurānatha, ed. Kāmākhyanatha Tarkavāgies, Bibliotheca Indica, 1974, p. 163.

68. See *Rahasya* of Mathuranatha, p. 185.

69. See *TC*. p. 166.

70. ibid. p. 166.

71. See *TC*. pp. 116-17.

72. See *Rahasya* of Mathurānātha p. 117.

73. See *TC*. p. 316.

74. See *Prakāśa* of Rucidatta on *TC*. p. 340.

75. ibid. pp. 340-41.
76. See *Rahasya* of Mathurānātha, p. 316.
77. *Nyāyakusumāñjali* of Udayanācārya ed. Padmaprasadopadhyaya and Dhundirajashastri, Kashi Sanskrit Granthamāla, 30, Benares, 1957, p. 120.
78. See TC. p. 189.
79. See *Prakāśa* on TC. p. 189.
80. See *Nyāyaśikhāmaṇi* on *Prakāśa on* TC. p. 189.
81. See *TC*. p. 510.
82. See *Rahasya* on TC. p. 479.
83. See *TC*. pp. 316-17.
84. See Rahasya on TC. p. 300.
85. See *TC*. p. 184.
86. See Rahasya on *TC*. p. 180.
87. *Prakāśa* on *Nyāyakusumāñjali* of Vardhamāna p. 220.
88. See Rahasya on TC. p. 151.
89. ibid. p. 157.
90. See *Rahasya* p. 173.
91. ibid, p. 183.
92. See *Rahasya* p. 297.
93. For other passages from *Rahasya* see *TC*. pp. 126. 140, 143, 144, 146, 151, 153, 154, 156, 158, 161, 165, 167, 187, 195, 204, 217, 219, 239 and 247-48 etc.
94. *Nyāyasiddhāntamañjari* of Janakinatha Bhattacharya — ed. Gaurinath Shastri, Calcutta, 1885. p. 355. For the full text see the same edition.
95. *Nyāyasiddhāntamuktāvali* with *Kiranāvali*, Chowkhamba Sanskrit Series, Varanasi, 1972, pp. 436-37.
96. *Prabhā* of Rāya Narasimha, on *Siddhāntamuktāvali* ed. S. Shankararama Shastri, Sri Balamanorama Series No. 6, Madras, 1923, p. 750.
97. *Tarkāmṛta* of Jagadīśa with *Vivṛti* commentary, the Asiatic Society, 1974, pp. 70-71.

98. *Tarkadīpika* on *Tarkasaṅgraha* of Annambhaṭṭa, ed. Satkari Sharma Vangiya Chowkhamba Sanskrit Series No. 187, Varanasi 1969 pp. 358-59.

99. On *Tarkadīpikā* on *Tarkasaṅgraha* of Annambhatta, ed. Satkāri Sharma Vangiya Chowkhamba Sanskrit Series No. 187, Varanasi 1969, p. 359.

100. On *Tarkadīpikā on Tarkasaṅgraha* of Annambhaṭṭa, ed. Satkari Sharma Vangiya Chowkhamba Sanskrit Series No. 187, Varanasi 1969. pp. 359-60.

101. *Bhāṭṭacintāmaṇi* of Gāgābhaṭṭa ed. Pt. Sūryanārāyana Śukla, Chowkhamba Sanskrit Granthamālā, No. 6, Varanasi, 1933, p. 14.

102. *Nyāyasūtram*, ed. Gaṅgānātha Jhā, Oriental Book Agency, Pune, 1939, p. 16.

103. See Section 4.2 of the Introduction, para. (g).

104. ibid, para (g. 1).

105. See Part II of this volume, Text 93.

106. See Umeśa Miśra (1930) p. 980.

107. *Mānameyodaya* of Narayana, ed. C. Kunhan Raja, The Adyar Library, Madras, 1975. p. 8.

108. *Prakaraṇapañcikā* of Śalikanātha Miśra ed. A. Subrahmanya Shastri, Benares Hindu University, 1961, p. 104.

109. See Part II of this volumc, Text 27.

110. ibid, Text 51.

111. ibid, Text 1.

112. *Mantrādhikaraṇa* of Murâri.

113. *Mānameyodaya* p. 9.

114. ibid. p. 9.

115. ibid. pp. 13-14.

116. *Prakaraṇapañcikā* p. 146.

117. *Sākṣātpratītiḥ pratyakṣam meya-mâtṛ-pramāsu sā* ibid, pp. 146-47.

118. See Ganganatha Jha (1964) p. 82. Also (1978) p. 33.

119. See Part II of this volume, Text 27.
120. See *Mānameyodaya*, p. 27.
121. ibid. p. 66.
122. See Ganganatha Jha, 1978, p. 49.
123. See Part II of this volume, Text 19.
124. ibid, Text 51.
125. Vide *Ekādaśādyādhikaraṇa* of Murāri.
126. See *Mānameyodaya* p. 93.
127. ibid, p. 105.
128. See Ganganatha Jha, 1978 p. 52.
129. ibid. p. 63.
130. ibid. p. 63.
131. She Part II of this volume, Text 51.
132. ibid, Text 93.
133. ibid, Text 67.
134. ibid, Text 65.
135. See *Mānameyodaya*, p. 110.
136. ibid, p. 120.
137. See Ganganatha Jha, 1978, p. 71.
138. ibid, p. 70.
139. See Part II of this volume, Text 35.
140. ibid, Text 52.
141. ibid, Text 53.
142. See *Ekādaśādyādhikaraṇa* of Murāri.
143. *Prābhākarāstu 'dṛṣṭaḥ śruto vā' iti Bhāṣyam laukikam abhidhānāntaram eva idam upalabdhivācanam iti varṇayantaḥ śrutārthāpattim pratyācakṣate. Nyāyamañjari* of Jayantabhaṭṭa ed. K.S, Vardācārya, Oriental Research Institute, Mysore, 1969, p. 124.
144. *Mānameyodaya*. p. 133.
145. See Ganganatha Jha, 1978, pp. 72-73
146. See *Smṛtyadhikaraṇa* of Murāri.

147. See *Mānameyodaya*, p. 151.

148. ibid, p. 244.

149. ibid, p. 282.

150. ibid, p. 289.

151. ibid, p. 298.

152. See Ganganatha Jha, 1978, pp. 88-89.

153. ibid. pp. 92-93.

154. See *Tantrarahasya* of Ramanujacarya, ed. R. Shama Shastri, Oriental Institute, Baroda, 1956, p. 18.

155. See Ganganatha Jha, 1978, p. 91.

156. ibid, p. 95.

157. ibid, p. 92.

158. ibid. p. 89.

159. ibid. pp, 89-90.

160. ibid. p. 90.

161. See Part II of this volume, Text 79.

162. See, Introduction of this volume section (4.2), para (d)

163. ibid, section (4.2), para (e)

164. See section (5.2) of the Introduction 'Validity of knowledge'.

165. *Katham punaḥ prāmāṇyasya svataḥ prāptiḥ ? Tadarthamidam sarvajñānāni adhikṛtya cintyate kim prāmāṇyam aprāmāṇyam ca ubhayam svata eva avagamyate ? Sastradipika*, Chowkhamba Sanskrit series. No. 188 p. 54.

166. *Athavā anyatarad api svabhāvena anirūpitam Kāraṇagunadoṣa-pratyayābhyām avagamyate ?* ibid p. 54.

167. *Āhosvid aprāmāṇyam svatovagamvate prāmāṇyam tu kāraṇa-guṇajñānat saṁvādajñānād arthakriyājñānād vā avadhāryate ?* ibid p. 54.

168. *Uta prāmāṇyam svataḥ prāptam sad artha anyathātva-kāraṇado-ṣajñanābhyām avagamya-mānena aprāmāṇyena apodyate* iti ? ibid p. 54.

169. *Svatogrāhyam iti. Jñānagrāhakasāmagrī-anya-grahaviṣaya ityarthaḥ* ! *Nilakanthaprakasika* (comm on *Tarkadipika*) The Kashi Sanskrit series 187. p. 358.

170. *Aprakāśasvabhāvāni 'meyāni, māta ca prakāśam apekṣyantām. Prakāśastu prakāśātmakatvāt nānyam apekṣyate.* Prakarana *Panika*, Banaras Hindu University Darsana Series No. 4. p. 172.

Also :—*Svata eva yad upapadyate, na tatra parāpekṣā yuktā. Meyānām mātuś ca svayam prakāśo nopapadyate iti yuktā tayoḥ parāpekṣā. Mitau ca kācid anupapattir nāsti iti svayamprakāśā eva mitiḥ.* ibid p. 173.

171. *Prābhākara—Mīmāṁsakāstu sarvadā jñānam utpadyamānam viṣayātmānau prakāśayadeva prakāśate dīpavat iti vadantaḥ saviṣayaka-vijñāna—svaprakāśatām manyante.* ibid. p. 172. See footnote by A. Subrahmanya Sastri.

172. *Tatra gurunaye jñānam svaprakāśam iti vyavasāyajanaka-sāmagryā eva vyavasāyo gṛhyate. Tathā ca ayam ghaṭa iti jānāmi ityeva vyavasāyaḥ. Na tu Kevalam ayam ghaṭa iti. Rāmarudrīyam* on *Tarkadīpikā*. Kashi Sanskrit Series 187. p. 359.

173. *Ghaṭaḥ ghaṭatvavad-viśeṣyaka ghaṭatva-prakāraka-jñānaviṣayaḥ. Ghaṭatvaprakāraka-jñātatāvatvāt. Nilakaṇṭhaprakāśikā* on *Tarkadīpikā*. p. 360.

174. *Svataḥ sarvapramāṇānām prāmāṇyam iti gṛhyatām. Ślokavārtika* Madras University Sanskrit Series p. 48.

175. *Svottaravarti-svaviṣayaka-laukikapratyakṣasya svaniṣṭhaprāmā-ṇyaviṣayakatayā svajanya-svaviṣayakapratyakṣasāmargī svaniṣ-ṭhaprāmāṇvaṇiścāyikā iti Miśrāh. Rahasya on TC.* Bibliotheca Indica : A collection of Oriental works. p. 126.

176. Vide *TC*, pp. 121-122.

177. *Nanu sāmagryām yāvatvaviśeṣaṇam ayuktam, yāvatsāmagrījanya-graha-aprasiddheḥ. Na hi sarvābhir jñānasāmagrībhir ekam jñānam janyate.* Nilakanthaprakāśikā on *Tarkadipikā* pp. 360-61.

178. *Idam jñanam pramā, saphalapravṛtti-janakatvāt.*

179. *Anumānādi-grāhyatvena siddhasādhanatvavāraṇāya yāvaditi. Tarkadipika.* Pp. 359-60.

180. *Tasmād jñāne prāmāṇyam anumeyam. Tathā hi, idam jñānam pramā. Samvādi-pravṛtti-janakatvāt. Yanna evam tanna evam, yathā apramā. Siddhāntamuktāvali.* Kashi Sanskrit Series 212 p. 438.

181. *Vyavasāyarūpā sāmagryeva tanmate jñānagrāhikā. Tanniṣṭham ghaṭaviśeṣyakaghaṭatva-prakārakatvam api tadgrāhyameva iti guravaḥ. Rāmarudrīyam* on *Tarkadipika.* p. 359.

182. Vide foot-note 173 above.

183. *Jñātatāliṅgakānumitirūpa eya etanmate grahaḥ. Tajjanikā ca sāmagrī parāmarśādighaṭitā, Tadgrāhyameva vyavasāyaniṣṭha-prāmāṇyam, iti Bhāṭṭāḥ. Rāmarudriyam* on *Tarkadipika,* p. 360.

184. *Indriyārthasannikarṣotpannam jñānam avyapadeśyam avyabhicāri vyavasāyātmakam, pratyakṣam. Nyāya-sūtra* 1.1.4.

185. *Miśramate tu anuvyavasāyagrāhyo vyavasāyah. Anuvyavasāyaśca vyavasāyapratyakṣam. Tajjanikā sāmagrī manas saṁyukta-samavāyādighaṭitā. Tadgrāhyam eva vyavasāyanisṭha-prāmāṇyam iti miśrāḥ. Rāmarudriyam* on *Tarkadipikā* p, 360.

186. See the section 'References to Murāri' of the Introduction of this volume.

187. *Manasā eva jñāna-svarūpavat tat-prāmāṇyagrahaḥ iti Murāri Miśrāḥ.* Vardhamāna's *Prakāśa* on *Kusumāñjali prakaraṇa.* p. 219.

Quoted by Umesa Misra. Proceedings. Fifth All India Oriental Conference, II. p. 986.

188. This is an independent commentary on the *JS* 1.2.1, 1.2.31 & 1.3.1.

189. For the elaborate discussion on this issue one may refer to an article, 'Adjectives and Substantives as a single class in the 'parts of speech' by Dr. S.D. Joshi.

190. *Na hi apratīte viśeṣaṇe viśiṣṭam kecana pratyetum arhanti. Sābarabhāsya* on JS. 1.3.33. Edn, Anandasrama Sanskrit Granthavali No. 97 pp. 247-48.

191. Vide *ŚBh* on *JS* 1.3.33, ibid p. 265.

192. Vide *Tantravārtika* on *ŚBh* on *JS* 1.3.33 ibid p. 265.

193. Vide *Tantravārtika* on *ŚBh* on *JS* 1.3.33 ibid p. 256.

194. Vide Bṛhatī of Prabhākara. edn. Madras University Sanskrit series No. 24, 1962, p. 165.
195. ibid p. 165.
196. ibid p. 165.
197. *Ṛjuvimalā* on *Bṛhatī* ibid p. 156.
198. Bṛhatī p. 166.
199. ibid p. 169.
200. ibid, p. 164.
201. *Nāgṛhītaviśeṣaṇā viśiṣṭe buddhiḥ*, ibid p. 173.
202. This work is referred to by Murāri very often.
203. Vide *Mīmāṁsānayaviveka*. edn. Rastriya Sanskrit Samsthanam. 1977 p. 156.
204. *Dharmāntareṇa vyāvṛttatayā dhīsthe dharmiṇi dharmāntaram pratīyamānam upalakṣaṇam* ibid p. 156.
205. i e. that of *daṇḍī puruṣaḥ*, as explained above, ibid p. 157.
206. Vide *Kiraṇāvalī*. edn. Gaekwad's Oriental series No. 154 p. 130.
207. The process is given as follows : *apekṣābudhi→dvitvotpatti→ dvitvatva—dvitva viṣayaka-nirvikalpaka→dvitvasavikalpaka→ dvitva—viśiṣṭa—dravya—savikalpaka.* Vide *Vaiśesika upaskāra*, edn. Haridas Sanskrit Granthamalā Vaisesika vibhaga—3, No. 1, 1923 p. 176.
208. *Viśeṣanam hi viśiṣṭa-jñāna-kāraṇam na tu viṣayaḥ.* Vide *Kiraṇāvalī.* p. 130.
209. *Tathā ca viśiṣṭa-jñānotpattikāle 'sato' pi pūrvabhāvinaḥ tattvama-virduddham.* ibid p. 130.
210. ibid, p. 130.
211. ibid, p. 130.
212. ibid, p. 130.
213. Vide *Saptapadārthī* edn. Theosophical Publishing House, Adyar, Madras, 1932. pp. 149-150.
214. The influence of Grammar is quite apparent on this interpretation of Sivāditya Miśra.

215. ibid, p. 149.

216. ibid, p. 150.

217. These examples are offered by the commentator. ibid., p, 149 .

218. *Nāpi viśeṣya-samāna-vibhaktikatvam viśeṣaṇatvam. Kākavad Devadattagṛhamityādau upalakṣane' pi gatatvāt.* Vide *TC* edn. Kendriya Sanskrit Vidyapith Granthamala, No. 20, 1973, p. 870.

219. *Ghaṭaḥ paṭaḥ ityabhidhānāt tayorapi anyonyaviśeṣaṇatāpāta ityapi bodhyam*, ibid. p. 870.

220. *pratyāyya-vyāvṛtty adhikaraṇatā puruṣasya daṇḍena avacchidyate na puruṣatvena, ativyāpteḥ*, ibid, pp. 874-875.

221. *Upalakṣaṇe tu gṛhatāpasādiniṣṭha prattyāyya-vyāvṛtty adhikaraṇatā na kākajaṭādibhir-avacchidyate, tadabhāvavaty-api vyāvṛttipratīteḥ*, ibid, p. 875.

222. *Evan ca pratyāyya-vyāvṛtty-adhikaraṇatā avacchedakatve sati vyāvartakam viśeṣaṇam, tadanyavyāvartakam upalakṣaṇam*, ibid, p. 875.

223. Vide *Vyutpattivāda* edn. Chowkhamba Sanskrit Series Office. 1933. p. 233.

224. *Viśeṣaṇasya sambandhaḥ matubādibhiḥ prattyāyyate*, ibid p. 234.

225. ibid, p. 234.

226. Vide *Upaskāra* p. 177.

227. Vide *Arthavādādhikaraṇa* of *Tripādīnītinayanam* of Murāri. Published in JORM 1928.

228. ibid.

229. ibid.

230. TS. 1.1.4.

231. *Padam iva vākyam api lakṣakam Nyāyakoṣa* pp. 694-695.

232. See Part II of this volume, Text 89.

233. ibid, Text 86.

234. ibid, Text 87.

235. ibid, Text 44.

236. ibid, Text 45.
237. ibid, Text 65.
238. ibid, Text 65.
239. Mādhavācārya, however, in his *Jaiminīyanyāyamālāvistara* says that there is *vākyaikavākyatā* between the *vidhi* and the *arthavāda*. See *Jaiminīyanyāyamlavāvistara* of Mādhavacārya, ed. Jivananda Vidya Sagar, Calcutta, 1883, p. 27.
   Also see 'On the Mīmāṁsā Doctrine of Ekavākyatā' by P.D. Navathe, Proceedings of the Winter Institute, on Ancient Indian Theories on Sentence-meaning, Poona University, 1980, pp. 189-193.
240. Ed. Bibliotheca Indica p. 704.
241. *Viṣayo viśayaś caiva*
   Pūrvapakṣas tathottaram l
   Nirṇayaś ceti pañcāṅgam
   Śāstre, dhikaraṇam smṛtam ll

PART II

Introduction

The *Arthavādādhikaraṇa* is written in the *adhikaraṇa*-style. The entire discussion is presented in a dialogue form. Hence I have split the Sanskrit text into a number of paragraphs, as per the dialogue so that the arguments become clear. The Sanskrit text is followed by the English translation which is followed by elaborate notes. The translation is not a word-to-word translation but a free translation.

While translating I had to introduce, at some places, some amendations to the Sanskrit text without which the text did not become clear.

To be frank, the translation and explanation presented here are my own interpretations of the texts as I understood them. I do not claim that my interpretation is final. It is indeed open for revision. However, I have seen that whatever interpretation I have presented here does have cogency in the discussion and hence I carried out my translation in the way I have given it here.

While fixing the reading of the text I have mostly accepted the suggestions made by the editor S.K. Ramanath Sastri. However, some additional corrections of the text became obligatory and hence, I have introduced the following amendations in the text. Without these amendations the text does not give cogent meaning.

	Printed Text	*Amended Text*
(1)	*Na cātītasya ca odanādeḥ vartamānasya ca vāyukṣepiṣṭhatvādeḥ*	*Na cātītasya ca rodanādeḥ* . . . . . (See Text 14).
(2)	. . . . . . *Sarvasya vedasya prayojanavadarthaparatvāpādānāt*	. . . . *prayojanavadattha-paratvāpādanāt* . . . . (See Text 15).

(3)	. . . . *siddhasiddhārthasādhyārthānvayayoḥ*	*Siddhārthasādhyārthānvayayoḥ* . . . . (See Text 45).
(4)	. . . . *siddhante prāśastyopanayapadānām*	. . . . *prāśastyopanayaḥ padānām* . . . . . . (See Text 65).
(5)	. . . *Upalakṣaṇam anyavyavacchedakam na bhavati*	. . . . *anyavyavacchedakam bhavati.* (See Text 77).
(6)	*Na ca lākṣaṇikatvād anuvādānām nābhidhānāparyavasānam*	. . . . . *nābhidhānaparyavasānam* (See Text 80).
(7)	. . . . . *tātparyāparyavasānam tu tatra* . . .	. . . . *tātparyaparyavasānam* . . . . . . (See Text 81).
(8)	*Yadyākāṅkṣākalpane nānvitabhidhānam*	*Yadyākaṅkṣākalpanenānvitābhidhānam* . . . . (See Text 82).
(9)	. . . . *sa cānvayābhidhāne na*	. . . . *sa cānvayābhidhānena* . . . . . (See Text 86).
(10)	. . . . *vidhyuddeśanā ucyate*	. . . . . *vidhyuddeśena ubyate* . . . . . (Text 93).

॥ त्रिपादीनीतिनयनम् ॥

मुरारिमिश्रप्रणीतम्

॥ अर्थवादाधिकरणम् ॥

॥ आम्नायस्य क्रियार्थत्वात् आनर्थक्यमतदर्थानां तस्मादनित्यमुच्यते ॥
(१. २. १.)

Text : 1

उक्तं कार्यमर्थं प्रतिपादयतो वेदस्य प्रामाण्यम् । न चार्थवादानां कार्यर्थिता, विधिना सहैकवाक्यत्वे प्रमाणाभावात् । तस्मादप्रामाण्यम् इति परेषां पूर्वपक्षः ।

Tr. *ARTHAVDĀDHIKARAṆAM*

It has already been stated that the Vedic sentences which convey an injunctive meaning are authoritative. And the *arthavādas* do not convey the injunctive meaning, because there is no ground to construe the *arthavādas* with the injunctions as a single sentence.

Thus, the Veda becomes inauthoritative. This is what others (i.e. Prabhākara Miśra) have stated in their *pūrvapakṣa*.

Notes

The whole vada is divided into five parts such as—(1) *Vidhi* (2) *mantra* (3) *nāmadheya* (4) *niṣedha* and (5) *arthavāda*. *Vidhis* are direct injunctions which induce a man into some action. They reveal some meaning which was not revealed by any other means before.[1]

Mantras are invocations to the deities which serve the purpose of reminding the *arthas* (i.e. the deities) at the time of sacrifice.[2] *Nāmadheyas* are the proper names of the sacrifices, by which the sacrifices are known.[3] *Niṣedhas* are prohibitions from some actions,[4] and *arthavādas* are merely narrative sentences which are aimed at either praising some action or decrying some action.[5]

In the first *pāda* of the First Chapter of *JS*, the authoritativeness of the *vidhis* i.e. the injunctive sentences, which convey, 'some action to be performed', has been established. Although unanimously it is accepted by both the prominent schools of *PM* namely the Bhāṭṭa as well as the Prābhākara that the *vidhis* are authoritative, still they have come to this conclusion on two different grounds. While the Bhattas say that a *vidhi* is authoritative because it is injunctive, Prabhakaras hold that a *vidhi* is authoritative since a *vidhi* expresses *kārya*.[6] Nonetheless both of them have a common ground namely, a *vidhi* involves an action to be performed.

The point that the opponent wants to make here is, the first *pāda* of the first chapter of *JS* has established a vedic sentence authoritative only when it conveys *kārya* (i.e. an action to be performed) and the *arthavādas* do not convey any such action. They convey only such things which are already established, and never induce a person into action. If it is argued that even-though the *arthavāda*—sentences are narrative sentences and even if they do not inform of any activity, they can be authoritative provided they are construed as the single sentence with the injunctive sentence, but the *arthavādas* cannot be construed with any injunctive sentence to form a sentence-unity,[7] for want of sufficient proof. Thus the objection remains that the *arthavādas* are inauthoritative, and since a part of the veda is inauthoritative, thereby the entire veda is inauthoritative.

Here, the opponent seems to be the follower of the Prabhakara School because it is that school which claims that *vidhis* express *kārya*. As a matter of fact, it is interesting to note that the very first sentence in the *Bṛhatī* on *ŚBh* on *JS* 1.2.1 is, *Uktam Kāryam artham pratipādayato vedasya prāmāṇyam*;[8] which is formed in the same form here in Murāri's text.

From the above discussion the following points imerge, which the opponent wants to emphasize :

(1) The Veda is authoritative because it expresses *kārya*.

(2) The *arthavādas* are narrative sentences and do not inform of any *kārya*.

(3) Since they do not convey any *kārya* they are not capable of being construed with the injunctive sentences by which the *arthavāda*—sentences also would have been treated as informing *kārya*.

(4) Since the *arthavādas* cannot be construed with the injunctive sentences they are not authoritative.

Text : 2

ननु तेषां सिद्धेऽपि व्युत्पत्तेः कथं कार्यार्थत्वम् एव ?

Tr. :

Well, some may raise a doubt here that, when the *arthavādas* are understood as having *siddha* meanings, how (do you say) only *kārya* meaning (is the basis of validity of the veda ? (i.e. how can this be an argument that the veda is *pramāṇa* only because it conveys *karya* meaning ? In other words, how do you say that *arthavādas* (should) convey *kārya* sense ?)

Notes :

Such a doubt can be raised even by the Naiyāyikas.

The word *siddha* means a thing which is already accomplished, and which is not to be accomplished i.e. which is not *sādhya*.

The word *kārya* is exactly opposite of the word *siddha*. It is something which is to be accomplished.

Text : 3

तत्राध्ययनविधिबलात्; सिद्धस्यार्थस्य निष्प्रयोजनत्वादिति केचित् ।

Tr. :

To this question some reply that, the *kāryarthatā* of the *arthavādas* is obtained on the strength of the *adhyayanavidhi* (i.e. the injunction which induces a person to study the entire veda), because otherwise a thing which is already accomplished has no purpose to serve.

Notes :

The argument is that in reality the *arthavadas* do not inform of any activity to be undertaken, and if the *kāryārthatā* of *arthavādas* is not obtained from any source then it will result into the purposelessness of the *arthavādas*, since no one will be prompted to undertake any action by the *arthavāda*—sentences, as they are just narrative sentences and not injunctive ones. In other words, one will be at a loss to know what should one do after knowing that, say '*Vayu* is the swiftest diety',[9] and the like. Naturally, purposelessness is the result. And if it is purposeless then no one will take the trouble to learn it by heart. Therefore, it is argued that the *svādhyāya-vidhi* makes the entire veda purposeful, of which the *arthavādas* form a part. How ? Let us see :

'*Svādhyāyo, dhyetavyaḥ*' is known as *svādhyāya-vidhi* which enjoins the learning of the veda as a whole. Now, no one will go to take up such a trouble unless the learning of the entire veda has some purpose because as it is well said by Kumārila that even a fool does not undertake any activity unless he is informed of the purpose of such activity. Moreover, the *vidhi*-form '*adhyetavyaḥ*' expresses that 'the learning of the entire veda is the means of one's desired goal (i.e. the knowledge of the meaning of the veda). Now, when the entire veda is purposeful in this way, and since the entire veda is meant for the performance of sacrifices (*Kārya*), it is but natural that the *arthavādas* are also meant for *kārya*. Thus, the *svādhyāya-vidhi* makes the *arthavādas* purposeful.

From the above discussion the following issues imerge :

(1) One need not think that the *arthavādas* are not authoritative because they inform only accomplished things and not the things which are to be accomplished like activity.

(2) Because the *arthavādas* too are meant for the activity, (sacrifice) on the strength of the *svādhyāya-vidhi*.

Text : 4

तदयुक्तं, तथा सति तद्बलादेव एकवाक्यत्वप्रसङ्गात् । तस्माद्धर्मे प्रामाण्यं सिद्धार्थतया न सम्भवति; तच्चिन्तनीयमित्यभिप्रायः ।

Tr. :

This is not a good answer. Because, had it been the case, then there would arise the contingency that, on the strength of the same *svādhyāya-vidhi* the unity of the *arthavāda*-sentences with the injunctions can also be formed.

Therefore, the statement that the *arthavādas* are not authoritative with reference to *Dharma* because they convey the meanings which are already accomplished, has to be reconsidered. This is what is intended (by the *pūrvapakṣa*).

Notes :

From this argument of Murāri it seems that he does not think that the unity of the *arthavādas* with the injunctions is achieved on the strength of *svādhyāya-vidhi* He observes that although it is true that the *svādhyāya-vidhi* makes the *arthavādas* purposeful, it does not mean that it makes the *arthavādas* expressive of *kārya*. Once it is accepted that the *arthavādas* are expressive of *kārya* on the strength of *svādhyāya-vidhi*, one can easily say that the same *vidhi* can cause the unity of the *arthavādas* with the injunctive sentences also, which is not a desirable proposition. Because mutual expectancy between the *arthavādas* and the injunctive sentences has been accepted as the ground for their unity. Thus, the stand of the *kecit* cannot be accepted.

Text : 4A.

कथमेकवाक्यताविरहः ?

Tr. :

(But a doubt arises in our mind that how do you say that) the sentence-unity (*ekavākyatā*) of the *arthavādas* and *vidhis* is not possible ?

Notes :

It has been argued in the *pūrvapakṣa* of *Prabhākara* that since there is no sentence-unity between the *arthavādas* and the *vidhis* because the *arthavādas* are not expressive of *kārya* and therefore the *arthavādas* are inauthoritative. Murāri wants to know why there can be no sentence-unity at all. In other words, he wants that Prabhakara must reveal his mind clearly why he does not think that there can be sentence-unity between them. The Prabhakara must give the ground for it.

Text : 5

कार्यस्य कार्येणैवान्वयात्, अर्थवादार्थस्य च सिद्धत्वात् ।

Tr. :

Because a *kārya* can be related to a *kārya* only, and the meaning of *arthavāda* however, is (not *kārya* but) *siddha.*

Notes :

Prabhakara reveals his mind here. He thinks that the meaning of an injunctive sentence is *kārya* and that of an *arthavāda* is *siddha.* He further thinks that a *kārya* should be related to another *kārya.* For instance, the *aṅgavidhis* are related to the *pradhāna-vidhi* because both are expressive of *kārya.* Thus, an *aṅgavidhi* can form sentence-unity with *pradhāna-vidhi* which is known as *viniyoga-vidhi.*

In other words, the *pradhāna-vidhi* enjoins a sacrifice for some results. But the sacrifice can be complete only when the subsediary rites are performed. Naturally, there is expectancy between them and hence there can be sentence-unity. But it is not the case with activity to be performed. Thus, there is no possibility of any sentence-unity between the *arthavādas* and *vidhis.*

Text : 6

कथं तर्हि नियोज्यान्वयः ? नियोज्यस्य अकार्यत्वात् ?

Tr. :

(If so then,) how a *niyojya* (i.e. a person who undertakes an action) is connected (with the injunctions i.e., the *karya* meanings conveyed by the injunctive suffix) ? Because, *niyojya* also is not a *kārya* (but it is an established entity i.e. *siddha*).

Notes :

Sentence-unity depends upon the relations among various meaning-elements coming from a sentence. The relations are understood in a verbal understanding arising from a sentence. Granting that a verbal understanding arises from an injunctive sentence only, it is not the fact that all the elements in a verbal understanding are only actions. Some are actions to be accomplished while some others are already accomplished or established. Yet the understanding takes place. But the under-standing cannot take place unless the action is related to rest of the elements. In the present context also, *niyojya* is a person who performs the *yāga*. Naturally he has to be connected with the *yāga* directly. Now a person is, no doubt, an established entity. And he is connected with the sacrifice which is the meaning of an injunction and which is yet to be accomplished by an action of the *niyojya* himself. Thus, in such cases it is seen that a *siddha* (*niyojya*) and a *kārya* (*yāga*) are related directly to each other. Therefore, the question is raised that why an *arthavāda* (the meaning of which is *siddha*) and an injunction (the meaning of which is *kārya*) cannot form a sentence-unity i.e. why they cannot be related to each other.

Text : 7

तत्र निरूढे नियोगे न सिद्धार्थान्वयः नियोज्यान्वयस्त्वनिरूढे एवार्थे इति केचित् ।

Tr. :

Here, some answer (may be the followers of Prabhakara), that, an established meaning is not connected with the established *niyoga* but it i.e. *niyojya* is connected with that which is not established (i.e. which is *sādhya*).

Notes :

Niyoga means *apūrva* (according to the Prabhakaras). *Apūrya* is the result produced by sacrifice. When a particular sacrifice is performed it produces *apūrva* (i.e. *puṇya*) as a link between the *yāga* and the *ultimate iṣṭa* i.e. heaven etc. *Apūrva* can be *siddha* or *sādhya*. It is *siddha* after the sacrifice is performed and it is *sādhya* when the sacrifice is being performed and before that also. *Niyojya* is connected directly with the *yāga* which is yet to be accomplished by his action and this *yāga* will produce the *niyoga*. A person performs a sacrifice and that produces *niyoga* i. e. *apūrva*. Thus a person (i.e. *niyojya*) is directly connected with an action and through *yāga* he is connected with *niyoga* which is yet to come.

Text : 8

तन्न, नियुंक्तितकत्वात् । तथाप्यर्थवादानाम् अनिरूढे एवान्वयोऽस्त्विति चोद्यानिवृत्तेः ।

Tr. :

This cannot be held since it lacks (good) reasoning. Because even if what you say is accepted, the objection that let the meaning of the *arthavādas* be related to *anirūḍha* (*asiddha* action) remains unanswered.

Notes :

The point is, if this is accepted that the *niyojya* (i.e. a *siddha* entity) is related to *kriyā* (which is not *siddha*)—then on the same ground one can say that let the meaning of *arthavāda* (which is *siddha*) be related to the *kārya* i.e. the meanings of injunctions which is not acceptable to the Prabhakaras. Moreover, the question, (why the *arthavādas* cannot form sentence-unity with the injunctions', remains unanswered. In other words, where the *niyojya* (i.e. a *siddha* entity) can be related, to the same, the meaning of the *arthavadas* can also be related.

Text : 9

अनिर्वाहकत्वादनिरूढ़िदशायां नान्वय इति चेत्

Tr. :

Well, since (the *arthavādas* are) not capable of serving any purpose to produce an action they cannot be related to (*kriyā*).

Notes

This is the answer to the question that how a *niyojya*, even if *siddha* gets connected to the *kriyā* i.e. *yāga*. The follower of the *Prabhakara* school argues that, *niyojya* although being *siddha*, is capable of helping in some way or the other to bring the action into existence. So it can be related to a *kārya* even if it is *siddha* but the *arthavādas* do not possess such a capability and therefore they simply cannot form a connection with the injunctions i.e. *kāryas*. Thus, even a *siddha* entity can be related to a *sādhya* one provided, the *siddha* brings about some effect in the *sādhya* In other words, the *siddha* must be a *kāraka*.

Text : 10

एवं तर्हि सिद्धत्वं न हेतुः स्यात् ।

Tr. :

If so then *siddhatva* (being an established thing) would not be the ground (for showing incapability on the part of the *arthavādas* for forming sentence-unity).

Notes

If the argument above has to be accepted then the ground (*hetu*) for the non-validity of the *arthavādas* with reference to Dharma, through the impossibility of their forming a sentence-unity with the injunctions, should not be *siddhatva*. In other words, one need not say that, because the *arthavādas* are *siddha* they cannot form sentence-unity with the injunctions and that is why *arthavādas* are not valid with reference to *Dharma*. In other words, some other ground namely *anirvāhakatva* and the like, should have been given to prove the absence of sentence-unity between the *arthavādas* and the *vidhis* and thereby the absence of their authoritativeness.

Text 11

तथापि निरूढिदशायामनन्वये सिद्धत्वं हेतुरितिचेत्,

Tr. :

Still (we can say that), with reference to the non-connection (of *arthavādas* i.e. the meanings of them) with the already effected *kriyā* (i.e. *nirūḍha* or *siddha*), the *hetu* is *siddhatva*.

Notes

The Prābhākara tries to clarify his position. Granting that I should have used the ground of *anirvāhakatva* to show the absence of sentence-unity between *arthvādas* and injunctions i e. *vidhis*, still, *siddhatva* can very well be the ground with reference to the relation of the *siddha* or already effected *kriyā* and it is not the ground to prove the inauthoritativeness of the *arthavādas* with reference to Dharma. In other words, he wants to say that a *siddha* cannot be connected with another *siddha* because it is *siddha*.

Text : 12

न; कालादेरप्यन्वयदर्शनात् ।

Tr. :

This cannot be acceptable (as well), because the connection of time etc. (which are *siddha*, with an action which is already effected) is observed (by all).

Notes

The Prābhākara said that a *siddha* cannot be related to another *siddha* entity. This is refuted here by showing the fact that a *siddha* is some times related to another *siddha*. For instance, Time is a *siddha* entity. As it is related to a future action, as it is related to a present action, so it is related to an action which is already effected. Thus we often see people using, '*Devadattaḥ pakṣyati*', '*Devadattaḥ pacati*' and '*Devadattaḥ a-pacat*'. In all these three situations time is related to the action of cooking. When the cooking is ready then also we say that *pākaḥ sampannaḥ*, where the time is related to the already effected cooking (*siddhapāka*). Thus, it cannot be maintained that a *siddha* is never related to another *siddha*.

Text : 13

तेषामपि क्रियान्वयेन साध्यता इति चेत्,

Tr. :

(As a matter of fact), these (*siddha* things i.e. time etc,) become *sādhya* when they come in contact with the *kriyā* (and hence our stand that a *siddha* cannot be related to another *siddha* remains intact).

Notes :

The implication in this argument is that a *siddha* object becomes *sādhya* when it comes in contact with *kriyā*. In that case, nothing prevents it from getting related to even such *kriyā* which is already effected. Because, in that case, both the entities which are to be related, do not remain *siddha*. Hence, the statement that a *siddha* cannot be related to another *siddha* remains unaffected claims the Prābhākara.

Text : 14

न; अन्योन्याश्रयापत्तेः क्रियान्वये साध्यता, साध्यत्वे च क्रियान्वय इति । तस्मादेवं वाच्यम् । कृत्यनुरञ्जनयोग्यं कार्यमत्राभिप्रेतम् । तच्च द्वयम् नियोज्यकोटिः विषयकोटिश्चेति । कोटिद्वयबहिर्भूतं सिद्धमभिप्रेतम् ।14A

Tr. :

No. If this accepted, then this will result into mutual dependency, namely; because of the connection with *kriyā*, *siddha* entities will become *sādhya* and after they have become *sādhya* they can be connected to *kriyā*. Therefore it should be said as follows : (actually), a *kārya* intended here is that which is fit to be associated with the volition (*kṛti*). That (*Kārya*) will fall under the category of either *niyojya* or under the category of *viṣaya* i.e. object (of *kṛti*).

And that which falls outside the field of these two is intended (to be known) as *siddha.*

Notes :

Mutual dependency is a fault in logical analysis. What is this fault? It is defined as, *svagraha-sāpekṣa—grahasāpekṣagrahaviṣayatvam anyonyāśrayatvam,*[10] i.e. if it is a case that the knowledge of 'A' depends upon the knowledge of 'B' and the knowledge of 'B' depends upon the knowledge of 'A', then it is said that there is mutual dependency between 'A' and 'B'.

Murāri points out that here too after the relation with the *kriyā* is known, something can be known as *sādhya*; and after that is known as *sādhya* then only the relation of that with the *kriyā* can be known. Hence, here is the case of mutual dependency. This is why Murāri says that let us first define in what sense the terms *kārya* and *siddha* are used here, so that ambiguity can be avoided.

Thus, *Kārya* or *Sādhya* is to be understood in the sense of '*Kṛtyanurañjanayogya*'. What does it mean ? It simply means that that which is fit to be related to the *kṛti* (i.e. volition of a person) is called *kārya* or *sādhya.* This may fall into two categories :

(1) The category of *nivojya* (*niyojyakoṭi*) and

(2) The category of *viṣaya* (*viṣayakoṭi*).

What is *niyojya* ? *Niyojya* is a person who is employed to undertake an action. It is interesting to note that by this definition of *kārya* Murāri has included a *niyojya* or a person who is *siddha* in true sense of the term, in the category of *sādhya* or *kārya.*

Now let us turn to the *viṣayakoṭi viṣaya* is an object of the action.

Since *kṛti* or volition exists in the person and since it is the person who takes up the activity, *kṛti* acts as a link between the person and the object of his volition.

Niyojya-Kṛti-Yāga

This is how *kārya* could be understood and in that case there will be no fault of mutual dependency as pointed out above.

Anything that is outside these two categories is to be called *Siddha.*

Text : 14A

न चातीतस्य च रोदनादेर्वर्तमानस्य च वायुक्षेपिष्ठत्वादेः कोटिद्वये योग्यता विद्यते इति नैकवाक्यत्वम् । इति ।

Tr. :

Neither the crying which occurred in the past, nor the present fastness of the deity *Vāyu* is fit to be included in either of these two categories (of *kārya*), and therefore there cannct be the sentence-unity (of the *arthavādas* with the injunctive sentences).

Notes :

It has been already made clear what a *sādhya* is and what a *siddha* is, and so there is no chance of any confusion now. It is clear that the fastness of the *Vāyu* which is true for all the three times or the weeping of the *Rudra* which occurred in the past can neither be a *niyojya* nor can it be the object of any action of the performer and that is why it cannot fall in the category of *sādhya*. And once it is decided that these are not *sādhya*, they cannot be connected with the *kārya*- sentences i.e. the injuuctions.

Text : 15

राद्धान्तस्तु—यद्यप्येकवाक्यता न प्रतीयते; तथाप्यध्ययनविधिना सर्वस्य वेदस्य प्रयोजनवदर्थपरत्वापादनादर्थवादानां तात्सिद्ध्यर्थं रूपभङ्गेनाप्येकवाक्यत्वं लक्षणयाङ्गीकर्तव्यं, विधेरपि इतिकर्तव्यतात्वेन प्राशस्त्यस्यापेक्षणादिति ।

Tr. :

The conslusion (of Prabhakara and his followers) is as follows :

Though there is no sentence-unity (between the injunctions and the *arthavādas*) apparently, even then, since the *svādhyāyavidhi* makes (the study of) the whole Veda purposeful because the whole Veda expresses the meaning which is purposeful (*kriyā*), (because it leads to heaven etc. and only a purposeful activity can be taken up by a person and not any purposeless activity) and in order to extend that purposefulness to the *arthavādas* too, one must accept the sentence-unity (of the *arthavādas* with the injunctions) even at the cost of changing their original form by resorting to secondary relation of words (*lakṣaṇā*). Moreover, the injunctions also require **some praise as an inducing factor.**

Notes :

As it has been already pointed out that the *pūrvapakṣa* which Murāri mentioned as *pareṣām* while initiating his discussion at the very beginning is the corresponding *pūrvapakṣa* of Prabhākara as attested in the *Bṛhati.* Similarly, the *rāddhānta* or conclusion given here by Murāri also corresponds to the *siddhānta* or conclusion of Prabhākara.[11] Thus, *rāddhāntastu* should be read here along with the word *pareṣām.* It is the style of Murāri that he has given both the *pūrvapakṣa* and *rāddhānta* of Prabhākara in the beginning and it will be seen later that he would point out that the construction of *pūrvapakṣa* as done by the opponent should not have been done so. Rather it should have been constructed as suggested by him.

Naturally, when Murāri does not find any logical frame in the opponent's *pūrvapakṣa,* he also does not find any logical deduction in the *siddhānta* of the opponent.

The opponent's conclusion makes the following points :

(1) Although the reality cannot be denied that there can be no sentence-unity of the *arthavāda* sentences with the injunctions if taken in their original form, still we should not forget that unless the *arthavādas* too have some purpose, they cannot be the object of study. The *adhyayana-vidhi* cannot induce any person unless what is studied has some purpose. It has been already discussed by the *Mīmāṃsakas* that one should study the entire veda on the ground of the *adhyayana-vidhi* because veda informs of some activity which leads the performer of that activity to the result mentioned in the vedic injunction.

(2) To achieve the purposefulness of the *arthavādas* one must try to form their sentence-unity with the injunctions. Otherwise, it is not possible to argue that they are purposeful.

(3) Once it is realised that without sentence-unity the *arthavādas* cannot be declared as purposeful one must achieve that even at the cost of bringing the sentences to the level of word by *lakṣaṇā.* But in any case the sentence-unity must be achieved.

Text : 16

तदयुक्तं; एवं विचारे प्रतिज्ञातप्रामाण्यानाक्षेपत् पूर्वपक्षसङ्गतिर्न स्यात्।

Tr. :

This is not proper, Because if we discuss the matter in the way presented by the opponent (i.e. if the *pūrvapakṣa* and *siddhānta* are presented in the manner presented by Prabhakara then since the *pūrvapakṣa* of the opponent does not object to the proposition (of the previous *pāda*) namely, the authoritativeness of the injunctive sentences (*codanā*) of the Veda, the relevance of the *pūrvapakṣa* (of this *adhikaraṇa* with the conclusion of the earlier *adhikaraṇa*) cannot be established.

Notes :

Murāri does not agree with the *pūrvapakṣa* and the *siddhānta* of Prabhākara. He wants to reconstruct both the *pūrvapakṣa* and the *siddhānta* in a different way.

The reason for his not aceepting opponent's *pūrvapakṣa* is the non-relevance of the *pūrvapakṣa* of the opponent with the conclusion of the earlier chapter. The structure of the discussion in a shastric text follows certain frame-work. It is a normal structure that first of all, there will be a proposition on which there will be the *pūrvapakṣa* or objections which will be followed by the *siddhānta* or conclusion by refuting the grounds of the opponent. Now when a new chapter begins, again there will be a *pūrvapakṣa* and *siddhānta*. But, while framing the *pūrvapakṣa*, it is necessary, according to Murāri, that the link of this *pūrvapakṣa* should be shown with the *siddhānta* of the last chapter. Here too, Murāri wants that such a link should be shown by raising objection to the *siddhānta* of the last chapter. In the last chapter it was established that the injunctive sentences which form a part of the entire veda are authoritative. Thus, while beginning a new chapter that very conclusion should be questioned in framing the *pūrvapakṣa*. Otherwise, there can be no *adhikaraṇa—saṅgati* (the link between the *pūrvapakṣa* and the last *adhikaraṇa*).

The *pūrvapakṣa* of the opponent, however, frames the *pūrvapakṣa* by raising objection on the authoritativeness of the *arthavādas* taking it for granted that the authoritativeness of the entire veda was established by the previous chapter, which is not a fact.

Text : 17

ननु न प्रतिज्ञाक्षेपेण सर्वत्र सङ्गतिः; न हि ग्रहाधिकरणे, 'शेषः परार्थत्वात्' ३. १. २. इति प्रतिज्ञा निर्विषया भवति, एकग्रहशेषत्वेऽपि

संमार्गस्य प्रतिज्ञया अविरोधात् । सङ्गतिस्तु प्रतिज्ञाया निर्वाहे अपि—यद्विचार्यतया प्रतिज्ञातम्, तद्विचारे एवं भवति; प्रतिज्ञातश्चात्र वेदप्रामाण्य विचारः; अर्थवादा अपि वेदा एवेति कथमसङ्गतिः?

Tr. :

(The opponent argues), there is no such hard and fast rule that this relevance must be established only by objecting to the previous concluded proposition. (Contrary examples can be cited. For instance), in *grahādhikaraṇa* the proposition, *śeṣeḥ parārthatvāt'*, 'what is meant for others is auxiliary one' is not without any scope, because even if the cleansing (of the soma-cups) is auxiliary to one cup, there is no contradiction of the cleansing with the proposition.

The relevance between *pūrvapakṣa* and earlier *siddhānta* is possible even if there is scope for the application of the proposition through the discussion of the theme which was proposed to be discussed. Here, (i e. in the first *pāda*) what was proposed to be discussed was the discussion of the authoritativeness of the veda and the *arthavādas* are also the veda and so how (can you say that) there is no connection (between the opponent's *pūrvapakṣa* and the *siddhānta* of the last chapter) ?

Notes .

The opponent pointed out the defect in Murāri's argument. Had it been the case that everywhere the relevance of the following discussion is shown only by raising objection to the immediately preceding conclusion, then what Murāri says could have been accepted. But there is *vyabhicāra* to this rule. In spite of any such objection, the *pūrvapakṣa* is attested to be framed. For instance, the *JS* 3.1.2 concludes that, 'if 'X' is meant for 'Y', then 'X' is auxiliary or subsediary to 'Y''. This is the definition of *śeṣa* 'subsediary entity'. Now in a subsequent *adhikaraṇa* called *grahasammārjanādhikaraṇa* or *grahaikatvādhikaraṇa*, the *pūrvapakṣa* says that as in the sentence '*paśunā yajeta*', 'one should sacrifice with one animal,' number one is significant, similarly, in the injunction, '*Daśāpavitreṇa graham sammārṣṭi*', 'one should cleanse the soma-cup with washing cloth', the singular number in *graham* should be significant and as such one should cleanse only one soma-cup and not all. The *siddhāntin* concludes that the number in the subject (*uddeśya*) which is prominent is not significant. In *paśunā yajeta*, however, the animal is subordinate to the sacrifice. Hence, not only one cup should be cleansed, but all the cups should be cleansed.

Here if we give a close look to the *pūrvapakṣa*, we find that cleansing is meant for the cups and hence it is subordinate to the cup. In fact, this is what is known as *śeṣa* and so the proposition of Jaimini 3.1.2 is very much applicable to the cleansing even if the cleansing is done of only one cup. There is no contradiction, therefore, of the *pūrvapakṣa* with the proposition of jaimini 3.1.2. And still the *pūrvapakṣa* has been framed in the subsequent *adhikaraṇa* under Jaimini 3.1.13-15. So, it is not a necessary condition that *pūrvapakṣa* must contradict or object to the proposition. This is what the opponent wants to point out.

The opponent further points out that whether there is a link between the following *pūrvapakṣa* and the earlier proposition should be tested on the ground whether the topic of discussion in the earlier proposition is the topic of discussion in the following *pūrvapakṣa* or not. Nothing more nothing less. Thus, the authoritativeness of the veda was the topic of discussion in the earlier *adhikaraṇa*, the same is the theme of discussion in the following *pūrvapakṣa* since the *arthavādas* also are veda. Hence, there is no inconsistency.

Text : 18

एतमन्तरेणापि प्रतिज्ञासिद्धेः प्रतिज्ञायां नायमर्थवादसिद्धान्तहेतु सम्बन्धः स्यादिति चेत्,

Tr. :

(We say so) because even without this (argument about the *arthavādas*), the proposition can be proved (on the basis of the reason, not depending on anything else'). The reason which is given for the establishment of the validity of *arthavādas* cannot get connected with the original proposition.

Notes :

Murari argues that even if what the opponent says is accepted i.e. even if it is accepted that in framing a *pūrvapakṣa*, there is no obligatory rule that the conclusion of the earlier *pāda* has to be objected, still it remains a fact that there is no link or consistency of thought between the proposition, *codanālakṣano'rtho dharmaḥ* and the validity of the *arthavādas*. Because even without this discussion about the validity of *arthavādas* the earlier proposition is very well established on the ground of *nirapekṣatva*. (It has been already concluded in the earlier *pāda* that the injunctions are authoritative because they do not depend upon any other *pramāṇa* for their operation. They directly induce a man into action). And that is why we say that there is no link as such between the *hetu* to establish the authoritativeness of the *arthavādas* and the proposition.

Murari thinks that *codanālakṣaṇo'rtho dharmaḥ* is the main proposition and to call it valid, the validity of the injunctions has to be established. So, whatever discussion follows after this *sūtra* is in a way to support the validity of the injunctions. One ground has been already given in the earlier *pāda*, namely, 'not depending on any other *pramāṇa*', and this is a sufficient ground to declare the injunctions as valid. The discussion on the validity of the *arthavādas* has nothing to do with the main proposition.

Text : 19

न; अनुमानैकदेशभूता हि प्रतिज्ञा तत्साधकेन हेतुना सम्बध्यते; इह तु विचारस्य प्रतिज्ञासम्बन्धः सङ्गतिनिमित्तम्; सोऽपि च न हेतुत्व-लक्षणः किन्तु विषयरूपः, तेन प्रतिज्ञायाः प्रामाण्यविचारविषयत्वादस्ति प्रामाण्यविचारस्य प्रतिज्ञायां सङ्गतिः हेतुस्तु सिद्धान्तस्य सिद्धान्तेनैव सम्बध्यते न प्रतिज्ञया ।

Tr. :

What you say is not correct. Because the proposition which is a part of a five-member syllogism is always related to the reason (*hetu*) which establishes it. But here, the relation between the discussion and the proposition is the cause of the link (between the earlier *pāda* and the *pūrvapakṣa* of the present *pāda*) and that connection also is not of the nature of a reason (in the technical sense) but here the connection is of the nature of having one and the same topic for discussion. Since the (main) proposition proposes to discuss the validity of the veda there is a relation between the discussion of the authoritativeness of the *arthavādas* and the main proposition. The reason to establish some particular conclusion is to be connected with that particular conclusion and not with the main proposition.

Notes :

The opponent once again tries to show the link between the conclusion of the first *pāda* and the *pūrvapakṣa* presented by him. He clarifies his stand as follows :

Murari said in the earlier passage that there can be no relation with the discussion of the opponent's *pūrvapakṣa* and the main proposition. The opponent now points out that what Murari thinks is that for having a relation it is necessary to be a ground for the main proposition. But there is no such rule. The relation can be of various types. No doubt a *hetu* can also be a relation to a *pratijñā*, but that is possible only when one puts forth his argument in the form of a five-member syllogism.[12] There is no such *vyāpti* that wherever there is a relation it is a *hetu* to the *pratijñā*. Thus, as there can be a relation of *hetu*, there can also be a relation of 'having one and the same topic for discussion'. We can very easily say that 'A' and 'B' are related in the sense that both 'A' and 'B' have one and the same topic for discussion. Therefore, the relation between the *pūrvapakṣa* and the main *pratijñā* is of this type of 'A' and 'B' and not of the type of the *hetu* in a five-member syllogism.

In our present context also the main proposition proposed the discussion about the authoritativeness (of the Veda) and the *pūrvapakṣa* also discusses the authoritativeness (of the veda since *arthavādas* are also the veda) and thus there is a link between the proposition and this discussion.

Moreover, in each unit of an argument (five-member syllogism) a particular *hetu* is used and that *hetu* is related to the conclusion of that particular argument only and not with the proposition of another argument. Each unit of argument is independent as it were. Thus, the *hetu* of *pūrvapakṣa* will be related to the conclusion of the *pūrvapakṣa* and not with the conclusion of the *siddhānta*. Similarly, the *hetu* of the *siddhānta* is related to the conclusion of the *siddhānta* and not with the *pūrvapaksa*. From this point of view also there is no chance of relating, the *pūrvapakṣa* with the main proposition of the earlier chapter in the form of the five—member syllogism. Nevertheless, there is an indirect relation of the type of 'A' and 'B' stated above.

Text : *20*

स्यादेतदेवम् तर्हि 'तस्य निमित्तपरीष्टिः (१.१.३) इत्यध्यायप्रतिज्ञया सम्बन्धः स्यात् । चोदनासूत्रे (१.१.२) तु वस्तुप्रतिज्ञा, न तु विचार प्रतिज्ञा; तत् कथमिदमधिकरणं विनापि सिद्धन्त्या प्रतिज्ञया सङ्गतं स्यात् ?

Tr. :

If it were so, then (the discussion about the validity of the *arthavādas*) could be related to the proposition of the (first) chapter, namely, '*tasya nimittaparīṣṭiḥ* (i.e. the examination of the authoritativeness of it i.e.Dharma). Because in the *codanāsūtra* (i.e. Jaimini 1.1.2 : *Codanālaksaṇo'rtho Dharmaḥ*) what is statad or proposed is the mere object of discussion (or topic for discussion namely, *Dharma*) and this rule (1.1.2) does not propose to discuss the authoritativeness of the veda. That is why (we ask you) how this discussion about the *arthavādas* can be connected with the proposition (*codanālaksaṇo'rtho Dharmaḥ*) which has not been established yet ?

Notes :

Murāri argues, that if the stand of the opponent is accepted in toto for the purpose of discussion, then it will mean that the link of thought (between the following *pūrvapakṣa* and the earlier proposition) is proved on the strength of having the same topic for discussion. In that case, the *pūrvapakṣa* presented by the opponent can be connected at the most with the rule, *tasya nimittaparīṣṭiḥ*—because this rule proposes to discuss the authoritativeness (of *codanā* which is stated in the rule Jaimini 1.1.2). Thus this rule (*JS* 1.1.3) has the same topic for discussion as that of the *arthavādādhikarsṇa* which examines the authoritativeness of the veda. But in any case this *adhikaraṇa* cannot be connected with the rule 1.1.2 since that rule proposes only the object of discussion, and the discussion about the validity of that object does not come under the perview of that proposition. Therefore, our question remains as it is—that how can this *adhikaraṇa* (on the basis of the opponent's *purvāpaksa*) be relevant to a proposition which is yet to be established ?

According to this statement it becomes clear that for Murāri *JS* 1.1.2 states that object which is to be discussed in the *JS* and *JS* 1.1.3 begins to examine what could be the proof for *Dharma* defined in *JS* 1.1.2. All subsequent *sūtras* are in some way or the other to examine that proof for *Dharma* and in this sense only the relevance of the subsequent sūtras has to be shown. There is no relevance in showing any link of any discussion to the discussion of *JS* 1.1.2.

Text : *21*

मैवम्, तत्सम्बन्धस्य सङ्गत्यनुपयुक्तत्वात् । द्वादशाध्यायी च तया प्रतिज्ञया सम्बद्धा न तु प्रथमाध्यायमात्रम् । अतश्च तस्मिन् सूत्रे यावद् वक्ष्यमाणविशेषों धर्मश्चोदनात्मक सम्पूर्णवेदलक्षणक इति प्रतिज्ञा । तत्र यथेतरेषामध्यायानां सामान्यतो धर्मनाक्षेपेऽपि सम्बन्धः, तथास्यापि सामान्यतः चोदनाप्रामाण्यानाक्षेपेऽपि ।

Tr. :

You should not argue in th's way, because the connection (of the *arthavādādhikarṇa* with the rule, *tasya nimittaparīsṭiḥ* will serve no special purpose with reference to the relevance of the *pūrvapaksa* (presented by us). As a matter of fact all the twelve chapters (of the *JS*) are related to that proposition and not only the first chapter. Therefore, in the rule 1.1.2 what is proposed is the Dharma which is of the nature of having the characteristics that are to be narrated later (in the remaining chapters) and which has the entire veda in the form of *codanā*, as its authority or proof. To that proposition as all the chapters are related in a general way, even though, no objection is raised against *dharma* in these chapters, similarly, this *arthavādādhikaraṇa* can be related to this proposition in a general way, even if, the authoritativeness of the injuctions is not challenged.

Notes :

The opponent argues that the relation of this discussion about the *arthavādas* with the rule 1.1.3 will not serve any purpose with reference to the consistency of argument. Moreover, the proposition of *JS* 1.1.2 pervades the entire text of Jaimini and it is not restricted to only the first chapter. Again it is not the case that before constructing each *adhikaraṇa*, *Dharma* has been challenged and then only the *adhikaraṇa-siddhānta* has been reached. As a matter of fact it has not been done so. In spite of that the *adhikaraṇas* have been framed. But this does not mean that the discussion in the following chapters have no relevence to the main proposition whatsoever. In fact, there is relation in general on which the *adhikaraṇas* have been framed. Similarly, it cannot be made an obligatory rule that without objecting to the authoritativeness of the injunctive sentences one can not frame any *pūrvapakṣa* to discuss the authoritativeness of a portion of the veda, namely, the *arthavādas* in our present context.

Thus, even if there is no specific relation possible, the general relation itself would suffice to make the two discussions relevant.

Text : 22

स्यादेतत् यदि ‘तस्य निमित्तपरीष्टिः १. १. ३. इति सूत्रे प्रामाण्यमात्र प्रतिज्ञा स्यात् । किन्तु तच्छब्दस्य प्रकृतमात्रवाचित्वात् चोदनाप्रमाणकस्य धर्मस्य प्रकृतत्वात् तन्निमित्तचोदनाप्रामाण्यमेवाध्यायार्थतया प्रतिज्ञातमिति कथमचोदनात्मकस्यानुवादस्य चिन्ता सङ्गता स्यात् ?

Tr. :

What you say would have been true, if in the rule, '*tasya nimittaparīṣṭiḥ*', authoritativeness of the entire veda were proposed. But (in reality) the pronoun *tat* (in *tasya*) expresses that which has been just mentioned, and since what has been just mentioned (in the immediately proceding sutra *JS* 1.1.2) is *Dharma* which is based on the injunctive sentences, the authoritativeness of the injunctive sentences alone, which are the basis of that (*Dharma*) is proposed as the subject matter of the entire chapter. Therefore, (the question that), how can it be relevant to discuss the authoritativeness of *anuvāda* (i.e. *arthavāda*—) sentences which are of the nature of the non-injunction ?

Notes :

Murāri says—what the opponent intends to say would have been true if the rule 1.1.3 had proposed to examine the authoritativeness of the entire veda. Because, in that case, the discussion about the validity of the *arthavādas* would have been quite relevant since they also form one part of the veda. But such is not the case. The *JS* 1.1.3 does not propose to prove the authoritativeness of the entire veda. How ? Let us see : The *JS* 1.1.3 runs as—'*tasya nimittaparīṣṭiḥ*.' Here, the word 'tasya' in this rule is a derivative of the pronoun 'tat'. Murāri argues that a pronoun always refers to something which has just appeared before. (c.f. *sarvanāmnaḥ pūrvaparāmarśitvāt*').[13] Accordingly, in the present context what has appeared just before *JS* 1.1.3 ? It is *Dharma* expressed by an injunctive sentence (*codanā*) which has been just presented in *JS* 1.1.2. Therefore, the rule 1.1.3 proposes to examine the authority of *codanā* only referred to by the pronoun *tat*. Obviously, the *arthavādas* are not *codanā*. Hence the doubt is very apparent that how the discussion about the authoritativeness of the *arthavādas* can be relevant to or consistent with what has been proposed by the proposition ?

The crux of the problem is as follows : From above argument of Murāri it is clear that to him the word *codanā* in *JS* 1.1.2 means only injunctions or *vidhis* and not the entire veda and that is why he raises the objection mentioned above. Whereas Prabhakara has argued before by taking that *codanā* to stand for the entire *veda*—or all types of vedic sentences—including the *arthavādas* and that is why we find the difference of opinion between Prabhākara and Murāri about forming the *pūrvapaksa* to the *arthavādādhikaraṇa*.

Text 23

अस्यापि चोदनात्मत्वेन प्रामाण्यं व्युत्पाद्यमिति चेत्,

Tr. :

The authoritativeness of this (*anuvāda*-portion) also is to be established by transforming them as injunctions (by bringing about the sentence-unity with the injunctive sentences).

Notes :

To the objection of Murāri, now the opponent replies as follows : Accepting what you say we can maintain that our *pūrva-pakṣa* is proper. Because, what we are going to do is establishing the authoritativeness of the *arthavādas* which form the part of the veda. Because it is not proper to accept some part of the veda as inauthoritative and some part as authoritative. But we are not going to establish the authoritativeness of the *arthavādas* directly or independently, but first we would bring about the sentence-unity of these *arthavādas* with the *vidhis* and once they are united with the *vidhis* they also attain the character of an injunction and in that form they can be authoritative. So where is the defect in discussing the authoritativeness of the *arthavādas* ?

Text : 24

न; न व्युत्पाद्यवशात् सङ्गतिः, किन्तु विचार्यवशात्; विचार्यत्वं चोदनात्वे सतीति कथं सङ्गतिः स्यात् ?

Tr. :

No. (It is not correct). Relevance is not shown (by you) on the ground of the future establishment of the authoritativeness but on the ground of their being an object of discussion (regarding their authoritativeness). And such a discussion is possible only if the sentences are injunctive sentences. Therefore, how is the discussion of the *arthavādas* relevant (to the proposition) ?

Notes :

Murāri reacts to the opponent's clarification in the following manner : He points out to the opponent that the opponent is arguing about the relevance between the two discussions on the ground that the object of the proposition and that of the *arthavādādhikaraṇa* is one and the same namely, to establish the authoritativeness of the veda. In fact this is what the opponent has been maintaining from the very beginning. But while clarifying Murāri's objection the opponent provided another ground to show the relevance. This is not fair. Moreover, even if the clarified ground is taken to establish the relevance, it does not help at all—points out Murāri. Because what is proposed in *JS* 1.1.3 is not being discussed in the *arthavādādhikaraṇa*. The authoritativeness of *codanā* alone was proposed to be discussed in 1.1.3, whereas the authoritativeness of *arthavādas* is being discussed here in 1.2.1. Thus, different topics are being discussed in *JS* 1.1.3 and the *pūrvapaksa* of 1.2.1. Hence, there can be no relevance between the two. Thus, Murari cornered the opponent on the very ground the opponent tried to show the relevance.

Text : 25

नन्वेवमेकचोदनाप्रामाण्याक्षेपेऽपि इतराध्यायवत् सङ्गतिसिद्धिः किं सर्वाक्षेपेण ?

Tr. :

Well, then, even if the authoritativeness of a single injunctive sentence is objected to, (the discussion about the authoritativeness of the *arthavāda*—portion) can be related (to the main proposition) just as all the other chapters (are related to the proposition and thus), where is the need to object to (the authoritativeness of) all (the injunctive sentences in order to relate this section to the proposition) ?

Notes :

The opponent has raised a new point here. He says, even if it is accepted that it is necessary to object to the authoritativeness of *codanā*, which was the main theme of discussion in the previous *pāda*, we do not understand why you say that the authoritativeness of all the *codanās* is to be challenged. Because, even if the authority of one *codanā* is challenged it is sufficient to link up this section with the main proposition of the previous *pāda*.

To be more specific, in the *JS* 1.1.3 the authoritativeness of *codanā* was proposed to be examined. Accepting that the previous proposition must be challenged in framing a *pūrvapakṣa*, one can fulfill this condition by merely objecting to a single *codanā* and that is sufficient to maintain the rule of showing consistency of arguments. There is no need to raise objection to the authoritativeness of all the injunctive sentences.

Text : 26

सत्यम अतिप्रौदिस्तु सेति केचित् ।

Tr. :

What you say is true. But according to some, it will be too bold a step.

Note :

Actually, the point is well taken and the suggestion of the opponent is quite acceptable. But according to some people, it will be a very bold step. They think that since in the first *pāda* it is not proposed to examine the authoritativeness of any one or two *codanās* but of all *codanās*, it is necessary to object to the authoritativeness of the *codanās* in general and not only the authority of any one *codanā*. This is the proper norm and hence that is ought to be followed.

Text : 27

अन्ये तु—चोदनासूत्रे' को धर्मः (शा. भा. १. १. २) इत्येतस्मिन् प्रश्ने 'न प्रत्यक्षादिगम्यः किन्तु चोदनागम्यः इत्युक्ते 'तस्य निमित्त-परीष्टिः' १. १. ३. इति सूत्रेण प्रतिज्ञानिर्वाहोचितमेव प्रामाण्यं जिज्ञासितम्, न तु चोदनाप्रामाण्यमात्रम्, तन्निरपेक्षतया प्रामाण्यमात्रस्य अध्यायार्थतयाभिधानानुपपत्तेः 'अथातः शेषलक्षणम् (३. १. ३.) इति तु न प्रतिज्ञानन्तरमध्यायार्थप्रतिज्ञानम् इत्यतः शेषत्वमात्रमेवाध्यायार्थः, इह तु न तथा। ततश्च पूर्वपक्षेऽपि प्रतिज्ञायाः साधुत्वे कथं सङ्गतिरिति ।

Text : 27 A

न च—प्रथमे एवं पादेप्रामाण्यं व्युत्पाद्यम्; द्वितीये विध्यनुवाद-मन्त्राणामुपयोगकथनम् तृतीये तु स्मृतिप्रामाण्यं; चतुर्थे नामधेयोपयोग इति। ततश्चौदुम्बरमन्त्रानुवादाद्यधिकरणानां नासङ्गतिः इति वाच्यम् ।

Text : 27 B

तथा सत्येकाध्यायार्थत्वानुपपत्तेः। तस्मादेकवाक्यतयैव पूर्वपक्षः तथा सति साक्षाद् अङ्गद्वारा वा सर्वेषामनुवादैकवाक्यतया प्रामाण्याक्षेपात् प्रतिज्ञाया निर्विषयत्वेन असाधुत्वात्। यद्यपि किञ्चिन्निरनुवादकमपि वाक्यम्; तथाप्येकस्या अपि चोदनायाः प्रामाण्याक्षेपेण स्वभावसिद्धमेव शब्दस्याप्रामाण्य .... पौरुषेयत्वस्याप्यप्रामाण्यउपाधित्वव्या-भिचारादिति सर्वेषामेवाप्रामाण्यम् ।

Tr. : 27

But some others argue as follows : When a question is asked, what is referred to by 'dharma' in the *codanā-sūtra* (*JS* 1.1.2), the answer is given, 'that which is not known by perception etc. but which is known from injunctions only, (is Dharma). (And from this we conclude that) what was desired to be known by the rule, *tasya nimittaparīṣṭiḥ* (*JS* 1.1.3) was the authority of that part of the veda which is just mentioned in the proposition (*JS* 1.1.2) and not the authority of the whole veda. Because it is not proper to say that the discussion of the validity of the entire veda independent of the *codanā* is the subject matter of the first chapter. *Athātaḥ śesalaksaṇam*' (*JS* 3.1.3) however, does not forward any fresh proposition for the whole chapter, after the main proposition has been stated, and therefore, only the concept of *śesatva* (a property of being auxiliary to something) comes under the range of the discussion in this chapter, but such is not the case under discussion here. And hence, the proposition (here) remains valid in the *pūrvapaksa* also, then how (can one establish) the link (between the proposition and *pūrvapaksa*) ?

Tr. 27A

Neither can you argue as follows :

"In the first *pāda* alone the authority of the veda is discussed, in the second *pāda* the utility of *vidhi*, *anuvāda* and *mantras* is discussed, in the third *pāda* the authoritativeness of *smṛtis* is established and in the fourth *pāda* the purpose of *nāmadheyas* is thought out, and hence there is no inconsistency between the proposition and the following *adhikaraṇas* namely *audumbarā-dhikaraṇa*, *mantrādhikaraṇa*, *arthavādādhikaraṇa*. etc."

Tr. : 27B

Because, if this argument is accepted then their forming the subject matter of one chapter cannot be justified. And so (we say that) a *pūrvapaksa* should be formed on the basis of sentence-unity only.

If (the *pūrvapaksa* is framed) like this, since all (the injunctive sentences) are connected with the *anuvādas* either directly or indirectly the validity (of all the injunctive sentences) will become questionable and in that case the proposition will become faulty because it will lose its object itself. Even though there are some sentences (i.e. injunctive sentences) which are not at all connected with the *anuvādas*, still on the very ground that the authority of one single injunction is questioned, the whole veda automatically becomes inauthoritative. Not only that, even the *pauruṣeyatva* (i.e. the human authorship of the vedas) also cannot be maintained as the ground for inauthoritativeness (of the vedas) and thereby, each and every sentence of the veda is proved to be inauthoritative.

Notes : 27

Here some people (*anye*) take objection to the formation of *pūrvapaksa* by Prabhākara in a different way. He has given another ground for not accepting the *pūrvapaksa* of Prabhakara.

Firstly, he says, *JS* 1.1.2 (i.e. *codanālaksano'rtho Dharmaḥ*) proposes *Dharma* as being known from *codanā* i.e. injunctive sentences, only, and which is not known by any other means of knowing, namely, perception, inference etc. Therefore, when the rule '*tasya nimittaparīṣṭiḥ*' (*JS* 1.1.3) proposes to examine the authority of *Dharma* it must examine the authority of *codanās* only. Because, if the authority of *codanās* which is just proposed in the previous rule, is not discussed then examining the authority of remaining veda has no meaning. Moreover, it is not proper to discuss something which was not proposed to be discussed. What was proposed was the examination of the validity of *codanā* only, and if it is said that the discussion of the validity of the entire veda is the subject matter of the first chapter, it will be unfair, and therefore, there is no connection of the *pūrvapakṣa* of Prabhākara with the main proposition.

Another point is, this chapter should not be compared with the chapter III. Why ? Because, in case of Chapter III '*athātaḥ śesalaksaṇam*' is a main proposition. It is not a second proposition which states the purpose of the whole chapter. And therefore, only the concept of auxiliariness comes under the topic of discussion there. But here, such is not the case. Here the *JS* 1.1.2 is the main proposition whereas *JS* 1.1.3 states the purpose of the whole chapter, Hence it (1.1.3) must be consistent with the main proposition (i.e. 1.1.2). Now, the main proposition taks of *codanā* only, (i.e. not of the *arthavādas* etc. also). And therefore, the rule 1.1.3 must examine the authoritativeness of *codanā* only.

Now, (if this is accepted then), the proposition beomes valid to the *pūrvapakṣa* (of Prabhākara) also, since he accepts that *kārya* part of the veda is authoritative. And if so, i.e. if the proposition is quite valid and there is no objection to it by the *pūrvapakṣa*, the question arises how to link the two i.e. the proposition and this *arthavādādhikaraṇa* ?

Notes : 27A

The opponent (i.e. Prabhakara) may try to show that each *pāda* has a separate theme to discuss and hence it is not necessary to establish any link between the *pūrvapakṣa* of the *Arthavādādhikaraṇa* and the proposition of the previous *pāda*. According to him the first *pāda* discusses the authority of the veda only, the second *pāda* tries to establish the utility of *vidhis*, *mantras* and *anuvādas* in the third *pāda* the authoritativeness of *smṛtis* only has been established, and the fourth *pāda* establishes the purposefulness of the *nāmadheyas*. In this way each *pāda* has independent topic to discuss and thus there is no inconsistency between them because the question of the link does not arise at all. Therefore, all your attempt to link them is futile and unnecessary.

Notes : 27B

But this argument cannot be accepted because in that case the topics of the four *pādas* coming under one chapter cannot be justified unless there is mutual link among them.

In other words, if the four topics discussed in the four *pādas* are considered as independent and unconnected they cannot be included in one chapter. Unless there is *Adhyāya-saṅgati* they cannot be treated as forming the part of one and the same chapter. So, the suggestion of the arguer cannot stand logic. And that is why we have said that your argument cannot be held valid.

In order to overcome this difficulty and to form a good *pūrvapakṣa* there is only one way left and that is, to form the *pūrvapakṣa* by showing the sentence-unity of *vidhis* and *arthavādas*.

If the *pūrvapakṣa* is formed like this i.e. on the basis of the sentence-unity of the injunctions and the *arthavādas* then since the *arthavādas* also become the part and parcel of the injunctive sentence and since they are not expressive of *kārya*, there arises the contingency of declaring them inauthoritative. So one can very well object to the authority of injunctive sentence (*codanā*) itself of which the *arthavāda* forms one part and thence the consistency in the argument could very well be shown. So this would be the proper way to form a *pūrvapakṣa* according to our argument.

The arguers represented by *anye tu* point out to the further implications of his stand. He gives the reason why he wants to form the *pūrvapakṣa* by accepting the sentence-unity of the *arthavādas* with the *vidhis*. They think that by adopting the above suggestion the *arthavādas* would not remain isolated since they have become one with the *vidhis*. In that case, the authority of the *vidhis* (i.e. *codanās*) can be very easily questioned because a part of *vidhi* has become inauthoritative. When a part is inauthoritative, the whole is automatically so. In that case, no *codanā* will remain authoritative. If so, then the proposition *codanālakṣāṇo'rtho Dharmaḥ* (*JS* 1.1.2) no longer stands valid. Because there is no object for this proposition. So the proposition becomes objectless.

Actually speaking, this is what is to be achieved by the *pūrvapakṣin*. By some way or the other, he has to prove that the proposition declared previously is not valid. Once it is shown by the opponent he can frame the *pūrvapakṣa* very well.

Still there remains another difficulty even after accepting the sentence-unity of *vidhis* and *arthavādas* in the *pūrvapakṣa*. And that difficulty is, of those injunctions which do not have any relation with the *arthavādas*, either directly or indirectly. How to take objection regarding the authoritativeness of those ? Because there is nothing which can invalidate them.

The proposers of the above theory meet this difficulty as follows : They say : We do not deny that there are such injunctions. But once you prove the nonvalidity of one injunction, where there is *arthavāda*, there is no way to protect the authoritativeness of any other injunctive sentence. Because if one *codanā* is not valid, whatever is known as *codanā* will become non-valid.

Another important point is, that if the invalidity of the injunctive sentences is proved this way, the argument that 'for the invalidity of any sentence (i.e. *śabdapramāṇa*) the reason is its being composed by a human being' is also falsified, because these injunctions which are *a-puruṣeya*[14] (i.e. which are not composed by any human being) are proved to be inauthoritative. In other words—it can be observed from above argument that it is not at all the case that a sentence must be valid, if it is *a-pauruṣeya*. And so we may object all i.e. each and every sentence of the veda—which is *apauruṣeya*.

Text : 28

नन्वेकवाक्यताभावेऽपि अर्थवादाप्रामाण्ये चोदनाया अपि किं न स्यात् ?

Tr. :

Even if the sentence-unity is not accepted (between the *vidhis* and the *arthavādas*), since the *arthavādas* are not valid, why can we not say that the injunctive sentences also are inauthoritative ?

Notes :

It seems that the Prabhakaras raise a doubt here. They do not think that it is necessary to frame the *pūrvapakṣa* on the basis of the sentence-unity of *vidhis* and *arthavādas*. Because even without that it can be shown that the *vidhis* are inauthoritative which is required for framing the *pūrvapakṣa* (according to some). They think that even if there is no sentence-unity, the validity of the injunctions can be objected on the very ground that the validity of the *arthavādas* is doubtful. How ? Let us see. Both, the injunctions and the *arthavādas* are the parts of the veda. Now, if one of the parts (i.e. the *arthavādas*) is not valid, automatically the whole becomes invalid. Thus, one can readily argue that if the authority of *arthavādas* is doubtful, the validity of the injunctions is also doubtful. If this much was necessary to form the Pp. it could be achieved in this way also. And so, according to our line of thought, there is no necessity of forming the Pp. on the basis of the sentence-unity of *vidhis* and *arthavādas*.

Text : 29

न, सिद्धार्थानाम् अनुवादानामप्रामाण्ये व्युत्पत्त्यभावस्य एवोपाधित्वात् !

Tr. :

No, (the validity of *codanā* cannot be objected if there is no sentence-unity. In isolation, only the *arthavādas* are non-valid). Because, the condition for the invalidity of the *arthavādas* is *vyutpatty abhāva* (non-intelligibility of the sentence-meaning).

Notes :

Here, someone who advocates that the *Pp.* should be framed on the basis of sentence-unity replies to the question of Prabhakara. He reminds him that the ground for the inauthoritativeness of the *arthavādas* is their incapability to express any sentence-meaning. In other words the *arthavādas* do not enjoin any activity to be undertaken by a man. But this is not the case with the injunctions since they are fully capable of expressing an activity to be undertaken by a man. Thus, how can the *codanās* be declared as inauthoritative simply on the ground that the *arthavādas*, which have no relation with the injunctions, are not authoritative ?

Thus, it is clear from the above argument that the view of '*Anye tu*' is to press for the sentence-unity. This is the reason why the arguer has suggested the *Pp.* to be formed on the basis of sentence-unity of the *arthavādas*. Because, if the *arthavādas* are in no way related to the injunctions, there is no possibility of showing the non-authority of injunctions. And thereby it is difficult to show relevance between the *Pp.* and the proposition of the first chapter.

Here the term *upādhi* seems to be technical in sense. It is a logical term which is used in inference to show a fallacious ground. It is defined as, *sādhya-vyāpaktve sati sadhanāvyāpakatvam upādhiḥ*[15]. An *upādhi* or condition is that which pervades the probandum but which does not pervade the probans. Here, the argument can be put in the following inferential form :

The *arthavādas* are not authoritative, because they are mere narrative sentences. Here, the probans is, 'being narrative sentences' and the probandum is, 'being non-authoritative'. The 'non-intelligibility' is the 'condition', because, it pervades the probandum but does not pervade the probans. Thus, on the ground of 'being non-intelligible' the inauthoritativeness of the *arthavādas* cannot be established because the ground is faulty.

Vyutpatti-abhāva means absence of intelligibility. *Vyutpatti* means the knowledge of relations among word-meanings or verbal understanding.

Prabhākaras hold the view that no verbal understanding takes place from a narrative ((*siddhārtha*) sentence (because, such sentences do not express any activity to be undertaken.)

But the Naiyayikas have criticized this view of the Prabhakaras, saying that one does get verbal understanding even from a narrative sentence.

Text : 30

परेषां सिद्धेऽपि व्युत्पत्तिरस्ति इति चेत्,

Tr. :

(But) according to some (philosophers) the verbal understanding does arise from narrative sentences even (and so the *arthavādas* do cause verbal understanding).

Note :

The objector continues his argument by saying that it may be that the *arthavādas* are not capable of expressing any activity which man can undertake, but they are not meaningless, they do convey their literal meanings which are *siddha* or already accomplished entities.

It seems that this objector is trying to argue that the *arthavādas* may be unauthoritative but it is not because they do not convey any (*sādhya*) meaning !

Text : 31

न; तथापि व्युत्पत्तेर्भावाद्धर्मेऽपि नानुवादानाम् अप्रामाण्येन देशनाया अपि स्यात् ।

(Construe: *Na Tathāpi vyutpatter bhāvād dharma api anuvādānām aprāmāṇyena deśanāyā api na syāt*).

Tr. :

No. (This argument of yours is not acceptable).

Eventhough, the *arthavādas* generate some understanding, they cannot be held authoritative with reference to *Dharma* also. And only on this ground of inauthoritativeness of the *arthavādas* the injunctions cannot become inauthoritative.

Notes :

The *Siddhāntin* (of *Anye tu*) argues that he does not deny that *arthavādas* are capable of generating verbal understanding. But that is not the sufficient qualification for their being authoritative, with reference to *Dharma*, since the definition of *Dharma* is, 'that which is conveyed by *codanā* and which is of the nature of activity to be undertaken by a person is *Dharma*' (cf. *JS* 1.1.2.) Moreover, it is not proper to argu that since the *arthavādas* generate verbal understanding they are authoritative with reference to *Dharma*, and since they are not authoritative, they cannot affect the authority of injunctions. Because, injunctions are in no way related to them, in case you do not accept their sentence-unity. So the injunctions do remain valid and hence there is no link to be shown between your *Pp* and the main proposition, (i.e. *JS* 1.1.2).

Text : 32

अनुवादानामप्रामाण्ये तदनुवादकतया नार्थज्ञानं स्वाध्यायाध्ययनविधिः प्रयोजनतया गृह्णाति, किन्तु स्वर्गादि; ततश्चान्यपरत्वात् सर्वा एव चोदना न प्रमाणमिति चेत्

Tr. :

When the *arthavādas* are not valid, the purpose of the *swādhyāyavidhi* cannot be the understanding of the meaning of the veda, but it would be heaven etc. And since, (in that case), the injunctions would convey something else (and not their own meaning), all the injunctions become inauthoritative.

Notes :

Some follower of Prabhakara, here, takes an attempt to show the non-authority of the injunctions even in the absence of their sentence-unity with the *arthavādas*.

Prabhākara does not want to accept the sentence-unity of them (i.e. injunctions and *arthavādas*) in the *Pp*. The basic stand of Prabhakara is as follows: The *Kārya* part of the veda is fully authoritative. In other words, the authority of that part of the veda has been proved beyond doubt in the first *pāda* of the first chapter. Another important stand taken by him is, there is nothing which can invalidate these injunctions. His argument is that on the ground of the non-authoritativeness of the *arthavādas* one cannot prove the non-authority of the injunctions[16].

On the other hand, according to his *siddhānta*, because of the association of the authoritative injunctions, the *arthavādas* become authoritative. So the present arguer may be the follower of Prabhakara who tries to show the invalidity of *codanās* independent of the ground of their sentence-unity with *arthavādas*. He says if the *arthavādas* are not authoritative. then since one part of the veda is non-authoritative, hence purposeless and meaningless, the *svādhyāya-vidhi* cannot prescribe the study of the whole veda for the purpose of understanding its meaning, namely, the sacrifice. That means the purpose of the study of the *vidhis* also is not to know their meaning but something else, like heaven etc. And so they too are meant for some other purpose and hence not authoritative with reference to *Dharma*.

Text : 33

न, विधेः प्रयोजनान्तरानपेक्षणात् । अत एवं नियोगस्य प्रयोजकत्वात् कामाधिकारेऽपि न स्वर्गादेः प्रयोजनतयान्वयः, किन्तु नियोज्यविशेषणतयैव ।

Tr. :

What you say is not correct because *vidhi* i.e. an injunctive sentence has no expectation of any other purpose. Therefore, since the *niyoga* is the inducer (of the performer into action), heaven etc. are not related (to *bhāvanā*[17]) as the purpose of the injunctive sentence even in the section dealing with the relation of the purpose or result, (but they are connected) only as a qualification of the *niyojya* i.e. the sacrificer.

Notes :

Prabhākara plainly denies the possibility, thought out by the arguer above, that the injunctions have some other purpose (like heaven etc) than their own meaning and so they become inauthoritative. Prabhakara says this is not possible because the injunctions do not except anything else as their purpose—to prove their authority. In other words, these injunctions are valid just as they convey their own meaning, namely, an activity to be performed. Let us examine one injunctive sentence, like '*Svargakāmo yajeta*'. Here, heaven is not construed as the purpose of this injunction with the *bhāvanā* but it is just the qualification of the sacrificer who is going to take up the activity of performing that particular (*yāga*) sacrifice. Had it been the case that injunctions have some other purpose to convey like 'heaven' etc., then in the above-mentioned example, heaven would have been construed as the purpose and not the *niyoga*. But in reality, the *niyoga*, i.e. *apūrva*, i.e. the fruit of *yāga* prompts the man to some action and the man desirous of some specific result (like heaven etc) takes up the performance of that particular *yāga*.

In any case the injunctions are valid because they convey their own meaning, (*kārya*). And thus, the question of their being non-authoritative on account of conveying some other purpose does not arise at all.

Text : 34

कथं तर्हि वेदस्यार्थपरत्वमिति चेत्,

Tr. :

Then, how to maintain that the veda has meaning (i.e. it is studied for the understanding of its meaning ?)

Notes :

Here, the follower of the Bhāṭṭa school of *PM* raises a doubt. He says, that according to the Bhāṭṭa school, the learning of the Veda is for the understanding of its meaning. But if you maintain that *niyoga* is the inducer of a man into action and the *svādhyāya-vidhi* will be considered purposeful just after one learns the Veda by heart then how to maintain the stand that the learning of the Veda is meant, for the understanding of its meaning namely, *yāga* ? In other words, if an injunction does not expect its meaning to be known and if it is purposeful only after it is learnt by heart the above-mentioned question has to be answered.

According to Prabhākara the meaning of *vidhi* is *niyoga*. It is this knowledge of *niyoga* that prompts a man into action. Thus, the study of Veda is not for acquiring the knowledge of the meaning of the Veda, but to obtain *niyoga* only. And once a person learns the Veda by heart the function of injunction is performed as it were.

If this is the case, then how to account for the meaningfulness of the Veda is the question, This implies that the Veda becomes un-authoritative since it does not convey the meaning required to be conveyed by it.

Text : 35

न; यतोऽर्थाज्जातस्यार्थज्ञानस्य विधिना पश्चादधिकारपर्यवसानार्थं स्वीकारात्। तच्च यथाजातमेव स्वीकारोचितं व्यापकमव्यापकं वा, सिध्दान्तेऽपि 'हुम्' इत्यादीनामव्यापनात्।

Tr :

No, (your doubt has no scope), because the knowledge of the meaning of the Veda is obtained by implication here andt his implied understanding of the meaning is accepted by the injunctions to make a person ultimately qualified for the performance of a particular sacrifice. Moreover, that understanding of the meaning of the Veda has to be accepted in the same form as it arises i.e. it may be *vyāpaka* or *sādhya* (i.e. it may be an activity (*yāga*) or it may be *avyāpaka* or *siddha* (i.e. already accomplished things). Because, the *siddhāntin* also accepts that the words like 'hum' etc. do not convey any meaning to prompt a man into action.

Notes :

The Prābhākara explains his view on the doubt raised by the Bhāṭṭas. He says that the understanding of the meaning of the Veda does arise in the person who learns the Veda and performs some particular sacrifice. It is implied, since there can be no inducement in a man in the absence of the knowledge of the meaning of the Veda. So what we say is, by implication this knowledge has to be there. We do not deny this fact. Nevertheless this is not the purpose of the *vidhi*. Moreover, this knowledge of meaning should be accepted as it is understood from the respective vedic sentences. Some sentence may convey a *sādhya* sence and some other may convey *siddha*. It is not the case that all sentences of the Veda convey *ṣādhya* sense only. Because there some words like 'hum' etc. which may not convey any particular sense but still they have some specific purpose, to serve. That they are otherwise meaningless is accepted even in the *siddhānta*.

It should be noted that according to the school of Prābhakara, the *adhyayana-vidhi* is prompted by the *ācāryakaraṇavidhi*. This *ācāryakaraṇa-vidhi* is based on the following *smṛti* sentence :

Upanīya tu yaḥ ṣiṣyam Vedam adhyāpayed dvijaḥ
Sāṅgam ca sarahasyam ca tam ācāryam pracakṣate.[18]

According to this a teacher has to teach Veda to a student after his *upanayana-saṁskāra* is completed. Now this *ācāryakaraṇa-vidhi* cannot be said to have operated unless the student learns the Veda. This vidhi prompts the operation of *svādhyāya-vidhi*, '*svādhyāyo 'dhyetavyaḥ*'. At this juncture the question arises what for the student should learn the Veda by heart. Prābhākaras maintain that the direct purpose of his study is not the knowledge of the meaning of the Veda, but some unseen result arising out of his study is the purpose which induces the student to learn the Veda.

Since in future the student has to perform sacrifice and that performance is not possible without the knowledge of the Veda, the knowledge of the meaning of the Veda is obtained by implication (i.e. by *arthāpatti-pramāṇa*)[19] in order to qualify the student to become a sacrificer. Directly the knowledge of the meaning of the Veda is not the purpose of the *vidhi.*

Text : 36

न च स्वर्गवन्नियोज्यविशेषणत्वमेवार्थज्ञानस्य, अनियोगफलत्वात् वैतुष्यवत्, आचार्यविधिलब्धानुष्ठाने अध्ययने नियोज्याभावात् ।

Tr :

And one need not argue that, if such is the case then let the understanding of the meaning of the Veda be the qualification of *niyojya* i.e. the sacrificer. Because the result i.e. the understanding of the meaning of the Veda is different from *niyoga*, which is *adṛṣṭa* (and so it is realisable) just as the removal of the husks (which is visible or realisable while husking the paddy-grains).

Moreover, the learning of the Veda, which is enjoined by the *ācārya-vidhi* does not have any *niyojya* as such.

Notes :

Now, if one tries to argue that "if such is the case, i.e. unless there is an understanding of the meaning of the Veda, there cannot be an inducement as well as the performing a *Yāga* on part of the person who has learnt the Veda by heart, then let this knowledge of meaning be a qualification of that person just as heaven etc., are the qualifications of that man", it cannot be a proper argument. Why ? Because the result namely, the 'Heaven' and the result namely, the '*arthajñāna*' cannot be compared with each other, since *arthajñāna* is a visible or readily realisable result whereas *svarga* is invisible or not readily realisable one.

This is the nature of man that he takes up an activity **only when** he knows that, that activity will lead him to obtain pleasure. Thus, the knowledge of pleasure can be the inducer. Here, *svarga* is pleasure, and so that will induce him into action. A pleasure is defined as, *itarecchānadhīnecchāviṣayatvam sukham*[20] i.e. that is called pleasure, the desire of which does not depend on the desire of anything else. The desire of heaven' alone can be the pleasure according to this definition. Hence it is the inducer. The knowledge of the meaning of the Veda cannot be called *sukha* and hence it cannot be the inducer and hence it cannot be a qualifier of the performer of the sacrifice.

And if one still tries to make a general rule of this type that *arthajñāna* is a qualification of a *niyojya* then there will arise a Very practical difficulty in the case of the learning of the Veda which is enjoined by the *ācāryavidhi* as we have observed above. The *niyojya* of the *ācāryavidhi* is the teacher and not the student. And so the student who is to undertake the study of the Veda is not the niyojya of the study of the Veda prompted by the *ācārya-karaṇavidhi*. Hence, how can one qualify the student with the knowledge of the meaning of the veda when he is not prompted by any injunction like, '*vedartha—jñānakāmaḥ vedādhyayanam kuryāt*' or even the teacher who is prompted in teaching for making himself a teacher by teaching that student and not by any injunction like, '*vedārthjñānakāmaḥ adhyāpayet*' ?

Thus, the knowledge of the meaning of the Veda cannot be the qualification of a sacrificer.

Text : 37

न च वेदार्थज्ञानकामनापि युज्यते; यदि प्रागसौ ज्ञातः किमर्थं काम्यते ? न चेत् तथापि न कामना, तस्या ज्ञातविषयत्वात् ।

Tr. :

There, even the desire for the understanding of the meaning of the Veda is not proper, because if the meaning of the Veda is already known then how can there be a desire to know it ? And if the meaning is not known then also the desire to know it is impossible because only a known thing could be the object of desire.

Notes :

Prabhākara here takes into account all the possibilities by which 'the understanding of the meaning of the Veda, could be a qualification to the sacrificer and then refutes them one by one.

Firstly, he says, let us take it for granted that there can be a desire to know the meaning of the Veda. But before that let me ask whether that meaning of the Veda is a known entity or an unknown entity. If the meaning of the Veda is already a known fact, there can be no more desire to know it. Again, if the meaning is not at all known then also there is no possibility of there being any desire to know it because, something becomes an object of desire only if it is known in some form or the other. In other words, desire must be preceded by knowledge. The object of the knowledge can be the object of the desire. And if such is not the case then the existence of desire itself is not possible.

Text : 38

सामान्यतो ज्ञातं विशेषतो ज्ञानार्थं काम्यते काव्यालङ्कारार्थवदिति चेत्,

Tr. :

If one argues that the meaning of the Veda is known in a general way and in order to know that in a specific way like in case of poetry, *alaṅkāra* etc. that *vedārtha* is desired (and so the desire to know the *vedārtha* is not improper).

Notes :

There can be another possibility to justify the occurance of desire. Let us assume that one knows the meaning of the Veda in a general way and now there arises a desire to know its specific meaning.

Text : *39*

न; सामान्यतो वेदार्थस्य नित्यनियोगरूपस्य वेदमन्तरेणाभ्युदयकारितया पुंवाक्यमात्रात् प्रमाणान्तरविरोधेन प्रत्येतुमशक्तेः ।

Tr. :

Our answer to this argument is, 'no'- Because, the meaning of the Veda is nothing but durable *niyoga* i.e. *kārya* and that it leads to the obtainment of Bliss (*abhyudaya*) cannot be understood in a general way without the Veda from the ordinary human sentences which are likely to be contradicted by the other means of knowing (namely, perception etc.).

Notes :

(But) this possibility also is ruled out by Prabhakara as follows ;

There is no way to know the meaning of the Veda in a general way. Because, what is the meaning of the Veda? It is always durable *riyoga.* And it is known only from the Veda. There is no possibility of knowing *niyoga* in a general way. It cannot be known from the ordinary human sentences because human sentences are dependent upon the perception and other means of knowledge. Thus, there is a likelihood that these human sentences can be contradicted. So there is no other way to know the meaning of the Veda than the Veda. And thus, there is no possibility of there being a desire to know it. Since there can be no desire of the same, it cannot be the qualification of the sacrificer.

Text : 40

वेद एवानुमितः प्रमाणान्तरबाधेन बोधयतीति चेत्

Tr. :

Well, if we say, that the inferred Veda itself will causet he understanding (of the meaning of the Veda in general) by setting a-side the operation of other *pramāṇas.*

Notes :

The arguer continues his argument by making a suggestion on the argument of Prabhakara that the human sentences cannot cause an understanding of the meaning of the Veda in general because they are likely to be contradicted by other means of knowing.

So let the inferred Veda cause the knowledge of that. In this way the meaning of the Veda can be kaown in a general way and hence, it can be the object of desire to know it specifically.

Text : 41

न; तस्य विशेषशक्तस्य सामान्यबोधनासम्भवात् काव्ये तु पुंवाक्यलिङ्गकेनानुमानेनैव कश्चिदर्थोऽभ्युदयकारी इति लक्ष्यते। यदि च विधिनः पूर्वमेव स्वाध्यायस्यार्थवत्ता ज्ञायते तदा किं तदभङ्गिनोऽध्ययन-विधानेन ?

Tr. :

No, (this suggestion is not acceptable). Because the Veda is capable of expressing specific meaning (only), therefore, it is impossible that the Veda conveys some general meaning. In case of poetry. however, by an inference based on human sentences alone, it is known that there is some meaning which leads to the happiness.

Moreover, if before the operation of the *svādhyāvavidhi* it is known that the learning of the Veda is meaningful (i.e. the Veda has meaning) than what is the necessity of enjoining the study of that meaning i.e. the Veda ?

Notes :

The above-mentioned suggestion is not acceptable to Prābhākara. Because, the Veda always expresses a specific meaning only, and never any general meaning. A sentence which expresses a specific meaning cannot at the same time express some general meaning also. e.g. if someone says, 'give me the black pen', then what general meaning can the hearer understand from this sentence ? This sentence has its specific meaning only. So the listener has no chance to guess some general meaning from the sentence. Similarly, when the Veda expresses a specific meaning, namely, *niyoga*, what general meaning is expected to be understood from the Veda ?

Secondly, the Veda shold not be compared with poetry etc., which is composed by a human being. Only for a simple reason that, in case of poetry, that it leads to the happiness is inferred on the basis of human language only. But this is not possible in case of the Veda for the reasons already discussed above.

Another very important point is, if it is known that the Veda and the learning of the Veda is meaningful before the operation of the *svādhyāyavidhi*, namely, *svādhyāyo' dhyetavyaḥ*, then the very *vidhi* will become redundant. Why ? Because whatever was to be achieved by the *vidhi* is already achieved since the meaning of the Veda is already known in a general way according to you. To be more clear, the purpose of this *vidhi* is to show that the learning of the Veda is meaningful. Now, if this very thing is known before the operation of this *vidhi* i-e. *svādhyāyo'dhyetavyaḥ* then there does not exist any purpose for this *vidhi* to serve. And hence the *vidhi* becomes redundent. So to avoid this type of contingency also, it is necessary to maintain that the meaningfulness of the study of the Veda is known only from the Veda and not from any other means.

Text. 42 :

नियमार्थो वधिरिति चेत्,

Tr. :

If we say that the (*svādhyāya*) *vidhi* is for the niyama[21] i.e. restriction, then ?

Notes :

The arguer presents another suggestion, on the difficulty raised by the Prābhākara that the *svādhyāyavidhi* will have no purpose to serve if it is known that the veda has some meaning, before the operation of the *svādhyāyvidhi.* This doubt of the Prābhākaras will have no scope if it is accepted that the *svādhyāyavidhi* restricts the manner of the aquisition of *vedārtha.* In that case, the *svādhyāyavidhi,* becomes purposeful. In other words, let there be knowledge of the fact that the Veda has some meaning in general from some other means before the operation of the *vidhi,* even then the *vidhi* will be purposeful by restricting the manner of the aquisition of the meaning of the Veda. In this way, the contingency that the *vidhi* would become redundant is removed. Moreover, the possibility of the desire to know the meaning of the Veda is also maintained. After knowing that the Veda has some meaning—there can, very consistently, be the desire of knowing the specific meaning of the Veda.

Text : 43

न, लौकिकेऽर्थज्ञाने नियमाभावात्, क्रत्वर्थत्वे च निरधिकारत्वात् । किञ्चित्क्रियार्थज्ञानं तु न अधिकारिविशेषणं स्यात् । पुरूषार्थे च नियमेऽर्थज्ञानम् आश्रयः स्यात्; अधिकारी त्वन्य एव प्राङ्मुखभोजने इव आयुष्कामः । अर्थज्ञानप्रवृत्तिर्वा निमित्तं स्यात् प्रतिग्रहादाविवार्जनकामस्य प्रवृत्तिः, न त्वर्थज्ञानं फलम् । न च स्वाध्यायादेर्नियमः सम्भवति, अन्याप्रसक्तेः ।

Tr :

No. Because in the case of the knowledge of meaning arising from ordinary language (say, poetry etc) there can be no such restriction (that one should understand the meaning of such and such poetry only in some fixed way and not by any other means.) Now, if this restriction is intended for the purpose of the sacrifice then no man will be the *adhikārin* of the knowledge of the Veda (since it is not meant for him at all). If (one argues that), let there be the understanding of the meaning of the Veda for some particular purpose (other than the heaven) then again no one is going to study it because, such particular purpose cannot be a qualifier of the *adhikārin*. If (you say that) this restriction (is not meant for the sacrifice but) is meant for the person only then in that case, the understanding of the meaning will be the basis of such restriction, and again the person will not be the *adhikārin*, (on the contrary), the *adhikārin* will be somebody else, just like in the case of, one who is desirous of long life should take his food, facing towards the East. Or else, the understanding of the meaning of the Veda will be the cause for the inducement in the person, just as, one desirous of earning some wealth is induced to accept gifts-but in that case also, the knowledge of meaning cannot be the result (which can induce him into actio action). And (most important point is), in the case of the learning of the Veda, such restriction is not possible also, because there is no possibility at all that the meaning of the Veda could be understood by any other means (than from the Veda). (*Niyama* is possible only when more than one means for something are available).

Notes :

The suggestion put forward by the opponent (of Prābhākara), in order to avoid the contingency of *svādhyāyavidhi* becoming redundent is not acceptable. Why ? There are more than one reason.

First reason is that if the understanding of some ordinary text and the understanding of the vedic text do not differ then there should be no restriction about the understanding of an ordinary text at all. So naturally a doubt arises why should there be such restriction with reference to the vedic texts only ?

Secondly, it has to be considered that if at all there should be such a restriction with regard to the vedic text then what could be the purpose of such a restriction ? One answer to this question could be for the purpose of the *yāga*. Then we say if this is the case then no person will be *adhikārin* to understand the meaning of the Veda since it is not at all meant for him. whey should anyone take up an activity which is not meant for him ?

Now, if someone says that some purpose or the other is there for the man who attemps to understand the meaning of the Veda then this too cannot be the case. Why ? Because nothing unspecified can be the qualifier of the person namely, the performer of *yāga* and so on, because, an unspecified item cannot be the inducer.

Now, if you say that, not for *yāga* but for the person involved himself is this restriction then in that case the understanding of the meaning will be the basis for the said restriction. In other words, this restriction is not going to make the person *adhikārin* either for the performance of *yāga* or for the understanding of the meaning—for the reasons already discussed above. So the *arthajñāna* will only be the basis for which this restriction will come into existence but *adhikārin* will be somebody else only. This fact can be illustrated by our ordinary experience. Take, for instance, the following case : One is Induced to take food when one is hungry and wishes to satisfy his hunger. Although he is an *adhikārin* for taking food because he wants to satisfy his hunger, the person is not the *adhikārin* for taking food facing towards the East, because, if satisfaction of hunger is only the aim that could be achieved by eating food facing any direction. Then who is the *adhikārin*? Obviously, one who desires to live long will be the *adhikārin* for taking meals facing towards the East. In the same manner, here also, even if the restriction in the mode of learning the Veda is meant for the person concerned, the *arthajñāna* will be the basis for such a restriction and it will not result in making the same person an *adhikārin* to the performance of the sacrifice. It will be somebody else like one who is desirous of obtaining heaven and so on, who will be the *adhikārin*. In simple words, even if the above-said restriction is meant for the person, ultimately, it is not going to make the same person act.

Accepting that *arthajñāna* is not the basis for the above-mentioned restriction, let the *arthajñāna* be the cause for the inducement in the person, just like in case of a person desirous of earning wealth is induced to accept the gifts from others. But in any case, the *arthajñāna* cannot be the goal to be obtained or desired to be acquired. Hence, *arthajñāna* cannot induce a man into a troublesome activity like the study of the Veda.

And lastly, the most important point pointed out by the Prābhākara is, that there is no scope at all for such type of restriction in case of the learning of the Veda or to be precise, for the understanding of the meaning of the Veda, because, the restriction is possible only when there are more than one means available for achieving the result which is intended to be achieved by following the restricted mode of achieving that result. For example, in case of removing the husks of paddy, there are more than one way possible like removing the husks by nails, husking etc. In that case, the *vidhi 'vrīhīn avahanti'* restricts the way of removing the husks by saying that the husks should be removed only by husking the paddy (and not by any other way). Here, in our present context no such possibility can be even doubted since there is no other way to understand the meaning of the Veda than to understand it from the Veda itself.

In this way, by all these arguments and mainly from the last argument it is quite clear that the possibility of the restriction with regard to the mode of study for understanding the meaning of the Veda is completely ruled out by the Prābhākara.

Text : 44

नन्वेकवाक्यतयापि कथं पूर्वपक्षः ? सा हि क्रिया कारकादिपदेषु विभक्त्यादिबलाद्भवति ; विभक्त्या संनिहितपदार्थप्रतियोगिककारणत्वस्याभिधानात् । इह तु द्वयोरनुपहताख्यातयोर्न व्युत्पत्तिसिद्धा एकवाक्यता ; वाक्यभेद एव तु व्युत्पन्नः ।

Tr. :

Well, (our basic doubt is) how can there be the *pūrvapakṣa* framed on the basis of sentence-unity (of *vidhis* and *arthavādas*) ? Because such *ekavākyatā* or sentence-unity is possible on the basis of case terminations and personal suffixes occuring in inflected forms expressive of action and the (various) *kārakas* because the suffices express the relation of causality, the counter-corelative of which is the meaning of a word adjucent (to the suffix).

Whereas here the two sentences have two verbal forms, neither of which is subordinated and so there cannot be normal sentence-unity. On the contrary, it is clear that, they are two different sentences.

Notes :

We have already seen that Prābhākara had initiated his discussion on the very ground that there can be no sentence-unity between a *vidhi* and an *arthavāda*.

The opponent objected to it and pointed out, if sentence-unity is not accepted then the construction of the *pūrvapaksa* it self would become impossible and hence the whole discussion of the authoritativeness of the *arthavādas* would become irrelevant. Prābhākara tried to meet those objections by raising various points and now again they are raising their basic question that how it is possible at all to show the sentence-unity between *vidhis* and *arthavādas*. While initiating the discussion Prabhakara had said that such a sentence-unity is not possible because the *arthavādas* are expressive of already accomplished things (*siddhārthas*) and a *siddhārtha* cannot be related to a *sādhyārtha*. Now he is raising the same point from a different angle. He is pointing out now the formal linguistic difficulties for a sentence-unity. What is our ordinary experience about a sentence-unity ? A sentence-unity is found among various linguistic elements expressive of action and the *kārakas* and their relations. Take for instance the single sentence, *Jyotiṣṭomena svargakāmo yajeta*, here the *kriyā* or action is *yāga*, which is obtained from the root in *yajeta*. It is related to *Jyoti-ṣṭoma* by the relation of identity. The agent of this *kriyā* is *svargakāma*. The relations among these meaning elements are expressed by the respective suffixes added to the bases. Now, since the agent helps the action to come into existence, he is related to the action and the action is related to *bhāvanā* as its instrument. These relationships are expressed by the various suffixes. Thus there is *ekavākyatā* here.

But such is not the case with reference to the *arthavādas* and the *vidhis*. They are two different independent sentences having separate actions as well as the helpers to those actions no matter whether action is *siddha* or *sādhya*. Thus, how can there be an *ekavākyatā* between these two ? They are explicitly two different and independent sentences. From this point of view also, there can be no sentence-unity. This is what Prābhākara contends.

Text : 45

उच्यते – सिद्धार्थसाध्यार्थान्वययोरप्याख्यातयोः एकवाक्यत्वं व्युत्पन्नम् । हेतुहेतुमद्भावेन चान्वयः । यथा 'मलिनं ते वपुः वर्तते, स्नायाः इति । 'मलिनः स्नायाद्' इति तु नोदाहरणम्, तत्र मलिनस्य कर्तृत्वेन अधिकारित्वेन वान्वितस्य साध्यकोटित्वात् हेतुत्वेन अन्वयाभावात्, एकाख्यातत्वाच्च ।

Tr. :

Here is the reply : The sentence-unity is possible between two verbs (i.e. between two sentences having two separate verbal forms), one denoting the relation with the already accomplished thing and the other denoting the relation with something yet to be accomplished. Such a relation between the two (sentences) can be as probans and probandum—relationship as in the case, fori nstance, your body is dirty, you should take bath. Here, (in this context) one who is dirty should take bath cannot be an example (of the sentence-unity of two sentences, one narrative and the other injunctive), because, in the sentence (i.e. *malinaḥ shāyāt*), an unclean person is related as the agent (of the action of taking bath) as one who is eligible or *adhikārin* (for that action) and so he forms the part of the probandum and in that case it cannot be related as probans. Moreover, there is oniy one verb (in the sentence *malinaḥ snāyāt*, and not two as in the case of *vidhis* and the *arthavādas*).

Notes :

Murāri offers a solution to the question raised by Prābhākara that how a *vidhi* which expresses *sādhya* entity and an *arthavāda* which expresses *siddha* entity can be related. The answer given is—the two can be construed as a single sentence with each other and the relation between them will be the *hetu—hetumadbhāva* i.e. one will be the ground for the other. In other words, if there are two sentences of which one is a narrative sentence and the other an injunctive sentence, and if there is a relation of *hetu-hetumadbhāva* between the two sentence meanings, the two sentences can be construed as one single sentence. This is substantiated by an ordinary sentence cluster, namely, 'your body is dirty, you should take bath'. The same example is discussed in other texts like Bhavanatha's *Viveka*[22]. Here. *malinam te vapuḥ vartate*, is one sentence and *snāyaḥ* is another sentence which is an injunctive sentence. Now, how to relate these two sentences ? Obviously there is no syntactical relationship between the two. Both are syntactically independent. Still there is semantic relationship, i.e. the meaning of one sentence is the ground for the meaning of the other. The meaning of the first sentence, namely, 'your body is dirty', is the ground or reason for the meaning of the second sentence namely, 'you should take bath'. Because it is only when one is dirty, one can ask him to take bath. Thus, semantically these two sentences can be related to each other and in this way they can form a single sentence. The relation which unite the two sentences is *hetu-hetumadbhāva* or *nimitta-naimittika-bhāva* or prompter and prompted relationship. To put it in syllogistic form :

(i) You should take bath.
(ii) Because your body is dirty.
(iii) Whose body is dirty he takes bath.
(iv) Such is your body.
(v) Therefore, you should take bath.

The sentence *malinaḥ snāyāt* cannot be an example of such a relationship for two reasons. Firstly, the unclean person in the sentence *malinaḥ snāyāt* is desired to be an agent of the action of bathing or he is to be made eligible (*adhikārin*) for the action of bathing. Thus, the entire sentence, 'one who is unclean, should take bath,' is what is to be achieved. And so, consequently, the person who is unclean forms the part of the *sādhya* and what is *sādhya* cannot be the *hetu* obviously.

If it were the expression that, '*tvam malinaḥ, snāyāḥ*' 'you are dirty' you should take bath', then, '*tvam malinaḥ*' could have been related as ground and that could have been an example of *hetu-hetumad-bhāva.* In that case, the *hetu* or ground is expressed by a separate sentence and the *sādhya* or the effect is expressed by a different sentence. And so, the *malinaḥ snāyāt* is in no way an example of the sentence-unity on the ground of *hetu-hetumad-bhāva.* Here, the sentence-unity is governed by the normal syntactical relationship.

The second reason for its not being an example of *hetu-hetumad-bhāva* relationship is the fact that the expression, *malinaḥ snāyāt*, contains only one finite verbal form and not two. It is a single sentence on the ground of syntactical relationship and not on the ground of semantic relationship.

Thus, Murāri points out that *arthavādas* and the *vidhis* can be construed with each other not on syntactical grounds but on the ground of *hetu* and *hetumad* i.e. of their sentence-meanings and then the sentence-unity of the two can be easily achieved.

This reminds one of the *JS* : *Arthaikatvād ekam vākyam sākaṅkṣam cedvibhāge syāt*[23]. Two or more expressions are said to form one sentence if the meanings of the expressions are 'related whole' and if the separation of any one of them makes the other expectant.

'Related whole' is possible through the various relations. One such relation can be *hetu-hetumad-bhāva.*

Text : 46

तच्चेदं मलिनत्वस्य सिद्धिहैतुत्वमेव, न तु करणत्वादिकोटिबहिर्भूतत्वम्। अत एव न साध्यताप्रसङ्गः मलिनत्वं हि स्वापनयेच्छाद्वारा स्नानहेतुरिति केचित्।

Tr. :

Some say that (even in case of the sentence *malinaḥ snāyāt*) *malinatva* (being dirty) is the ground or probans for the accomplishment (of the action of bathing). It is not the case that the *malinatva* is excluded from being karaṇa etc. And that is why there is no contingency that (*malinatva*) would form the part of *sādhya* or a thing to be accomplished. The *malinatva* or dirt is the ground (*hetu*) for taking bath through the desire to get itself cleaned.

Notes :

Here someone tries to show that the stand taken by Murāri about the sentence *malinaḥ snāyāt* is not proper. He tries to justify that here too one can demonstrate that the *malinatva* is the ground (*hetu*) for the action of taking bath. How ? According to him it is not true that *malinatva* is excluded from being *karaṇa* (*apādāna*) etc. even in case of the sentence *malinaḥ snāyāt*.. And so, there is no question of its not being *sādhana* etc. It is indeed the ground for taking bath through the desire of its being cleaned.

This explanation of the objector implies that according to him, *malinaḥ snāyāt* can also be an example of the sentence-unity on the ground of *hetu-hetumad-bhāva* i.e. on the ground of the semantic relationship which was objected to by Murāri.

This implies that even within a single sentence which contains only one verbal form one semantic item (*siddhārtha*) can be related to another semantic item (action or *sādhyārtha*) by the relation of *hetu-hetumad-bhāva.* It is not necessary that for such a relationship there must be two distinct verbal forms.

This further implies that the objector interpretes *malinaḥ snāyāt*, as, *malinatvāpanayakāmaḥ snāyāt*, because he wants to relate *malinatva* as a ground for *snāna* through the desire of its being removed by taking bath.

Text : 47

तन्न, इच्छायामपि भूतायाम् इष्टसाधनताज्ञानामन्तरेण कर्त्तव्यताज्ञानाभावात् ज्ञप्तिसिद्धावेव व्यापारात् । ज्ञानं चैवं सिद्धिहेतुः स्यात्, न च मलिनत्वं तस्य चान्वयो वक्तव्यः, न तु ज्ञानस्य ।

Tr. :

No, (This not tenable). Because even if there is the desire, without the knowledge of being an instrument of desired goal, the knowledge of taking up some activity does not arise. The activity takes place only after the knowledge (of instrument) arises. Thus, the knowledge (of instrument) can be the ground for the action of bathing, (in case of *malinaḥ snāyāt*) and not mere *malinatva* or dirt. And (in the present context) what is required is the connection of the *malinatva* (with the action of bathing) and not of the knowledge (with that action).

Notes :

Murāri outright refutes the point the objector was trying to make. He seems to be influenced by the Naiyayikas' concept of *iṣṭasādhanatā* and argues that no activity can take place, unless one gets the knowledge of being the instrument of the desired goal in that activity. According to the Naiyāyikas the desire (to do something) is always preceded by the knowledge that such activity will lead to achieve the desired goal. Accordingly, Murāri says unless there is the knowledge that bathing is the instrument of removing the dirt, there cannot be any volition for the activity of bathing on the part of a person. It follows from this that the knowledge (of instrument) is the cause of the activity and not the *malinatva*. But this is not relevant because we are taking about the connection of *malinatva* as a cause or *hetu* for the action of taking bath and not about the knowledge as the cause of the same.

Thus, the proposal of the objector is not relevant in the present context and so it has to be rejected.

Text : 48

सिद्धिहेतोर्हेतुत्वेन अभिधानं किमर्थम् ?

Tr. :

Well, why should that which prompts the activity be called a cause or ground (*hetu*) ?

Notes :

There can be no doubt that the knowledge of *iṣṭasādhanatva* prompts a man into action. But is it necessary to call it by the name of *hetu* ? As the knowledge is the cause, so also the object of knowledge. Therefore, *malinatva* can also be the ground of taking bath. In other words a *prayojaka* can also be the prompter of action. Thus, *iṣṭa* is the removal of dirt (*malinatvāpanaya*) and its means is the bathing. In the knowledge of *iṣṭasādhanatva*. the *iṣṭa* as well as the *sādhanatva* are the objects. Thus, the knowledge is the *hetu* and its object is the *prayojaka*. Therefore, *malinatva* can be related to the action as the ground. This seems to be the idea in mind of the objector.

Text : 49

स्वरूपमात्रज्ञानस्यैवेच्छाऽजनकत्वात् । तस्मात् स्नाननिष्ठा साधनता अस्नानमलिनत्वादिति ज्ञप्तिहेतुतयैवान्वयः । अतोऽनुवादकस्यापि ज्ञप्तिहेतुतयैवान्वयः । तत्र यदि प्रतिबन्धग्राहकं प्रमाणमस्ति, तदानुमानप्रमेयप्रमाण तयाऽनुबोधयन्ती देशना न प्रमाणम्; अथ नास्ति, तथापि विपर्ययायातस्मृतिमात्रजनिका सापेक्षत्वान्न प्रमाणम् ।

Tr. :

Because knowledge of mere form of a thing cannot produce desire. Therefore, because the uncleanliness is caused by the absence of taking bath, it is known that the instrument (of removing dirt) is taking bath. In this way, (the *malinatva*) is related to the cause of knowing *iṣṭasādhanatva* in bathing.

That is why the *arthavādas* are also related to the *vidhis*, as the cause of knowledge. There, if there is any means to know the invariable concomitance (vyāpti) between the two (i.e. *vidhis* and *arthavādas*) then the *vidhi* cannot be authoritative since it causes the knowledge of the object of inference. And if there is no *vyāpti* between the two then the understanding of the meaning of the *vidhi* will be in the form of remembrance, which is obtained conversely and in that case it cannot again be authoritative because it will then be dependent upon experience.

Notes :

The answer given by Murâri to the question raised by the objector is interesting. Murāri explains that the knowledge of something in its own form cannot produce any desire. What does it mean? Let us take one example and see : Suppose one has the knowledge of water and he is feeling thirsty. Now, if he does not know that water will quench his thirst he is not going to fetch water. In other words, if one knows water as the means of satisfaction of thirst, then only there can arise a desire to fetch water when he feels thirsty, otherwise not.

This is what Murari means by stating, '*svarūpamātrajñānasya icchā 'janakatvāt*'. In the present context also, *malinatva* is the ground for taking bath. But the knowledge of mere *malinatva* will not generate any desire for taking bath. The dirty person should want to remove the dirt and he should know that without taking bath it cannot be removed. This is how by *anvaya* and *vyatireka* he knows that the means of removing dirt is taking bath, And that is why he knows that *malinatva* is the ground for taking bath. Thus, if *malinatva* is known as the ground then alone one will have desire for the means of its removal and not otherwise.

Some way, Murari says the *arthavādas* are related to *vidhi*, i.e. the *arthavādas* are the ground for the *vidhi*. For instance, since the *Vāvu* diety bestows one desired object very fast, one should perform the sacrifice[24] in which *Vāvu* is the main diety (*Yataḥ Vāyuḥ kṣepiṣṭhā devatā. ataḥ vāyavyam śvetam ālabheta*).

Now, once such a relation of *hetu* and *hetumat* is accepted between the *arthavādas* and the *vidhis*, there is no difficulty in showing the unauthoritativeness of the *vidhi* in the *pūrvapakṣa*—according to Murāri. He says, when such is the case then *arthavādas* will be the *hetu* and the *vidhis* will be the *sādhya*, and in that case, there should be invariable concomitance between the two and if that is known—then obviously the *vidhis* become the object of inferetial cognition. Now, whatever is conveyed by a *vidhi* will become the object of inferential cognition. And so it is not authoritative—because the content of a *vidhi* should never be known by any other means than the *vidhi*. If inference is allowed to operate in this case also, different persons will draw different conclusions. There is nothing by which the inference can be directed to yield an uniform conclusion. How ? Let us see : There is one narrative sentence (*arthavāda*) —So, rodit[25]—i.e. He cried. ('he' in this sentence is the deity *Agni.*)

Now, what type of inferential conclusion should one draw from this narrative sentence which is a ground for some *vidhi* ? Two altogether different inferences can be drawn from such a sentence (1) He cried so *let us also cry* or (2) He cried. It was not good. Inspite of that he cried. So, there can be such mistakes even on the part of such deities. But we must avoid such mistakes. And *we should not cry*.[26]

It is very clear that there is no means to restrict the operation of inference in any particular way. By no way we can predict an identical conclusion.

Thus, if the *vidhis* become the object of inference, they automatically become non-authoritative.

On the other hand if there is no means to know the invariable concomitance between the *vidhis* and the *arthavādas* then the meaning of *vidhis* is not known by inference. It is true. But in that case *vidhi* will be just remembered at random. Because there will be no ground to restrict the understanding of the meaning of the *vidhis*.

Thus, if the relation of *hetu-hetnmad-bhāva* is accepted between the *arthavādas* and the *vidhis*, the *vidhis* become unauthoritative and thence the *pūrvapakṣa* can very well be framed by objecting to the original proposition which is a necessary condition for forming a *pūrvapakṣa* according to Murari.

Text : 50

ननु शब्द एव प्रतिबन्धं बोधयिष्यति, अस्मिन्नेव अंशे प्रमाणं भविष्यति; अनुमेयत्वांशो भवत्वप्रमाणम् ।

Nr. :

Well, the invariable concomitance (i.e. *vyāpti* or *pratibandha* between *arthavādas* and *vidhis*) is known by the *śabdapramāṇa* itself—and it will be valid only with reference to this part (that is the *vidhi* part.) Let the inferred part of *vidhyartha* be invalid.

Notes :

Here, the Prabhakara in a way replies to Murari and suggests him that the first alternative is acceptable to us: we say that the *vyāpti* or invariable concomitence between the *arthavādas* and *vidhis* is known by the verbal testimony itself. We do not depend for this knowledge on any other *pramāṇa* and hence there will be no chance of *vidhis* becoming the object of inferential cognition, in entirity. The *śabdapramāṇa* will cause the knowledge of *vyāpti* and then inference will operate. It is true that some part will be the object of inference and we do not mind if that part is treated as unauthoritative, since the *vyāpti*—part is known by the *śabdapramāṇa* which alone is valid with reference to *vidhi.*

Text : 51

मैवम्; न ह्यनुमानवाक्यानि हेतुस्वरूपतत्प्रतिबन्धादिप्रतिपादकत्वेन व्युत्पन्नानि; किन्तु प्रमाणान्तरसिद्धहेतुस्वरूपतत्प्रतिबन्धादिस्मरणद्वारानुमानज्ञानोत्पादकानि। अतः शाब्द एवानुमानवाक्यस्य नास्ति, शब्दभावेन प्रामाण्ये प्रतिज्ञामात्रेण साध्यप्रतीतौ हेत्वादिप्रयोगवैय्यर्थ्यात्।]

Tr, :

You should not argue like this. Because it is not the fact that the syllogistic sentences are meant for revealing the nature of reason (*hetu*) and its inveriable concomitance (with *sādhya*). But they produce the inferential cognition through the remembrance of the nature of reason (*hetu*) and through the remembrance relation of *vyāpti* between the two (i.e. *hetu* and *sādhya*) both already known by some other means of valid cognition. Therefore, syllogistic sentence does not produce verbal understanding (in the sense of the *śabdapramāṇa* produces a verbal understanding) because if these sentences are treated as '*śabdapramāṇa* then since the *śādhya* is known just from the *pratijñā*, that is the first syllogistic sentences (proposition) the operation of the remaining syllogistic sentences namely *hetu-vākya* etc. would become redundant.

Notes :

Murāri refutes the suggestion of the Prabhākāra on the ground that if the suggestion of the Prābhākara is accepted then the very nature and purpose of syllogism will be lost.

Here Murāri points out a fundamental distinction between '*śabdapramāṇa* and *anumānapramāṇa.* The difference in the epistemology of both the *pramāṇas*. It is the difference in the process of generating a cognition that distinguishes one cognition from the other and thereby one *pramāṇa* from the other *pramāṇa*, The *parrāthānumāna* employs five sentences to generate the inferential cognition of *sādhya*. Now the question arises since the cogniton is generated by the sentences, why should it not be called a verbal understanding? In other words, why not the cognition given by the *pañcāvayavavākya* be called *śābdabodha*? Murāri defines the grounds why such a cognition cannot be called a verbal understanding. He says that the process involved in generating a verbal understanding is quite different from that involved in generating inferential cognition.

As a matter of fact, language comes to operate with reference to a thing after that thing is known by another means of knowing. After the nature of the thing is decided by perception etc. language simply conveys this fact to the receiver of that language. Nothing more nothing less. Thus, the nature of smoke and its invariable concomitance is already known by perception, the *hetuvākya* and *udāharaṇavākya* simply remind the hearer of these sentences, the *hetu* and the *vyāpti*. These sentences never decide the character of *hetu* or nature of *vyāpti*. Moreover, the function of a sentence is over after reminding the hearer of its meaning. It has no function to determine the nature of anything. But the inferential cognition is preceded by a different process—knowledge of *hetu*. remembrance of *vyāpti*, the *parāmarśa* and finally the *anumiti*.

Thus, in the present context, if *arthavādas* are the *hetuvākya*, they will simply remind one, of the *hetu* only, and they will never determine the *vyāpti*. Thus, Prābhākaras will be wrong if they say that by *śabdapramāṇa vyāpti* would be known.

If this distinction is not accepted, there will be no necessity of drawing the conclusion after employing five sentences, because the very first sentence, namely, the *pratijñāvākya* will be enough to reach a conclusion. The other sentences will become thus redundant.

Text . 52

सहेतुकं कार्यं प्रतिपन्नं सहेतुकत्वाय प्रतिबन्धम् आक्षिपति इति चेत्,

Tr. :

Whenever some effect is known as dependent upon some ground, in order to explain that it is dependent upon some ground (*hetu*), the effect implies the invariable relation (between the probans and the probandum) i.e. *vyāpti*.

Notes :

Now, since Murāri has refuted the point, Prābhākara wanted to make, fully and clearly, Prābhākara tries to clarify his statement and offers another suggestion. He says : Let not the *śabdapramāṇa* convey the *vyāpti* but we do not see any difficulty in obtaining *vyāptijñāna* by implication. How ? If something is known on the basis of some ground then it is obvious that it cannot be established to be so unless there is invariable relation between that 'something' and that Particular ground. That is why if it is to be maintained that some effect is established on the basis of some reason, it necessarily implies that the effect has an invariable concomitance with the reason. So now we say that let the *vyāpti* or invariable concomitance be known by implication only and not by *śabdapramāṇa*. Thus, this will serve two purposes : (1) The *vyāpti* need not be said to be known by *śabdapramāṇa* as we suggested before and (2) The *vyāptijñāna* obtained through implication will facilitate the operation of inference, which in turn will establish the *hetu-hetumadbhāva* relation between the *arthavādas* and the *vidhis* which again will establish the *ekavākyatā* between them.

Text : 53

न; प्रतिबन्धस्य प्रतीतिहेतुत्वात् तदाक्षेपमन्तरेण प्रतीतेरेवासिद्धत्वात् । न तु सर्वत्राक्षेपः सम्भवतिः रुद्ररोदनादिहेतुस्वरूपे नित्यानित्यसंयोगविरोधात् । प्रतिबन्धस्य रजतदानेऽपि संवत्सरादर्वाग्रोदनानुपलम्भेन बाधात्

Tr. :

No. Because the relation (*vyāpti*) is the cause of *anumiti* and without the implication of that (relation i.e. vyāpti) *the anumiti* itself will not come into existence. Moreover, this implication (of the *pratibandha* i.e. *vyāpti*) also is not possible everywhere. Because in the form of reason, namely, *rudrarodana* etc., its relation with the *kārya* is found to be irregular, because (it is observed that) even after offering silver in the *Barhis* sacrifice, there is no sad event (with the donator) within a year-and thus the *vyāpti* is absent here.

Notes :

Murāri does not accept the alternative suggestion of Prābhākara either, for two reasons. Firstly, if it is accepted that the *vyāpti* is known by implication then, there will arise the fault of mutual dependency. How ? Let us see : Murāri explains, if the *vyāpti* is implied by *anumiti* it is necessary that *anumiti* should come into existence. But the ground to have *anumiti* is the knowledge of *pratibandha*. So unless *pratibandha* is known *anumiti* cannot take place and unless *anumiti* takes place, *pratibandha* cannot be known by implication. Thus, the mutual dependency.

Secondly, even if it is aecepted that the *vyāpti* is implied there by the inferential cognition, this implication is not possible in each and every case of *arthavāda*. Because, sometimes the relation (*vyāpti*) cannot be demonstrated, for example in case of the *arihavāda* relating to *rudrarodana*, this *vyāpti* does not hold true. Why ? The story is as follows : *Rudra* i.e. *Agni* once cried and his tears became silver. So one should not give silver in the *Barhis* sacrifice. If one gives silver then he will have to face a sad event within one year. But in fact, this relation between the offering of silver in Barhis sacrifice and the occurrance of the sad event withine one year is not found to be regular or invariable. On the contrary it is contradicted clearly by the absence, of any sad event after the offering of silver in Barhis sacrifice.

Thus, no implication of *vyāpti* between the *hetu*, namely, the *rudrarodana* and the *sādhya* or *kārya* namely the occurrance of any sad event is possible in this case. And so it cannot be accepted that the *vyāpti* or *pratibandha* is known by implication.

This is how Murāri refutes the suggestion of Prābhākara that *vyāpti* could be known by implication.

Text : 54

केचितु ज्ञापकत्वातिरिक्त सम्बन्धाप्र (पे) क्षितत्वात् हेतुत्वस्य चानुवादेऽसम्भवात् न हेतुत्वा (पेक्षा) इत्याहुः ।

Tr. :

Here some hold the view that (*hetutva* means nothing but *jñāpakatva* and) no relation other than *jñāpakatva* is seen (to stand for *hetutva*) and (such) *hetutva* is not possible in the case of *anuvādas*. Therefore, *arthavādas* cannot be considered as *hetus* (for the *vidhis*).

Notes :

Here someone (probably the supporter of Prābhākara) argues that the *anuvādas* or *arthavādas* cannot at all serve the purpose of *hetus* for the injunctions. For (1) you have just now shown that there can be no *vyāpti* in case of the *rudrarodana* and the occurrance of any sad event within one year. That itself proves that the *anuvādas* cannot be the *hetus* or ground for the *vidhis*—so there is no possibility of there being *hetutva* in the *anuvādas* and (2) no relation other than the *hetutva* or *jñāpakatva* is found in case of the *anuvādas*. So we say better you give up your position that *anuvādas* are *hetus* for the *vidhis*.

Text : 55

तन्न; रोदनप्रभवबर्हिर्द्वारकरजतदानयोः रोदनजनकत्वाकर्तव्यतयोश्च कार्यकारणभावैकार्थसमवाययोः सम्भवात् ।

Tr. :

This is not (acceptable either). Because the relationship of cause and effect and of *sāmānādhikaraṇya* are possible between *rodanaprabhava-rajatadāna* (the giving of silver which is originated from the tears) and *akartavyatā* (the act of not giving) and between *barhirdvārakarajatadāna* (the giving of silver through the Barhis sacrifice) and *rodanajanakatva* (being the producer of tears) respectively.

Notes :

While refuting the point of opponent that no relation other than *hetutva* is possible in case of the *arthavādas* Murāri states that there is a possibility of other relations here namely, in the case of the same *arthavāda, so rodit* ...' i.e. in case of the Rudra-rodana. They are (1) *Kāryakāraṇa-bhāva* and (2) *ekārthasamavāya* or *sāmānādhikaraṇya*.

Murāri shows that there are the two possible relations between *rodanaprabhavarajatadāna* and *akartavyatā* and between *barhirdvārakarajatadāna* and *rodanajanakatā*. How ? Let us see. The prohibitive injunction says that one should not offer silver in the Barhis sacrifice. Why ? Because silver is produced from the weeping of Agnidevatā. And one should not offer somebody else the tears of somebody else. So there is *kārya-kāraṇabhāva* between the two. Not offering the silver is the *kārya* or effect and the *kāraṇa* is *rodanaprabhavatva* or being produced from the weeping of Agni. Similarly, there is the same relation of *kārya* and *Kāraṇa* in case of the *Barhirdvārakarajatadāna* and *rodanajanakatva*. How ? If silver is offered in the Barhis sacrifice the sacrificer will meet some sad event within one year from the time of the sacrifice, i.e. he will have to weep. So the offering of silver in Barhis sacrifice will produce weeping within one year. Here too there is cause—and—effect relationship. The sad event is the *kārya*, the *kāraṇa* of which is the offering of silver in the Barhis sacrifice. Thus, the relationship of cause—and—effect is seen in case of these two, as described above. Similarly *ekārthasamavāya* (i.e. being the locus of two properties) can be another such relation. And thus there is no scope for the opponent's argument that no relation other than *jnāpakatva* is possible in case of the *arthavādas* and on that ground they cannot be the *hetu* or ground for the *vidhis*. Thus, the *arthavādas* and the *vidhis* can be related to each other and they can form sentence-unity.

Text : 56

नन्वेवं हेतुत्वासम्भवात् कथमन्विताभिधानम् ? तदभावे च प्रतीत्यभावात् कथमेकार्थप्रतीतीजनकत्वात् एकवाक्यता ?

Tr. :

Well, in this way, when *hetutva* is not possible (in case of the *arthavādas*) then how do you say that (the two i.e. *vidhis* and *arthavādas*) can be construed with each other (as one single sentence) ? Since they cannot be construed with each other there can arise no understanding. And thus, how could you claim that, on the ground that they produce the knowledge of one single object they constitute one single sentence ?

Notes :

The opponent again points out that there can be no sentence-unity on the ground of the relationship of *hetu-hetumad-bhāva*. He says that it has been clearly demonstrated that there are two relations other than *hetutva* with reference to the *arthavādas* namely, the *kāryakāraṇabhāva* and the *sāmānādhikaraṇya*. That itself proves that there is no *hetutva* in the *arthavādas*. Now, if there is no *hetutva*, there can be no *hetu-hetumad-bhava* between the *arthavādas* and the *vidhis*. If so, then they cannot produce an understanding of one single object. And if they cannot produce an understanding of one single object, it is obvious that they cannot form the sentence-unity.

Text : 57

आपाततः प्रतीतैकवाक्यता चरमं भज्येतैव इति केचित् ।

Tr. :

Some hold that the apparently known sentence unity (in the above case) will not stand scrutiny ultimately.

Notes :

Some think that the sentence-unity between the *arthavādas* and the *vidhis* is not real but illusory one and hence it simply appears to be there. But in reality it is going to be dissolved ultimately.

Text : 58

तन्न, चरममेकवाक्यताभङ्गे तन्निमित्तस्य अप्रामाण्यस्यापि भङ्ग-प्रसङ्गात् ।तद्भङ्गे चक्रकापत्तिरिति चेत्,

Tr. :

No. If the sentence-unity is dissolved ultimately then inauthoritativeness (of the *vidhis*) the ground of which is the sentence unity can also not be maintained (in the *pūrvapakṣa*). And it (the inauthoritativeness of the vidhis) is no more there then it will result into circularity only.

Notes :

Murāri is not prepared to accept that the sentence-unity in the present context is illusory. Because, once this is accepted, the whole building of the *pūrvapakṣa* will collapse and in addition to it there will arise the fault of circularity. The result of circularity is that it never allows the fact to be known. In the *pūrvapakṣa* Murāri needs that the *vidhis* should be brought to invalidity and that could be achieved by showing the unity of the *arthavādas* with the *vidhis*.

But if this unity is illusory the conclusions also will have to be illusory and then again the same circle of attempts will have to be continued which will have no end. Thus, the sentence-unity has to be treated as genuine.

Text : 59

तर्हि त्यज्यतामियमेकवाक्यता, चक्रकनिदानत्वात् ।

Tr. :

Then, please give up this (insistance for) sentence-unity because it will cause circularity.

Notes :

The opponent again insists that there need not be any such sentence-unity to frame the *pūrvapakṣa*. Moreover, Murāri has also pointed out that if this sentence-unity is accepted as suggested by him it will cause circularity. In such a situation it is better to give up the insistance of the sentence-unity, suggests the opponent.

Text : 60

व्युत्पत्तिसिद्धैकवाक्यता न हातुमर्हति

Tr. :

The sentence-unity which is so explicitly known cannot be abandoned.

Notes :

Murāri is not ready to form a *pūrvapakṣa* without accepting the sentence-unity between the *vidhis* and the *arthavādas*. He argues that the sentence-unity can be very explicitly known and that is why it is not proper to ignore it.

Text : 61

न वायोग्यात् प्रतीतिः सम्भवति इत्याशयेन विशीर्णान्येव वेदवाक्यानि इति कश्चित् ।

Tr. :

Since, it is not possible to have a verbal understanding from an expression which has no compatibility—from this point of view the vedic sentences (i.e. the *vidhis* and the *arthavādas*) are indeed separate only—this is what some people argue.

Notes :

Murāri records here the opinion of some supporter of Prābhākara.

There should be no two opinions that a verbal understanding arises from an expression which possesses compatibility. Since the *arthavādas* are narrations and the *vidhis* are injunctions, there is obviously no compatibility between the two, as in the case of *vahninā siñcati*. Hence, the suggestion of Murāri cannot be accepted.

Text : 62

तन्न, एवमध्यवसायेन पूर्वपक्षापत्तेः ।

Tr. :

No. If this is accepted then the thesis of *pūrvapakṣa* gets proved.

Notes :

Murāri argues that if what you say is accepted then there will arise a contingency of accepting the thesis of *pūrvapakṣa* that the *arthavādas* are not valid, what is the argument of *pūrvapakṣa* ? *Pūrvapakṣin* wants to establish that, the *vidhis* and the *arthavādas* cannot get connected on any logical ground, and the *arthavādas* themselves are not capable of expressing any *kārya*-sense and so they are not authoritative with reference to *Dharma*. This will have to be accepted in toto if what you say is accepted.

Text : 63

पूर्वपक्षिणां भ्रमज्ञानाङ्गीकारात् भ्रान्तैकप्रतीतिजनकतयैव एकवाक्यत्वमित्यन्ये ।

Tr. :

Here some others say that the opponent accepts illusory knowledge (*bhrama* in such cases) and thus, since (the group of the expressions of the *arthavādas* and the vidhis) generates illusory single knowledge, there is (illusory sentence-unity there.

Notes :

Some scholars tried to settle the matter by arguing that in such cases the Prābhākaras would accept the false knowledge and thereby a false sentence-unity-since Murāri insists to form the *pūrvapakṣa* on the basis of *ekavākyatā* between *vidhis* and *arthavādas*. So the arguer says, let there be *ekavākyatā*. How ? the Prabhakaras will accept false knowledge in such cases and so let us suppose that after reading the *vidhi* sentence and also the relevant *arthavāda*-sentence, there would arise a single knowledge. Nevertheless, this knowledge would be a false knowledge. And on the basis of this false knowledge, one can assume a sentence-unity between the *vidhis* and the *arthavādas*. Thus, let us say for the time being that the Prabhakaras also accept the sentenceunity but that unity is illusory and not real one.

Text : 64

तन्न, देशान्तरनिषिद्धस्य स्वीकारासम्भवात् स्वसिद्धान्ततन्मूलन्यायेतरन्यायदर्शित्वात् पूर्वपक्षिणो भ्रान्तेश्चाव्यवस्थितत्वात् भिन्नान्यपि वाक्यानि एवमेकवाक्यानि स्युः। अत एव भिन्नानामपि ज्ञानानां भेदाग्रहवत् एकार्थव्यवहारकारितयैकतामौपाधिकीमाश्रित्य तज्जनकतयैकवाक्यत्वं सम्भवति इति निरस्तम्।

Tr. :

This is not (proper). Because, (when illusion) is denied in some other place, the same cannot be accepted to be valid (here), also because that will lead to accept some other doctrine different from one's own doctrine. Moreover, it has not been very well established by the opponent that they accept *bhrama* (in such cases). (And if one accepts *bhrānti* here) then any two sentences could be connected with each other, (what to talk of the *vidhis* and the *arthavādas*. Because of this stand the following view is automatically refuted : As in the case of the knowledge (this is silver after seeing the conchshell) although there are two different knowledges still oneness is superimposed on that because it refers to one object due to not catching the difference between two knowledges, similarly, the sentence-unity can be there in the case of *arthavāda* and *vidhi* due to superimposed one-ness because of their causing the behaviour of a single object.

Notes :

Murāri, straight way, denies the *bhrānti* in an understanding of *ekavākyatā* between the *vidhis* and the *arthavādas*. He firstly points out that it is not possible on the part of the Prabhakara to say that at this juncture, they accept *bhrānti* or false knowledge. Why ? Because the Prābhākara has refuted the very existence of a false knowledge. Now, when that was denied in some place it cannot be accepted as valid in another place by the same person, says Murāri. This will imply two things; firstly, that it will lead to accept something which is not accepted by one's own school. And secondly, Prābhākara has not even established his *bhrānti* in this context, of *ekavākyatā* beyond any reasonable doubt.

By the above argument Murāri prevents the extension of the application of the *akhyātivāda* of the Prābhākara.

Now let us first see, what the *akhyātivada* of Prābhākara is. It will be clear from one example : Say, a person has a knowledge, '*idam rajatam*' after seeing a conch-shell. Now, according to Prābhākara the knowledge of a silver after seeing a conch-shell is not a false knowledge. But it is a true knowledge. It is a simple fact that the person could not know the difference between the knowledge of silver and the knowledge of conch-shell. As a matter of fact, the knowledge, 'this is silver' consists of two knowledges (1) the perception of 'this' and (2) the remembrance of 'silver'. Both are true. It is only the *vyavahāra* which is erroneous, and never the cognition.

This is what is called *akhyātivāda* of Prābhākara in short. Now, in the present context of ours Prabhakara may argue that just as in case of two different knowledges, one is unable to grasp the difference between the two and superimposes one-ness upon it, same way here, on the basis of the superimposed one-ness one can imply sentence-unity between *vidhis* and *arthavādas*.

Murāri turns down this possibility also.

Text : 65

उच्यते—नैकप्रतीतिकारित्वमेकवाक्यतावधारणहेतुः किन्त्वेकार्थप्रतीतिपरत्वम् । तच्च प्रतीत्यजननेऽप्यस्ति, फलशून्यस्यापि तात्पर्यस्यानाप्तवाक्येष्विव सम्भवात् । तदवधारणमपि योग्यतां नापेक्षते, अयोग्येष्वपि विप्रलम्भकवाक्येषु तदवधारणात् । सिद्धसाध्यसमभिव्याहारादिरेव तस्या अवधारणे हेतुः । अत एव गङ्गाघोषादौ लक्षणा; अन्यथा—योग्यत्वादेकवाक्यत्वं, तद्बलाच्च लक्षणया योग्यत्वं—इति दुरुत्तरमितरेतराश्रयं स्यात् । तस्मादन्विताभिधाने एव योग्यता कारणम् न तु एकवाक्यतावधारणे । यथा च सिद्धान्ते प्राशस्त्योपनयः पदानां सम्भूयः प्रत्येकं वा, तथा पूर्वपक्षे हेतूपनयः ।

65 A :

न चैवं प्राशस्त्योपनयं एवास्तु इति वाच्यम् लक्षणाप्रसक्तेः । प्रामाण्यार्थं लक्षणेति चेत्, न, अव्युत्पन्नत्वात् ।

Tr. :

Here is our answer. The state of producing 'one understanding' is not the ground for determining the sentence-unity but it is the state of producing the 'understanding of one object'. And that (state of expressing knowledge of one object) is present, even if there is no understanding just as an intention is found in the sentences of an unbelievable preson where the result (ie. successful activity) is not found.

The determination of the sentence-unity also does not require compatibility (as its cause) because it (the understanding of *ekavākyatā*) is determined even in the incompatible sentences of a cheat.

The juxtaposition of the *siddha* and *sādhya* words is the ground for determining the *ekavākyatā*. This is the reason for accepting *lakṣaṇā* (i.e. secondary relation) in the sentences like (*gaṅgāyām ghoṣaḥ*. Otherwise, (i.e. if compatibility would have been the ground for the sentence-unity) there will arise a contingency of mutual dependency which cannot be removed : Because of the compatibility, there will be sentence-unity and on the strength of the sentence-unity there will be compatibility through *lakṣaṇā*. Therefore, compatibility is the cause for (understanding) the relations between the meaning of the words of one single sentence, but it is not the cause or ground for determining the sentence-unity. (And thus,) as the *prāśastya* is known by either *padalakṣaṇā* or *vākyalakṣaṇā*, according to the *siddhānta*, in the same way, the understanding of the *hetu* is acquired according to the *pūrvapakṣa*.

65 A. :

Now here, one should not argue that the knowledge of *prāśastya* only could be accepted in the *pūrvapakṣa*, because that will lead one to resort to *lakṣaṇā*. Now, if one says that let there be *lakṣaṇā* in order to prove the authoritativeness (of the *arthavādas*) then that is also not acceptable. Because *lakṣaṇā* is not agreed upon (by both the parties in case of the *pūrvapakṣa*, whereas it is agreed for the sake of authoritativeness in the *siddhānta*.)

Notes :

Here Murāri clearly states his view about how the understanding of *ekavākyatā* takes place. He points out that *ekavākyatā* or sentence-unity is not known in a sentence simply because it produces one knowledge. Rather it is determined on the ground that it produces the knowledge of one single object. What does it mean ? Let us consider following two sentences ;

(1) There is a pen, a pencil, a note-book and a pen on the table.

and

(a) There is a blue pen on the table.

Now, in the first instance, though there arises one knowledge, it has many things as its object. This type of knowledge is called, *samūhālambana-jñāna* in the technical terminology. *Samūhālambana-jñāna* means a knowledge having a group of things as its object. Now from the point of view of the Mīmāṃsakas, the first sentence though it seems as one sentence apparently, it is not a one single sentence. But it is a combination of four different sentences underlying the surface construction of the sentence. Because according to the Mīmāṃsakas one sentence conveys only one thing (*viśeṣya*) and not more than one.

Now let us turn to the second sentence. The second sentence denotes only one qualified thing i.e. the blue pen. Now the knowledge arising from this sentence has only one object i.e. the blue pen.

From this it will be clear what Murārī means when he says that it is not one knowledge that contributes to deciding the sentence-unity but it is the knowledge of one single object that counts. So according to Murāri's opinion which is very much in keeping with the general opinion of the Mīmāṃsakas, the second sentence is a single sentence whereas the first sentence cannot be called one single sentence.

Now, further Murāri points out that even if it is not known that it is the knowledge of one single object it exists there alright (in one single sentence). Because, it cannot be argued that something does not exist simply because someone does not know it. For instance, in the case of a sentence of an unbelievable person, there may not be any successful activity as the result of the understanding of that sentence but still the sentence uttered by that person remains meaningful. The meaingfulness of the sentence has no expectancy of the consequence (i.e. a successful activity and so on).

Further Murāri makes an important point that the understanding of the sentence-unity has no expectancy of *yogyatā* or compatibility as its ground. In other words, *yogyatā* is not the criterion to determine the sentence-unity. How ? Murāri explains that a cheat's sentence may not be *yogya* or compatible but still that it is one single sentence is understood without any difficulty. This itself proves that the compatibility is not the cause or ground to determine an *ekavākyatā*.

Then the next question arises, what could be the ground on the basis of which the *ekavākyatā* is known ? Murāri gives a very simple answer : The juxtaposition of *siddha* and *sādhya* words (i e. nominal inflected forms and a finite verbal form) will decide the sentence-unity. To say it in other words, there are some words which denote siddha meanings and there are some words which denote *sādhya* meanings in one single sentence. A single sentence consists of some words denoting *siddha* meanings and some words denoting *sādhya* meanings. Now, this juxtaposition of these words is enough to determine the sentence-unity according to Murāri.

He further argues that had it not been the case then the *lakṣaṇā* in the sentence *Gaṅgāyām ghoṣaḥ* would have been difficult to explain. In the well-known example of *lakṣaṇā Gaṅgāyām ghoṣaḥ* (there is a milkman's house on the ganges) the expressed meaning of the word *Gaṅgā* i.e. the stream of the river cannot be construed with the other word *ghoṣa* i e. milkman's house. And so the word *Gaṅgā* is taken to mean the bank of the river by *lakṣaṇā* i.e. In other words, the secondary meaning of the word *gaṅgā* is accepted. This is how *lakṣaṇā* operates. But if the sentence-unity depended upon the compatibility, there is in fact no compatibility between the water and the milkman's house and so there would have been no sentence-unity and so, no need to resort to *lakṣaṇā*.

Murāri therefore argues, that had the criterion been *yogyatā* for the determination, a serious contingency of mutual dependency would have been the result, in case of the *lakṣaṇā*. How ? Let us take the same example which is explained above, to make the point more clear.

Now, the sentence is '*gaṅgāyâm ghoṣaā*. If the compatibility is to decide its one-ness then what will be the consequence ? Mutual dependency. How ? Murāri explains, on the basis of compatibility the sentence is one and on the other hand, because the sentence is one, there can be *lakṣaṇā* and through *lakṣaṇā* there comes compatibility. Needless to say, there is no compatibility in the sentence *gaṅgāyām ghoṣaḥ*, since the *ghoṣa* cannot exist on the stream of the river Ganges. (This compatibility is already explained earlier. (c.f.).

That is why, Murāri further says, compatibility is a ground to relate two meanings of the words in the same sentence but it cannot be a ground for determining the sentence-unity.

Thus, as the praise is understood from the *arthavādas* by accepting *padalaksaṇā* or *vākyalaksaṇā* in the *siddhānta*, in the same manner hetu is known in the *pūrvapakṣa.*

65 A.

One cannot argue that let the *prāśastya* be known in the *pūrvapakṣa* itself. Because that will mean going against the norm and to accept *laksaṇā* in the *pūrvapakṣa* itself is not an established fact. In the sense of *hetu*, however, the *arthavādas* can be understood by *lakṣaṇā* in the *pūrvapakṣa.*

Text : 66

राद्धान्तस्तु—शाङ्कितदोषाद्धि पुंवाक्यात् प्रतीतोऽर्थः प्रमाणभूतं हेतुमपेक्षते; निर्दोषात्तु वेदात् प्रतीतस्य विशेषतोऽपूर्वस्य न हेत्वपेक्षा। न च तदुत्थापनं शक्यम्, स्वरूपभङ्गप्रसंङ्गात्। न चानुवादानुरोधेन तत्स्वरूपमेव त्याज्यम्; अनुवादत्वात्, तस्य प्रधानत्वात्। अतो वाक्यार्थेऽपूर्वेऽनुवादार्थस्य सम्बन्धानुपपत्तेः प्राशस्त्यलक्षणैव; नैव ह्यप्रामाण्यार्थे लक्षणा। किं च अगृहीतप्रतिबन्धतयानुवादार्थो न मुख्यर्थान्वययोग्यो गङ्गापदार्थेव स्पदार्थइव इति लक्षणैव युक्ता। स्तावकत्वेन चान्वयो दृष्ट एव यथा इयं गौः क्रय्या, स्त्र्यपत्या—इत्यादौ।

Tr. :

The meaning which is understood from a sentence of a human-being the authoritativeness of which can be doubted does expect some reason in the form of proof, but with reference to the meaning which is understood from the faultless (i.e. self-valid) *vidhi*-sentences, which was not known earlier by any other means, there is no expectancy of any *hetu* or ground (as a proof for it). Moreover, if you somehow accept that there is an expectancy of ground there also, then the very nature of the Veda itself (i.e. not depending upon anything else) will be lost. And it is not proper to abandon the very nature of the *vidhis* just for the sake of *anuvāda*-sentences because after all, they are only *anuvādas* 'narrative sentences' whereas, a *vidhi* is, in any case, prominent. Therefore, since the expressed meaning of *anuvāda* cannot be fit to be connected with the meaning of the *vidhi* which was not known earlier, we have to accept *prāśastya-lakṣaṇā* (i.e. to understand the meaning of the *arthavādas* i.e. the praise by accepting secondary relation). The *lakṣaṇā* however is not accepted for the sake of (removing the inauthoritativeness of the *arthavādas*. Moreover, since the invariable relation between *viahis* and *arthavādas* is not known, the primary meaning of the *arthavādas* cannot be connected with the *vidhis* just like the (primary) meaning of *Gaṅgā-pada* (cannot be connected with the *ghoṣa* if the relation between the two is not known), therefore, it is quite proper to accept *lakṣaṇā* here.

Even in our common-parlance, it is seen that two sentences are related to each other, one being the priase of the other as in the sentences like, this cow is fit to be purchased. It has given birth to a female calf,

Notes :

Here, Murāri has stated the argument of the *siddhāntin*. *Siddhāntin* does not accept the proposal of *pūrvapakṣa* that the *anuvādas* can be related to the *vidhis* as their *hetu*, on the ground that there is no expectancy on the part of vidhis for any *hetu*. The *siddhāntin* argues that a ground is always expected as a proof for a sentence uttered by a human-being-since there is always a possibility of a mistake on the part of a human being. But such a situation does not arise at all in the case of *vidhis* since a vedic sentence is not uttered by any human being. And that is why the *vidhis* are absolutely faultless and self-valid which require no reason or ground for their validity.

Now, if someone attempts to say that the *arthavādas* can be related as the *hetus* to the vidhis by some way or the other, that is also not possible because this will mar the basic nature of the *vidhi*. How ? Just now we have seen that the vedas are free from any relation with any human agency and that is why the *vidhis* are absolutely self-valid. Now if we imagine that they have an expectancy for some ground for them then the very characteristic of the *vidhis* is lost. Because if they are dependent upon some ground then in what way will they be different from ordinary sentences ?

If someone goes one step further and says then give up this independent nature of the *vidhis* for the sake of the validity of the *arthavādas* then it is rediculous because the *vidhis* form the major part of the Veda and they are prominant-whereas the *arthavādas* are subordinate because they are narrative in nature.

Then how to relate the two—*vidhis* and *anuvādas* ? It is a fact that the possibility of relating the primary meaning of the *arthavādas* with that of the *vidhis* is not there and it is also a fact that unless the two are related there is no scope for the *arthavādas* being authoritative. These two facts by themselves imply that the secondary meaning of the *arthavādas* has to be accepted. There is no other way to settle the problem.

In this way, it is accepted that the praise is understood from the *arthavādas* by *lakṣaṇā*. Now, the *prāśastya* and the meaning of the *vidhis* can be related. The *yāga* is now worth-performing.

And similar examples of understanding praise by *lakṣaṅā* can be observed even in ordinary verbal behaviour of ours. The example is explained as follows : If a person wants to sell his cow he will naturally say that this cow is fit for buying—it gives birth to female progeny and so on. Now this is only for praise of the cow so that the person would feel like purchasing it.

Same way *arthavādas* could express the praise of *yāga* so that a person would be inclined to take up its performance.

Thus, from all this what is achieved is the idea of relating the *arthavādas* with the *vidhis* by *hetu-hetumadbhāva* relation is dropped, and so all earlier contingencies are automatically removed and a new proposal has been made namely, relating the *arthavādas* and the *vidhis* by the relation of 'the praiser-and-the praised'. This new relation has been corroborated by our daily experience.

Text : 66 A

तद्गुणस्वरूप कथनमेवेति चेत्, न; वाक्यभेददोषात् ।

Tr. :

If someone argues that (in the above-mentioned ordinary sentence) there is nothing more than the description of the qualities of the cow, it will not be proper. Because, in that case it will invite the fault of sentence-split.

Notes :

Sentence-split is a fault of which Mīmāṃsakas are afraid very much. According to them, one sentence expresses only one single thing (*vidheya*) and if there is a case of expressing more than one thinges (*vidheyas*) by a sentence it is a case of *vākyabheda* or sentence-split, which must be avoided as far as possible.

Here, if it is said that in the above-mentioned sentence, it is the description of the qualities of the cow then there will be the contingency of being more than one sentences, namely, the cow is purchaseable, the cow gives birth to female calf and so on. And so the suggestion is not acceptable to us.

Text : 66 B

हेतुत्वेन तत्रापि अन्वय इति चेत् न; असतोऽपि गुणस्य कीर्तनात् ।

Tr. :

Now if one argues that, there too (in those ordinary sentences, it has given birth to female calf) can be related to (the cow is purchaseable) as a ground (*hetu*), that too will not be a correet stand. Because, the qualities which the cow does not possess are also described there (so that the person will have inclination to buy it).

Notes :

The objector wants to say that what you say as the praise can also be said to be the ground and so let the *arthavādas* be related to the *vidhis as hetu* and so what is the need to resort to praise ? This suggestion is not acceptable to Murāri because a *hetu* has to be an existent entity and not that which is non-existent. But in praise this restriction is not there; even a non-existent quality can be mentioned in order to create an inclination. So a praise and a *hetu* do not go hand in hand.

Text : 66 C

विप्रलम्भ इति चेत् न; आप्तैरपि प्रयोगात्—एवं "वरं विषं भुङ्क्ष्व, मा वास्य गृहे भुङ्क्थाः–" इत्याद्युदाहार्यम् ।

Tr. :

If you argue that (if non-existent quality can also be mentioned to create inclination then) it is a *vipralambha* i.e. an act of cheating.

It is not correct. Because even reliable parsons (*āpta*) are found to use such type of sentences. For instance, take the following sentence and the like : "Better you eat poison than you take food in *his* house".

Notes :

The opponent tries to tie Murāri in his own words. He argues, if there is a description of the qualities which are not existent then it is clearly an utterrance of cheating. On this, Murāri simply points out to the fact that the people who are quite reliable also use such sentences. What he means to say is that the reliable people cannot use any sentence to cheat others. Murāri corroborates this by citing the following example :

'Better you eat poison than you take food in his house'. Let us imagine a situation in which this sentence might have been uttered. Suppose, a mother has some enemity with her neighbour and she does not want her son to go and eat in the house of her enemy and says the above sentence. Now, the implication of this sentence is not that her son should take poison. She simply wants to refrain her son from taking food in the house of her enemy. That is all. But nevertheless she says expressedly 'better you take poison'. So mere decrying is the meaning of this expression. Similarly, praise can be there even if non-existent qualities are mentioned.

So two main points imerge from the above explanation :

(1) Sentences like the example given above are not uttered to cheat others, and

(2) They are not to be taken at their face-value. i.e. in other words, their expressed sense is not important but the secondary sense which is intended by the speaker is significant and is to be taken into account.

Thus, from all this Murāri wants to show that the primary sense of the *arthavādas* is not important just like in the above explained example, and they are to be construed with the *vidhis* by accepting their secondary sense namely, a praise, by the relation of praiser-and-praised.

Text : 66 D

मुख्यार्थानुवादकतयैवानुवादानां प्रामाण्यमस्तु; किं प्राशस्त्यलक्षणया ? इति चेत्—

न एकस्मिन्वाक्ये प्रतीतिवदनुवादश्चेत्यङ्गीकारे वाक्यभेदप्रसङ्गात् इति केचित् ।

Tr. :

If you say let the *arthavādas* be valid because they repeat the main sense i.e. the *vidhyartha*. What is the need of accepting *laksaṇā* in the sense of praise ? Then some people deny it. Because if it is accepted then it will mean that the same sentence causes the knowledge of the main sense as well as it repeats the same and there will arise the contingency of the faulty of *vākyabheda*.

Notes :

Someone here suggests that instead of accepting *lakṣaṇā* to express the praise, we can prove the authority of the *arthavādas* by another way, let us say that the *arthavādas* only repeat the main sense of the injunctions and hence they are also valid.

But according to some, this cannot be accepted only because it will result into the fault of *vākyabheda*. Because if one and the same sentence expresses its meaning as well as it repeats the injunctive sense also then the fault of *vākyabheda* cannot be avoided which is a serious fault compared to resorting to *laksaṇā*.

Text : 66 E

कथं तर्हि 'सौर्यं चरुं निर्वपेत्' इति निर्वपतिः अनुवाद इति चेत्, न; तस्यापि स्तावकत्वात्, अविधेयान्वयितया त्वनुवादोक्तिः ।

Tr. :

Then how is it said that the *nirvāpa* in '*sauryam carum nirvapet*' is a repetition ?

No (this cannot be asked). Because (in fact) that too is the expression of praise and simply because it is connected with *avidheya*, that is *uddesya* it is said that it is a repetition.

Notes :

In the *Darśapūrṇamāsaprakṛtiyāga* the *nirvāpa* (measuring of the oblation) is already enjoined by the sentence, '...*evam eva anūpūrvam havīṃsi nirvapati*. The *saurayāga* is a *vikṛtiyāga* which is enjoined by the sentence, '*sauryam carum nirvapet Brahmavarcasakāmaḥ*'. In this sentence the verb *nirvapet* is used which literally means 'one should measure'. But this measuring is not required because *nirvāpa* is already enjoined by another sentence mentioned above. Hence *nirvapet* here is treated as *anuvāda*. In fact *nirvāpa* is not enjoined here but still the sacrifice is enjoined here by the word *nirvapet*. Thus we have to interpret that by *nirvapet* the *nirvāpa* enjoined by the earlier *vidhi* is being praised here and the sacrifice in which *Sūrya* is the deity is also enjoined here.

Text : 67

तन्न, क्रमेणान्विताभिधाने एकस्मिन्नपि वाक्ये प्राप्त्यनुवादयोः सम्भवात् । यदि नो वादः, तदा प्राशास्त्योपनयेऽपि का विधा स्यात् ? यदि च तदपि विधीयते, तदा स्वातन्त्र्येण वाक्यभेदः । तद्विशिष्टयागादि-विधावपि प्राशस्त्याङ्गत्वमनुवादानां विध्युद्देश्यत्वं प्रसज्येत । उपलक्षण-मिति चेत्, एवं तर्हि तत्प्रमाणान्तरप्रतीतमेव भवति, न तूपादेयम् । तदा च तस्य वादः कथमनुवादः स्यात् ?

Tr. :

This argument is not proper. Because, the understanding (of an expressed sense) and the repetition (of the same) are possible in one and the same sentence when the words express their meanings as connected (with the meanings of the other constituent words of the sentence). If there is no *anuvāda* i.e. repetition then what course could be adopted in the knowledge of praise ? If (you say) that (praise) also is enjoined there then the (fault of) *vākyabheda* will be quite explicitly seen there. Even if the sacrifice qualified by praise is enjoined (i.e. like *viśista-vidhi*), in that case the *anuvādas* will be accessory to the praise and the *anuvāda*-sentences will become injunctions. If you say that this praise is (not a viśeṣaṇa but) an *upalakṣaṇa* of *yāga*) then that is indeed known by another *pramāṇa*, but not enjoined. And then how the expression of it (praise) can be called *anuvāda* ?

Notes :

Here somebody (probably the Bhāṭṭas) points out to the fact that it is not the case that the primary sense and the secondary sense cannot be expressed by one single sentence. He argues that when a verbal understanding of a sentence takes place, what the process involved in it is ? First, the meaning of the words is known either by primary relation or by secondary relation and then the meanings of all the constituent words of the sentence get connected and then the sentence meaning is understood. Now, when the meanings of the words get related, at that time of course the word-meaning is repeated otherwise it is not possible for it to get related with others because knowledge lasts only for two moments. So, when the meaning of the next word is known the first understanding is destroyed by that time, So, naturally, the word-meanings are repeated at the time of their connections. Thus, it is possible that there can be the understanding and the repetition in one and the same process of verbal understanding.

If this were not the fact then how the knowledge of the praise could have taken place? Because to understand the secondary meaning, primary meaning must be known before.

Now, if someone says that the praise also is enjoined then *vākyabheda* will be the result. Because one and the same sentence will enjoin the praise as well as *yāga*. If you say that the praise qualifies the *yāga*, then naturally, the very nature of the *anuvādas* will be lost. Since they enjoin praise, they will become the injunctions and will not remain the *anuvādas*.

Now, if you say that the praise is an *upalakṣaṇa* and not *viśeṣaṇa* then it should be known by some other means of knowledge before because *upalakṣaṇa* is always known before. If it is known then it need not be enjoined obviously. If it is not at all enjoine then there is no question of its being a repetition.

So the point that the arguer wants to make is that it is quite possible and acceptable that there is *prāpti* i.e. first understanding and the *anuvāda* i e. the repetition of the same in one and the same sentence.

Text : 68

विध्युद्देशप्रवृत्तकृतौ हि सिद्ध्यन्त्यां (तां) पश्चादङ्गोपकारार्थं प्राप्तानां वादोऽनुवादो भवति। (वे) रोदनादि तु न तथेति केचित्।

Tr. :

Some hold that once an inducement is caused by an injunction, and some sacrifice is to be undertaken (by some person), the sentences, expressing something needed as the help to the performance of *aṅga*-rites are called *anuvādas* And *rodanādi* sentences are not like those (sentences).

Notes :

Here somebody tries to define what actually is an *anuvāda* sentence. Let us take one example to make the definition clear :

There is one *utpattividhi* which prescribes the *agnihotra homa* for the first time : *Agnihotram juhoti*. Now after reading this sentence, a person is induced to take up *homa* named *Agnihotra*. When actually he goes to perform the rite, he faces a question : With what substance should he perform the sacrifice i.e. in other words, what oblation is to be offered in this sacrifice ? Now there is another sentence of *guṇavidhi* which enjoins the *dravya* for the sacrifice. That sentence is '*Dadhnā juhoti*'. Now, there, curds is the *aṅga* or *gauṇa* to the sacrifice And the homa is only repeated in this sentence—because it is already enjoined by the sentence mentioned above. So the arguer here says that this second sentence i.e. *Dadhnā juhoti*' is called *anuvāda* which helps to perform the sacrifice, by prescribing the subordinate of the sacrifice and merely repeats the sacrifice.

Now the next point is, the *rodanādi* sentences (explained earlier cf) are not of the type, explained above. And so, it is not possible to call them *anuvādas* at all.

And thus, to discuss the authoritativeness of those sentences it is necessary to prove them to be the *anuvādas* before, according to the arguer.

Text : 69

तदयुक्तम्; यदि तस्य नानुवादः, तर्हि प्राशस्त्यस्वाभाविकायाः (कस्य) कृतेरसिद्धन्त्याः (सिध्यतः) कथं प्रथमवादोऽपि भवेत् ?

Tr.

We do not think that this is proper. If *rodana*-sentences are not (accepted as) *anuvādas* (then a contingency will arise that) since the volition itself (i e. to perform the *yāga*) which is very naturally to follow after (the knowledge of) the praise will be impossible. And in that case how to accept the first injunction (of the same) ?

Notes :

The answer to the question raised by the arguer is given (probably by the Bhāṭṭas) as follows : If it is taken for granted for the sake of argument that the *rodanādi*-sentences are not the *anuvādas* then what will be the result ? If the *rodana*-sentence etc. are not the *arthavāda*-sentences then there will be no inducement by the injunctive sentences on the part of any person, and then there will be no performance of any sacrifice obviously. Because without an inducement no action can come into existence. Actually, the function of the *arthavāda*-sentences is to create inclination to take up an activity (in a man) by praising it or create non-inclination not to take up any bad action by condemning it. Now if it is not accepted that there are the *anuvādas* then there will be no inducement at all in any person. And thus, if there is no action at all then it cannot also be said that it is the first statement.

Text : 70

उच्यते—न वा च रोदनादीनां स्वरूपेण प्राप्तिरस्ति ; विध्यन्वयितया तु सुतरां दूरम् । तत् कथं मुख्यार्थस्यानुवादः स्यात् ? यत्र तु सम्भवति, तत्र भवतु तथा । तस्माज्लक्षणया प्राशस्त्यमेवोपनीयते कस्तस्यान्वयप्रकारः इति चिन्त्यम् ।

Tr. :

Now on this point we say the following : Weeping in its own form is not possible to obtain so (that it should be obtained) as connected with the injunctions is out of question. Then how can there be the re-statement of *mukhyārtha* (of *vidhis*) ? Wherever it is possible, let it be there Therefore, *prāśastya* alone is understood from the *arthavādas* by *lakṣaṇā* (there is no question about it), the matter to be considered is only this that how to connect this *prāśastya* or praise with the *vidhis*.

Notes :

Murāri here tries to settle the point raised in the above argument by explaining that, there is no possibility of obtaining (i.e. performing) *rodana* i e. weeping readily. What does it mean ? It means if there is no cause for weeping, there will be no weeping at any cost, i.e. unless there is some cause present like the *iṣṭaviraha* (going away from the beloved one) etc. there is no possibility of occurrence of weeping. Thus, when the weeping itself is not existent, what is the point in talking about its getting connected with the injunctive sentences, at all ? And if it has no relation with the injunction how can it repeat the primary meaning of the *vidhīs* ? That also is not possible. So, it must be accepted that the *arthavādas* only convey the praise through secondary relationship (*lakṣaṇā*). The next question will arise how to connect this praise with the meaning of the injunctive sentences-which requires serious consideration.

Text : 71

अन्वय एवायं विभक्त्यन्वयिकरणत्वादिवत्; न त्वस्याप्यन्वयान्तरापेक्षा विद्यते इत्येके ।

Tr. :

Here some people (think that), the relation (of the *arthavādas* with the *vidhis*) is just like that of the meaning of the *vibhaktis* like *karaṇatva* etc. (with the meaning of the *prātipadika*) it does not require another relation (to get related with the *vidhis*).

Notes :

Here someone argues that actually there is no necessity of postulating any relation for connecting the *prāśastya* with the meaning of *vidhis*. Because, he says that they are connected just as the meaning of *vibhakti* is connected with that of the base (*prātipadika*). As the meaning of a suffix is related to the meaning of the base to which the suffix is added simply by juxtaposition, similarly, the *prāśastya* and the meaning of the *vidhis* can be connected and so no extra relation is required to connect them.

Let us take one example to make our point clear. *Jalena siñcati* is one sentence. In this sentence instrumental case-ending is added after the *prātipadika* 'jala'. Now the meaning of that case-ending namely, *karaṇatva* or instrumentality is connected with *jala* naturally. No relation other than juxtaposition is required to connect them. Similarly, the arguer wants to say that the meaning of the *arthavādas* namely, *prāśastya* can be connected with the meaning of *vidhis* by juxtaposition.

Text : 72

तन्न; एवं तर्हि विध्युद्देशतापत्तेः विभक्तिवत् । न च फलसाधनत्वं प्राशस्त्यं; येनान्वये प्रकारता स्यात्; किं तु तद्वशादन्योत्कृष्टत्वम् ।

Tr. :

This is not (acceptable). Because, if this is the case then just **as** the *vibhakti* (forms a part and parcel of the same sentence, **similarly, the** *prāśastya*) will become the *vidhi* (which is an unwanted situation. Had *prāśastya* been an instrument of the ultimate goal it could have been construed as the *prakāra* i.e. qualifier in the verbal understanding arising from the injunctive sentence. But it is simply the indicator that such and such *yāga* is worthy to be performed.

Notes :

The suggestion of *eke* cannot be accepted. Because, if that is accepted, one has to accept that the *arthavādas* are the part and parcel of the *vidhis*. In other words, the *arthavādas* will become *vidhis* which is not true.

Now, to explain it a bit elaborately, let us see what is the function of *prāśastya* i.e. the secondary meaning of the *arthavādas*. The function of this *prāśastya* (i.e. the act of praising) is simply to praise some particular *yāga* through praising its deity and to convey the excellence of the *yāga* thereby so that one will be inclined to take up that sacrifice for performance. That is all. In no case this *prāśastya* can act as an instrument of the ultimate goal. The instrument however is only that what is conveyed by the *vidhis* themselves. If the nature of the *prāśastya* had been that of an instrument of *iṣṭa* i.e. *svarga* etc., it would have been very easy to construe it as the qualifier in the verbal understanding arising from a *vidhi*-sentence (connected with praise). But such is not the fact. And so there is no way to relate *prāśastya* as a *prakāra* in the verbal understanding of *vidhi* like a *vibhakti*. So the suggestion is totally unacceptable and the position remains the same that it is necessary to think in what way should the praise get related to *vidhis*.

Text : 73

भवतु तर्हि विधेयविशेषत्वमेव प्राशस्त्यस्य; ननु तस्य प्रयत्नविशेषानपेक्षस्य तदुपनेया स्तुतिरेव विधेयास्तु, प्राशस्त्येन स्वज्ञानस्योपस्थापनासम्भवात्। न चैवं विध्युद्देशत्वापातः इति वाच्यम्; तस्य प्रयोजनत्वात् इति चेत्,

Tr. :

Then let the *prāśastya* be a particular *vidheya*. In that case let the *stuti* or praise itself which is presented to the mind from that *prāśastya* be enjoined since the *prāśastya* is capable to present its own knowledge. And one need not worry that it will lead to (the contingency of *arthavāda*) becoming an injunction because it (*prāśastya*) is the *prayojana* (which cannot be a *vidheya*).

Notes :

Here somebody argues that let the *stuti* be a particular predicate which is understood from *prāśastya*. Because it is quite possible to know the praise from *prāśastya*. And even if the praise is predicated, there is no chance of its becoming an injunction because as it is said earlier, it is not an instrument of the ultimate goal like the *yāga* or sacrifice which is expressed by an injunction. Then what is *prāśastya* ? It will fall under the category of purpose and a purpose is never enjoined. It is only the means to attain a particular purpose that is enjoined. Hence, there is no chance of *prāśastya* being enjoined.

Text : 74

न ; [तथाप्यर्थप्रवणतां हित्वा] लक्षितलक्षणापत्तेः : प्राशस्त्योपस्थितिरेव स्तुतेरप्योपस्थितिः, स्वप्रकाशत्वात् ज्ञानस्येति चेत्,

Tr. :

No. Because this will involve *lakṣitalaksaṇā* (which has to be avoided as far as possible). (What we say is), the knowledge of *prāśastya* itself is the knowledge of *stuti* also because knowledge is self-illuminating.

Notes :

Here some (probably the Prābhākaras) take objection to the above-suggestion; since it involves *laksita-lakṣaṇā*. Now let us first see what is *lakṣita-laksaṇā* to understand the point more clearly. An example will make the point clear. *Dvirepha* is a name of a bee. Now how does one get this meaning from the word *dvirepha* ? Because the word *dvirepha* primarily means two 'r' S. So, by the secondary relationship it stands for a word which has two 'r's i.e. the word *bhramara*. But that also does not make much sense in a sentence like *dvirephaḥ guñjati*. So by another secondary relationship again we understand that *dvirepha* stands for the bee.

Thus, to understand the meaning of the word *dvirepha* twice we resorted to *laksaṇā*. So this kind of *lakṣaṇā* is called *laksita-laksaṇā*.

Now let us turn to our context. In our context also, if we accept that *stuti* is understood from *prāśastya* it will be a case of *lakṣitalaksaṇā*. How ? Firstly, the *prāśastya* is understood from the *arthavāda*-sentences, by *lakṣaṇā* or secondary relationship. And again to understand *stuti* or praise from the *prāśastya* we will have to accept *laksaṇā*.

If one says here, then accept two *lakṣaṇās*, what harm is there ? Then the answer to this question is, the *lakṣitalaksaṇā* is not something very desirable and acceptable. But it has to be accepted when there is no other go like the case of *dvirepha* explained above. But if the problem could be solved some other way, one need not resort to *lakṣita-lakṣaṇā*. It must be avoided otherwise.

So, the Prābhākara here points out this fault in the above suggestion and says, actually there is no necessity of accepting second *laksaṇā* here, because the knowledge of *prāśastya* itself is the knowledge of *stuti* because knowledge is self-illuminating. It does not require another knowledge to reveal it. Here *prāśastya-jñāna* is equated with *stuti* and since knowledge is self-illuminating *prāśastya-jñāna* is known by the same knowledge and hence *stuti* is also known.

The Prābhākara view of self-validity of knowledge[27] can be said in brief as follows : The knowledge reveals the object and at the same time it reveals itself just like a lamp which reveals an object and at the same time it reveals itself also.

Text : 75

न; तथाप्यर्थप्रवणतां हित्वा स्वप्रवणताकल्पने गौरवापत्तेः ।

Tr. :

No. giving up the position that knowledge reveals an object (which is an accepted fact) and imagining that it reveals itself involves the fault of *gaurava*.

Notes :

Murāri does not accept the stand of Prābhākara either. He says that it is a well known and accepted fact that knowledge reveals an object. Now if we give up this stand and say that the knowledge reveals itself then this stand will have to be established fully and then only it will be acceptable. This will involve *gaurava* i.e. a long way which should be avoided when other way is possible. And thus, *prāśastyajñāna* itself is *stutijñāna*' is not acceptable to us.

Text : 76

उच्यते—विधेयोपलक्षणतया प्राशस्त्योपनयः ।

Tr. :

(That is why) we say that the knowledge of *prāśastya* is to be accepted as an *upalakṣaṇa* of that which is enjoined (i.e. *yāga* by the *vidhi*).

Notes :

Our suggestion is *prāśastya* is an indicator of the *vidheya* i.e. *yāga*.

Text : 77

ननूक्तमु··· पलक्षणंमन्यब्यवच्छेदकं (न) भवति यथा—कमण्डलुना च्छात्रमानय – इति च्छात्रान्तरं व्यवच्छिद्यते । न चात्र तदस्ति, अप्रशस्तस्य बायोर्व्यवच्छेद्यस्याभावात् ।

Tr. :

Well, *upalakṣaṇa* is a differenciator of something from something else. For instance, when someone says, "Bring the student having the pitcher", (the pitcher) distinguishes that student from the other students. But here, such is not the case, because there is no *vāyu* which is not praised and which could be distinguished thereby.

Notes :

For detailed discussion on this topic, please see Introduction (Section 5.7).

Text : 78

नैवम्; न व्यावर्तकमुपलक्षणं विशेषणं वा, किं तु कार्याङ्गं सत् सम्बद्धं विशेषणम् कार्यानङ्गं सत् सम्बद्धं चोपलक्षणम्; व्यवच्छेदस्तु प्रयोजनमुभयोः । तदिह प्राशस्त्यस्य विधेयवाय्वादिसम्बन्धादुपलक्षणत्वम् उक्तम् । न च प्रयोजनाभावो दोषः ; न हि सर्वेण प्रयोजनवता भवितव्यम्: अस्ति तु तदिति सर्वत्र अतिरेके परिहारः ।

Tr. :

What you say is not correct. *Viśeṣaṇa* or *upalakṣaṇa* is not (defined as) a mere differentiater but that which is connected with (*viśeṣya*) being subsidiary to an action is *viśeṣaṇa* and that which is not subsidiary to an action, at the same time which is connected with (the *viśeṣya*) is called an *upalakṣaṇa.* Nevertheless, the purpose of both is differentiation. So we observe that here (in the present context) *prāśastya* is called *Upalakṣaṇa*, because it is connected with *vāyu* which is *vidheya.* (Now if someone argues here, that if the definition of *upalakṣaṇa* is accepted as you say then here, in case of *Vāyu* (and all the *arthavādas* also) the contingency will arise that there is no *prayojana* since there is no scope for *vyavaccheda* or differentiation because no *vāyu* is *apraśasta*, then our say is as follows :). To be purposeless is not a fault, because it is not necessary that each and everything must have some purpose. And here purpose is indeed there, so this is our argument wherever it is the question of distinction or differentiation.

Notes :

For detailed discussion on this topic please see Introduction (Section 5.7)

Text : 79

न 'चैवमनुवादानामधिकस्यानुष्ठेयस्यअनुपमेयत्वाच्चोदनान्तर्निवेशों न स्यादिति वाच्यम् ; सम्भूयकारित्वव्युत्पत्तेः अनुवादं विना कार्यज्ञानस्यासम्भवात् तस्यैवानुष्ठेय (त्व) प्रतिपादनात्। अत एवार्थवादानां प्रमाणकोटिपर्यवसायित्वमुच्यते । यद्यप्येतादृशं कार्यस्य स्वरूपे प्रमाणत्वं सर्वेषामेव विद्यते, तथापीतरेषामनुष्ठेयान्तरद्वारापि कार्ये व्यापार इति न तथा व्यपदेशः ।

Tr. :

One need not argue that in this way, since there is no action enjoined by the *arthavādas* in addition to *vidhis*, they cannot be said to be construed with the *vidhis.* Because both of them together generate the understanding of something which is to be performed and hence there cannot be the knowledge of what is to be performed without the *anuvādas*, and they cause the knowledge of something which is to be undertaken for performance. This is why the *arthavādas* are said to be included in the category of valid means.

Although all (the *mantras*, *nāmadheya* etc.) are valid with reference to the performance of the sacrifice as they help it in some way or the other, still, since others play their role through another subsidiary action also, through enjoining something more, therefore all of them are not designated in the same way.

Note :

Murāri further explains that, one need not again raise the question that *arthavādas* do not enjoin any action to be performed and so they cannot be related to the injunctive sentences, because as it is seen that, an action i.e. *yāga* is enjoined by the *arthavādas* and *vidhis* collectively. i.e. *Arthavādas* praise some sacrifice and that praised sacrifice is enjoined by the *vidhi*-sentences. Thus, since the action is enjoined by the *vidhis* with the help of the *arthavādas*, the *arthavādas* have to be valid.

Now, in this way, all the remaining types of vedic sentences a e valid by helping the performance of the sacrifice in some way or the other. But the help they provide is not of the same type as that of the *anuvādas* and that is why they are not called by the name of *anuvādas*.

Text : 79 A

न च विध्युद्देशेऽनाकाङ्क्षितत्वात् प्राशस्त्यस्य नान्वय इति वाच्यम्;

रक्तपटवदाकाङ्क्षोपस्थापनसम्भवात्। यथा पटपदं भवति, नैव निराकाङ्क्षं रक्तपदं पट (पद) मन्तरेण, साकाङ्क्षम् अतस्तद्बलात् पटस्यापि रक्ते आकाङ्क्षाकल्पनम्, तथात्रापि। न चात्रासम्भव एवाकाङ्-क्षायाः ; यथा हि पटस्य रक्तो गुणः तथा प्राशस्त्यमपि वाय्वादीनाम्।

Tr. :

Here one should not argue that since there is no expectancy on the part of the injunctions, *prāśastya* cannot be connected (with the *vidhis*). Because, it is quite possible to explain the expectancy (on the part of the *vidhis*) as in the case of *rakta-paṭa* (To make it clear), the word *rakta* is not without any expectancy without the word *paṭa*, so, on the strength of this we can postulate that the word *paṭa* also expects *rakta* in the same way. The same is the case here also (i.e. the *vidhi* expects *prāśastya*).

One should not say that here (in the present context) such an expectancy is not possible. Because as *rakta* is the quality of *paṭa*, *prāśastya* also is a quality of the deities like *Vāyu* etc. (which constitute the sacrifice).

Notes :

Murāri explains that one need not raise any question about the connection of the *prāśastya* with the *vidhis* on the ground that the *vidhi*-sentences are not at all expectant of the *arthavādas*. Because it is logically possible to show the expectancy on the part of the *vidhis*. Murāri explains it with the help of the example, *raktaḥ paṭaḥ*' (i.e. red cloth) Here, the word '*raktaḥ*' is not fully inexpectant of any other word. It does expect some other word to satisfy the expectancy. What does it mean ? It simply means that 'red' eannot be said to be an independent unit in the expression 'red cloth'. It does expect cloth to complete the meaning.

Now, on the strength of this fact one can say that the (word) 'cloth' also expects 'red' in the same way 'red' expects 'cloth', though in reality 'the cloth' is an independent unit to express its meaning.

Now, here also, even if *vidhis* are not dependent upon any thing else, only because the *prāśastya* excepts *vidhi* to make sense, *vidhis* can also be imagined to expect the *prāśastya*. And then the connection of the two is very easily possible since there is an expectancy on the part of both the relata.

Moreover, one need not raise a doubt whether the injunctions require the *prāśastya*. Because the example given above perfectly corresponds with the present case of *prāśastya*, and *vidhis*. In other words, as the red colour is the quality of the cloth same way here, *prāśastya* is the quality of the deities. Hence, as there is mutual expectancy between the red colour and the cloth in the same way there can be an expectancy between the *prāśastya* and the *vidhi*.

Text. 80

न च – लाक्षणिकत्वादनुवादानां नाभिधान (अ) पर्यवसानम्, अतश्च कथमाकाङ्क्षा – इति वाच्यम् ;

Tr. :

One should not argue that since the *anuvādas* are *lākṣaṇika* (i.e. they do not generate any *anubhava*) they do not result into expressing their primary sense and thus how can their be any *ākāṅkṣa* (for the *anuvādas* on the part of the *vidhis*).

Notes :

Here Murāri takes into consideration another possibility of objecting to the above solution. He says that one need not worry that the *arthavādas* are not expressive of their primary meaning and so how can there be *ākāṅksā* or expectancy between these two ? The implication behind this argument seems to be that since these two types of sentences do not convey one and the same type of meaning, they cannot be connected with each other.

Text : *81*

यतः सर्वलक्षणासाधारणत्वात् । तस्मादभिधानग्रहणम् उपलक्षणं तत्र, तात्पर्य [अ] पर्यवसानं तु तत्र विवक्षितम् ।

Tr. :

Because this phenomenon is common to all cases of *lakṣaṇā*. Therefore the understanding of their primary meaning is only an indicatior (to the secondary meaning and) what is intended to be understood from them is only the intention of the speaker.

Notes :

Murāri answers the above question as follows : This is not a problem here. Because if it were so then the problem will be there in case of each and every *laksaṇā* because in any case of lakṣaṇā, the *lakṣyārtha* is obtained through primary sense only. The expression of primary meaning by a *lāksaṇika* word is just an indicator of the secondary meaning and above all the intention which is known from the context is the main factor which leads to go for the *lakṣyārtha*.

So, even if the *arthavādas* convey the secondary meaning by expressing the primary meaning, the expectancy can very well be there because otherwise the intention cannot be known.

Text : 82

यद्याकाङ्क्षाकल्पनेनान्विताभिधानमुभयाकाङ्क्षालक्षणत्वात् सम्बन्धस्य, तर्हि हविरुभयत्वेऽप्याकाङ्क्षाकल्पनम्; अतः कथं तदविवक्षितमिति चेत्;

Tr. :

Now if someone argues here that if you connect (the *vidhis* and the *arthavādas*) on the strength of the postulation of expectancy because expectancy on the part of both sides is the definition of a relation, then in case of "*yasya ubhayam haviḥ* " also one should postulate an expectancy. And then how is it said that it (the expectancy) is not intended there (to be postulated) ?

Notes :

Here somebody raises a doubt. He says that if there is a connection between the *arthavādas* and the *vidhis* on the ground of the postulated expectancy as explained earlier, then the same will be the case in connection with *ubhayam haviḥ* and there also it would not be possible to say that the *ubhayatva* (of *havis*) is not intended. Because, there also, one can have a postulated expectancy. But that is not exactly what is desired. And so this will be the contingency if we accept the view that there can be a postulated expectancy as in the case of 'red cloth' already explained earlier.

Text : 83

न, विशेषणत्वमात्रेण हि तत्राकाङ्क्षाकल्पनम्, न तूद्देशकोटि-विशेषणत्वेनेत्यदोषः ।

Tr. :

No, it is not true. Because, (in case of "*yasya ubhayam*") the expectancy is postulated as mere adjunct and not as an adjunct of the subject (*uddeśya*), and so there is no fault.

Notes :

To understand Murāri's answer to this doubt, let us first see what is the context of *ubhayam haviḥ*. In *Darśapūrṇamāsa* sacrifice, it is enjoined that if the two oblations get spoiled then one should measure five cups of rice (*Yasya ubhayam havih ārtim ārchet, pāñcaśarāvam odanam nirvapet*).

This is a *prāyaścitta-karma*. Now here the question is, whether the number 'two' in 'two oblations' is intended or not. And the answer to this question is that it is not intended.

Now, in our present context here, the arguer says that why should there be no expectancy of *ubhayatva* in *havis* ? Here, Murāri answers, the *viśesana* i e. *ubhayatva* is not the *viśesana* of the *uddeśya* but it is understood as a general viśeṣana in the verbal understanding. And that is why it is not intended. In other words, there is no expectancy between the two. Whereas here the *arthavādas* are not the *viśeṣaṇa* in general but they directly indicate to the sacrifice which is enjoined i.e. *vidheya* and thus the *ākāṅkṣā* can be very easily postulated between the *vidheya* and the *arthavāda*.

In other words, the case of *ubhayam haviḥ* and that of *arthavādas* and *vidhis* cannot be compared because they are of two different types. In the case of the *arthavādas*, the meaning of them is intended to be related with the *vidheya* whereas the *ubhayatra* is not intended to be related as the *viśeṣaṇa* of the *havis*. What is intended there is, 'if any one of the two oblations gets spoiled then one should perform the *prāyaścitta*'.

Text : 84

तत्र प्राशस्त्यं प्रतिपदमेव लक्ष्यते, अतो बह्वः स्तुतय इति केचित् ।

Tr. :

There, *prāśastya* is the secondary meaning of each and every word (of the *arthavāda* sentence) thus, there will be many praises (understood from one and single *arthavāda* sintence).

Notes:

This *kecit* may be some who do not accept *vākyalakṣoṇā* but only *padalakṣaṇā*. They have a doubt that if the *prāśastya* is the secondary meaning of the *arthavādas* then it is known from each word of the sentence and that means that as may words are there, so many will be the *stutis*, i.e. praises understood from one single *arthavāda*-sentence.

Now this situation is naturally not desired. Because, if there are many *stutis* one will be at a loss to select one from them and connect it up with the *vidhi*.

Text. : 85

तदयुक्तम्, एकस्मिन् पदे स्तुतिबुद्धेरनुपपत्तेः । अपि चैवं विध्यन्वये रोदनादीनां विधेयत्वमेव किं न स्यात् ? रूद्ररोदनं हि विधातुं न शक्यते, न तु रोदनमात्रम् । अपि चैवं क्रियाकारकभावेनान्वयः प्रतीयते, स भज्यते; तत्त्यागे वाक्यभेदतुल्यो दोषः स्यात् । तस्मात् सम्भूय प्राशस्त्यलक्षणा ।

Tr. :

This is not proper. Because, knowledge of praise cannot arise from one single word. Moreover, if it were so then why should the *rodana* not be enjoined ? Because it is true that *Rudrarodana* cannot be enjoined but such is not the case with *rodana* i.e. weeping in general, (i.e. it can be enjoined).

Again, another point is if your position is accepted (that from each word praise is understood) then our experience that verbal understanding arises from a sentence which consists of verbal form and the *kāraka* forms will be contradicted. And if that is allowed the fault of sentence-split will be unavoidable. And therefore, we say that the *lakṣaṇā* should be accepted collectively.

Notes :

The answer given by Murāri to the question raised by *kecit* is as follows : There is no possibility of knowing praise from any single word, he says. This is actually a practical difficulty. How ? Let us take an example. There is one *arthvāda*-sentence : *Vāyuḥ vai kṣepiṣṭhā devatā*'. Now the first word in this sentence is *vāyuḥ*. After hearing this word one understands deity *vāyu*—but what more does he understand from this word ? Certainly nothing. i.e. there is no possibilty of knowing praise from a single word. If we turn to the second word of the above mentioned sentence, the point will be further clear. So, the main point of Murāri is, there is no scope to understand praise from a single word.

Next he says, let us suppose, for the sake of discussion that it is possible to understand praise from one word by resorting to *lakṣaṇā*. Then the result will be two-fold. Firstly, there will be no excuse to deny the injunction of *rodana* i.e. weeping. If praise (or censure) is known from one single word of the *arthavāda* then why should not the weeping be enjoined ? It is not the case that weeping cannot be enjoined. It can be, The point is only that the weeping of Rudra cannot be enjoined. So one can say that *rodana* which is known to be praised from single word of the *arthavāda*,, should be enjoined, which is of course not a very sensible thing.

Secondly, if the praise was to be understood from each and every word of the *arthavāda*-sentence then it will mean that understanding does not show a structure which consists of an action and the *kārakas*. In other words, even without the syntactical structure there will arise the verbal understanding which is never the case.

Now, if you say that from every single word praise is understood then this structure of the sentence which consists of *kriyā* and *kārakas* will no more be there. And once it is not there, there is no single sentence one can say, i e. it amounts to the fault of *vākya-bheda*, or sentence-split which must be avoided as far as possible.

That is why we say that let the whole *arthavāda* sentence convey its secondary meaning i.e. praise collectively, which, in turn, will be connected with the meaning of the vidhi-sentence.

Text : 86

नन्वेवं विशकलितानां लक्षकत्वाभावादनुवादानां परस्परान्वयः प्रत्येतव्यः, स चान्वयाभिधानेन। न चान्विताभिधानकालीना लक्षणा सम्भवति, वाक्यार्थप्रतीतिहेतुकत्वाल्लक्षणायाः। वाक्यैकवाक्यता चैवमनुविध्युद्देशयोः स्यात् स्वार्थबोधे पर्यवसानात्।

Tr.

Now if your position is accepted then the words independently cannot denote the secondary meaning (i e- praise) so the connection among the words of *anuvādas* must be understood and that is possible only when the *anuvādas* generate verbal understanding.

It is not true that the *lakṣaṇā* is possible at the time when the relation among the word-meanings is being known, because, the cause or the ground for *lakṣaṇā* is the understanding of the sentence-meaning. And since it results into expressing the sentence-meaning (independently) there will be *vākyaikavākyatā* between the *vidhis* and the *anuvādas*.

Notes :

The Bhāṭṭas (probably) reply to the argument of Murāri in the above paragraph. They say, if the view of Murāri is accepted then we will have to accept *vākyaikavākyatā* betwcen the *vidhis* and *arthavādas*, which is not actually accepted by the Bhāṭṭas.

If the verbal understanding arising from the *arthavādas* is accepted as significant and then if it is related to the meaning of the *vidhis* it will mean that two sentence-meanings are related to each other which is a case of *vākyaikavākyata*. Thus, the contingency will arise that the *vākyaika-vākyatā*, will have to be accepted between the two.

Text : 87

अवान्तरव्यापारतया स्वान्वयावगतिः ; अतः पदार्थप्रतीतिस्थानीयत्वादत्रोपदेशवाक्यता एवेति चेत्,

Tr. :

The connection of the knowledge of the secondary meaning of the *arthavāda* (i e. *prāśastya*) with the meaning of *vidhi* is understood as some additional function (of the *arthavāda*). And so, as the knowledge of *prāśastya* is nothing but the knowledge of a word-meaning there is *padaikavākyata* only (between the *vidhis* and the *arthavādas*). This is what some hold.

Notes :

As the Bhāṭṭas are not willing to accept *vākyaikavākyatā* between the *vidhis* and the *arthavādas*, someone here suggests that there is no *vākyaikavākyatā* only but *padaika-vākyatā* only is there between them. How ? Let us see. The arguer explains that *prāśastya* is understood from the *arthavāda* by *lakṣaṇā* Now this *prāśastya* is just a single word-meaning and when it is connected with the meaning of the *vidhis*, it does not mean that two sentence-meanings are united together, and so there is no question of *vākyaikavākyatā*. It simply implies that one word-meaning is related to another word-meanning of a sentence and hence it is the case of *padaikavākyatā* only. Here knowledge of *prāśatya* itself acts as the function of the *arthavāda* to relate its meaning with the meaning of *vidhi*.

Text : 88

न, सर्वत्र वाक्यैकवाक्यतोच्छेदप्रसङ्गात् ।

Tr. :

No. (In this way) there will be no possibility of *vakyikavākyatā* anywhere.

Notes :

The above suggestion also is not acceptable to the Bhāṭṭas. because if the suggestion is accepted then there will be no *vākyaikavāyatā* in any case. Why? Because, just as it is explained above, every where one can understand word-meaning from the sentence by *lakṣaṇā* and then one can connect it up with the meaning of another sentence. And thence, there will be no occasion to connect two sentence-meanings. Thus the *vākyaikayākyatā* will vanish. Hence the suggestion cannot be accepted.

Text : 89

यत्र द्वयमेवान्विताभिधानं कार्यविषयम्, द्वयोश्च वाक्यार्थयोः परस्परान्वयः, तत्रैकवाक्यता यथा अधिकाराङ्गवाक्ययोः कार्याभिधानेन वाक्यपर्यवसानादिति चेत्,

Tr. :

(Our view i.e.) where both the understandings of the sentence-meanings *anvitābhidhāna*) have *kārya* as their object and both the sentence-meanings are mutually connected, there takes place *vākyaikavākyatā*. For instance, there is *vākyaikavākyatā* between *adhikāravidhi* and *aṅgavidhi*, since they result into one single sentence through conveying *kārya*.

Notes:

The Bhāṭṭas make their position clear. According to them, *vākyaikavākyatā* can be formed between two sentences referring to *kārya*. For example, *adhikāravidhi* and *aṅgavidhi* can form one sentence and there will be *vākaikavakyatā*. Let us take one *adhikāravidhi* and one *aṅgavidhi* to make the point clear. There is one *adhikaravidhi* namely, *agnihotram juhuyāt svargakāmaḥ* and after *aṅgavidhi*, namely, *dadhnā juhoti*. These two sentences indepenently generate verbal understandings of an activity (*kārya*) and hence they can be united into one single sentence. This will be a case of *vākyaikavākyatā* since the verbal understandings arising from both the sentences are significant and one understanding expects the other understanding for completion of the full activity.

Text : 90

एवं तर्हि अकार्यार्थानामनुवादानामन्विताभिधानमेव कथम् ?

Tr. :

If this is correct, then how can there be the knowledge of the sentence-meaning of the *arthavādas* at all which do not express any *kārya* ?

Notes :

Here, the point is that if there is a possibility of the verbal understanding only when the sentence expresses *kārya*-sense then since the *anuvādas* do not convey any *kārya*-sense how will there be the understanding of the sentence meaning at all ?

Text : 91

कार्यान्विताभिधाननियमात्तर्कात् सिद्धार्थानामन्वयावगतिः ततो लक्षणेति चेत्,

Tr. :

Since it is always a ease that (the meaning of the *arthavādas*) is understood in relation with the injunctive meaning, it implies that the narrative sentences also cause verbal understanding and after that *laksaṇā* operates.

Notes :

This a reply to the above objection. The very fact that verbal understanding cannot arise unless there is an association with a *kārya*, implies that the narrative sentences should give rise to verbal understanding. Because, that they are incapable of being associated with *kārya* can be understood only if they generate understanding. Thus, *tarka*[8] stands for 'reasoning' here.

Text : 92

न, तर्कस्य प्रमाणान्तरप्रमेयतयोपस्थापकत्वात् तस्मिश्च प्रमाणान्तर-प्रतीतेः । न च सा विशिष्टावगतिरेव युक्ता अयथात्रस्तुविषयत्वात् । न च तत्रापिल क्षणा तथा सति ताहशेन विशिष्टेन प्राशस्त्यबुद्ध्यभावात् ।

Tr. :

No. Tarka is that which causes knowledge being an object of some other means of valid cognition, and when there is some other means then the verbal understanding from the narrative *arthavādas* will be there by that other *pramāṇa* itself. One need not argue that this knowledge (arising from the narraive sentence) will be a qualified cognition because the object of that knowledge does not correspond to the fact. You cannot say that let there also be *lakṣaṇā* (to have the qualified cognition) because if it is so then by that kind of qualified (cognition obtained through *lakṣaṇā*) the knowledge of *prāśastya* cannot be (produced).

Notes :

Murāri refutes the view that the narrative sentences also generate significant verbal understanding and this fact is known by *tarka.* He says this is not possible because *tarka* is always an object of some other means of valid congnition. Now when there is that other means of cognition what is the necessity of *tarka* ? One can have, in that case, the verbal cognition from narrative sentences even by that other *pramāṇa*..

One cannot argue that let that understanding of the narrative sentence-meaning be the qualified cognition. Because the object of such cognition i.e. the meaning of the narrative sentence does not correspond to the fact.

Here, if one argues, going one step still further, that let there be *laksaṇā* for the understanding of the narrative-sentence-meaning, that will not hold ground. Because, in that case it will mean that the qualified cognition is significant and hence there will be no need to reject that understanding and go for the meaning of praise required for inducing a performer into the activity of a sacrifice

Notes :

Murāri ultimately tries to settle the problem of connecting the *arthavādas* with the *vidhis*. He explains the process of understanding the sentence-meaning of the *arthavādas*. The important point to be noted here is that he offers two different explanations to the understanding of the praising sentences and to that of decrying sentences.

In the case of *nindānuvādas* Murāri says it is an illusion just like it is so in the case of any erroneous cognition arising from a sentence which does not correspond to the fact. The process of understanding will be as follows : Firstly, the word-meanings are known and because of illusion they get connected in the knowledge and produce a qualified cognition thereby. Similarly, the word-meanings are known distinctly after hearing an *arthavāda*-sentence. Then an illusory qualified cognition arises from those word-meanings being connected. Such will be the understanding from the following *nindārthavāda* namely, *Barhiṣi rajatam na deyam. Rudraḥ kila ruroda. Yad arodīttadrudrasya rudratvam.*

And the form of the understanding will be *Rajatasya rodana-prabhavatayā taddānam rodanahetuḥ.*

In the case of *praśaṁsārthavādas* however, the process is not the same. When one reads a *praśaṁsānuvāda* he understands *prāśastya* by the secondary relationship (*lakśaṇā*).

Text : 93

उच्यते—प्रत्येकं पदार्थाः स्मर्यन्ते । तेषां त्र भेदाग्रहाद्विशिष्टैकार्थ-व्यवहारकारित्वं भ्रमतयावभाति । (यथा) तत्र भ्रमादभेदव्यवहारो जायते तथात्राभेदज्ञानोचितं स्मरणम्-रजतस्य रोदनप्रभवतया तद्यनं रोदनहेतुः -इति भ्रमावगते तस्यानुत्कृष्टत्वस्मरणम्, ततोऽदानस्य उत्कृष्टत्वम्, ततस्तदान्वितस्वार्थौ विध्युद्देशानोच्यते । एवमन्येषु निन्दानुवादेषु । प्रशंशार्थवादेषु तु‥‥[न] प्राशस्त्यमेव प्रथमं लक्षयते । तस्माद् भ्रमनिमित्ता लक्षणात्र व्युत्पाद्यते । यत्र विशिष्टोऽर्थः सत्य एव, तत्र भ्रमत्वं न भवति; किं तु तत्रापि नान्विताभिधानम् । अत एव भेदस्याग्रहत्वान्न भ्रमत्वम् अत एव पठन्ति, "सतावासतार्थे न स्तुतिः कर्तव्या" इति ।

Tr. :

Here we have the following to say : (in every case of non-factual sentence) a word-meaning is remembered from each word. And then because of not catching the difference among them by illusion it appears (to the hearer of the sentence) that the meaning understood from the sentence is one qualified object with which one can behave. (As in the above mentioned process) one behaves as if with one single object because of illusion, similarly, here (in the case of *nindārthavādas*) the word-meanings are remembered in such a way as to cause a qualified cognition of those meanings (In the case of *Rudraḥ Kila* ruroda...... *Barhiṣi rajatam na deyam* for instance) the understanding that arises out of illusion is, 'Since the silver is produced from the weeping (of Agni) the offering of it (to the priest in the Barhis sacrifice will cause weeping', and this (non-factual cognition) causes the remembrance that the offering of silver in that sacrifice is not good and from that it is understood that 'not offering (of silver in the sacrifice) is good, and (ultimately) the meaning of *vidhi* connected with that (*rajatadāna-utkṛṣṭatva*) is expressed by an injunctive sentence. The same will be the process of verbal understanding in all cases of the *nindānuvādas*.

In the case of the *praśaṃsārthavādas*, however, the *prāśastya* is understood first, by *lakṣaṇā*. Therefore, here we accept *lakṣaṇā* caused by illusion. Where this qualified object (i.e. the sentence-meaning) corresponds to a fact, there illusion is not accepted to occur, but there too, factual knowledge of sentence-meaning cannot be there. That is why, since the difference is understood it cannot be called an illusion.

Therefore, it is said that, one should praise something by a quality (or an entity) whether it exists in the object praised or not. But one more point Murāri adds to it and says, where the meaning of *arthavāda* corresponds to the fact there one need not say that it (the knowledge of the meaning i.e. *prāśastya*) is illusion. But there also the understanding of the sentence-meaning is not at par with that of a *vidhi* because the knowledge arising from narrative sentence does not involve *kārya*.

Finally, Murari concludes that for praising it is not an absolute necessity that all the properties pointed out by praise must be present in the object praised. At best some of the properties must be present but all need not be present.

Text : 94

अन्ये त्वाहुः – न प्राशस्त्यान्वितः स्वार्थो विध्युद्देशेनोच्यते। किन्त्वनुवादपदैरन्वितस्यैव प्राशस्त्यलक्षणा। क्षिप्रफलदातृत्वे वायोर्भ्रमादप्यवगते वायव्यागस्य क्षिप्रफलसाधनतारूपप्राशस्त्ययानुमन्मानभासरूपात् स्मरणाद् भवति। तच्च ज्ञानं लिङ्ग यत् कर्तव्यताभिधानमापूर्वस्य कार्यम्, तत्र दुःखमयकर्ममूलतया नेयस्य प्रतिबन्धं वारयति। अतः प्रमाणकोटित्वमेव स्तुतेः।

Tr. :

Some say, that an injunctive sentence does not express its meaning as connected with the *prāśastya*. But *prāśastya* is understood by *lakṣaṇā* from the *arthavādas* as connected with the *vidhi*-sentence. Even if the understanding that '*Vāyu*' is a diety that gives result very quickly' takes place by illusion, the knowledge that the sacrifice is praised as the instrument of the quick result, occurs by remembrance which is (in fact) an illusory inference. And this knowledge (of praise) debars the obstruction on the way of performance of the sacrifice which is a troublesome act and which is expressed by the *liṅ* as something to be done. And that is why praise is authoritative (and hence the *arthavadas* which convey praise are also authoritative).

Notes :

Here, Murāri states an opinion of some, which is different from his own. But it seems that he is not in favour of this view. The holder of this view tries to solve the problem by adopting a different means. Instead of saying that the *prāsastya* is understood from the *arthavāda*-sentence and then it is related to the *vidhyartha* why not say that the injunctive sentence in association with the *arthavāda*-sentence conveys praise by *laksaṇā* ? What he wants to say is that, that *vāyu* is a deity who gives result quickly, is understood by illusion and then the knowledge of the *vāyavya*-sacrifice being worthy of performance since it yields quick result occurs by an illusory inference. And ultimately, this knowledge of praise debars the obstruction on the way of performance of the sacrifice prescribed by the injunctive suffix. The obstruction is in the form of reluctance of a person to perform the sacrifice because of the tedious process of *yāga*. And this reluctance will be no more there when a man has the knowledge of praise, and he will be induced to perform it. Since the *arthavādas* perform this function of inducing a man to perform a sacrifice through the praise of the sacrifice, they are authoritative. This is what *anye* want to say.

Text : 95

नन्वनुवादाः प्रमेयमन्विताभिधाने न निवेशयन्ति; अत एवैषामप्रयोजनत्वम् । अनतिप्रयोजनत्वं तु परिभावनेनैव प्रेक्षावतां प्रतिबन्धनिवृत्तेः ।

Tr. :

(Someone objects to the view mentioned above as follows): The *arthavādas* do not supply any content in the verbal understanding (arising from an injunctive sentence). Henee, they have no purpose to serve. Now, the limited purpose (that you are telling) can be understood by wisemen by mere little thinking over it which can remove the obstruction (on the way of performance of the sacrifice).

Notes :

Someone here objects to the way of solving the problem, mentioned above. He says, the *arthavādas* are said to be non-authoritative simply because they do not contribute to the content of the *vidhi*-sentences. And hence the *arthavādas* are purposeless. And if someone argues that the *arthavādas* are required in order to praise the sacrifice, then it is not proper, but that could be achieved by other means also.

Text : 96

यदि सर्वथा निष्प्रयोजनत्वं स्यात्, ततः कथं लोके स्तुतिः स्यात् ?
न हि तत्रायं परिहारः, न च यं वेदकर्तार इति ।

Tr. :

If it is held that (the *arthavādas* serve) no purpose at all then how could there be praise (of anything) in this world ? And there it also is not the solution : *Na ca yam vedakartārah*.

Note :

The upholder of the view stated in *anye tu āhuh* above, replies to the objection merely by pointing out to the fact that the act of praising is a reality. If praising had no purpose why does one praise ? The very fact that people praise (something) implies that praise definitely serves some purpose. The *arthavādas* are also aimed at praising the sacrifice and hence they are purposeful.

The line that is quoted here, namely, '*na ca yam vedakartāraḥ*' could not be attested anywhere and so the context of this line could not be known and hence it could not be understood properly.

Text : 97

विवरणे तु – बाह्यहेतूत्थमप्रामाण्यं प्रथमपादे निरस्तम् । इदानीं तु वेदवाक्योत्थमेवाप्रामाण्यं निरस्यत इति पादभेदः पादावान्तरसङ्गतिश्च । पूर्वपक्षः हेतुसापेक्षकार्यप्रतिपादकत्वात् लिङ्स्तादृशस्वभावावधारणात्' यत्रापि हेतुर्नास्ति, तत्रापि सापेक्षमेव कार्यं प्रतिपाद्यमिति सकलवेदप्रामाण्याक्षेपः । न च स्तावकत्वेनान्वयः, तथापि हेतुत्वापरित्यागात् – यस्मात् प्रशस्तोऽयम्, तस्मात् कर्तव्य इति तदाप्यन्वयः ।

Tr. :

In *Vivaraṇa* (also called *laghvī* by Prabhākara Miśra) however, (the framing of the *pūrvapaksa* and *siddhānta* is as follows :)

The inauthoritativeness of the vedic sentences caused by some ground outside (i.e. other than the vedic text was refuted in the first *pādā* of the 1st Chapter of *Jaimini-sūtras*). But now the inauthoritativeness arising from the vedic sentences themselves is being refued and so the distinction of *pāda* (i.e. sub-chapter) is quite proper and there is also the link with the previous *pāda* (since the authority of the Veda is being discussed).

(Here) the *pūrvapaksa* (is construed as follows). Since the suffix *liṅ* expresses something to be performed which expects some ground, it is determined that such is the nature of the *liṅ*. (Now, once it is accepted) wherever there is no ground, there also (the suffix will express) the *kārya* which expects some ground and thus the whole veda will become inauthoritative. One cannot say that (the *arthavādas* do not serve the purpose of ground but) that of a praise, because even in that case they will not lose their nature as ground, because there also the sentence-meaning will be : since this is praised so it should be done.

Text : 98

राद्धन्तास्तु – यत एव हेतुत्वेनान्वये कार्यस्य कार्यत्वं नास्ति, अत एव स्तावकत्वेनान्वये न स्तुतितः कार्यम् । किं तु कार्यतः एव स्तुतिः । कार्यमेव

ह्यभिधीयमानं स्वावगमाय लिङादिसहकारितया स्तुतिमपेक्षते, न तु प्राशस्त्यं कार्यावगमे लिङ्गमिति ।

॥ इति त्रिपादीनीतिनयने अर्थवादाधिकरणम् ॥

Tr. :

The *rāddhānta* or *siddhānta* (conclusion) is as follows : Because of the very fact that if the *arthavādas* are related to the injunctions as ground, the *kārya* will not remain *kārya*, therefore if they are related to the *vidhis* as praising sentences, it will mean that something is *kāryā* not because of praise but it is a praise because something is a *kārya*. The *kāryā* being expressed (from the *vidhi*) requires praise as an auxiliary cause of the optative suffix in order to cause its own understanding. But in no case the praise is the ground for knowing the *kārya*.

(Here ends the *Arthavādādhikaraṇam of Tripādīnītinayanam*)

Notes :

In the end, Murāri just states the argument of Prabhākara from *Laghvī*. He does not express his own view regarding it. Perhaps it is his style which he has, most probably, picked up from Bhavanātha the author of *Nayaviveka*. Even if Murāri has not commented upon Prabhākara, we can very well observe that he is not in favour of the view of Prabhākara, since he has not accepted Prābhākara views elsewhere. We have already seen that he refutes the theory of Prabhākara according to which knowledge is self-illuminating.

An interesting point to be noted here is, that though both Bhavanātha and Murāri state Prabhākara view from *Laghvī* still they differ very much in doing so. What is stated as the *siddhānta* of Prabhākara in *Nayaviveka*, Murāri states it as the view of *Pūrvapakṣa*. Since *Laghvī* is not available today it is difficult to verify who correct is, whether Bhavanātha or Murāri. This kind of discrepancy is found also due to lack of a living tradition of both the Prābhākara school as well as the school of Murāri.

Bibliography

Anargharāghava of Murāri : Ed. Durgaprasad & K.P. Parab, Nirnaysagar Press, Bombay, 1887.

Aṅgatvanirukti of Murāri : Anandashram Sanskrit Granthavali, Granthanka—137, Pune, 1938.

Arthasaṅgraha of Laugakṣi Bhāskara : Ed. Narayanram Acharya, Chowkhamba Sanskrit Series, Varanasi, 1982.

Bhāṭṭcintāmaṇi of Gāgābhaṭṭa : Ed. Pt. Suryanarayan Shukla, Chowkhamba Sanskrit Granthamala-6, Varanasi, 1933.

Bṛhatī of Prabhākara Miśra : Ed. S. Subrahmanya Shastri, Madras University Sanskrit Series No. 24, 1962.

Bhāratīya Darśan (Hindi) of Umesh Mishra : Hindi Samiti Granthamala No. 10, Lucknow, 1958.

Epistemology of Bhāṭṭa School of Pūrvamīmāṁsā by Govardhan Bhatt: Chowkhamba Sanskrit Studies vol. xvii, Chowkhamba Sanskrit Series Office, Varanasi, 1962.

History of Indian Philosophy (vol. I) by S.N. Dasgupta : Motilal Banarsidass, Delhi, 1975.

History of Indian Philosophy by Umesh Mishra : Tirabhukti Publications, Allahabad, 1957.

Indian Philosophy by S. Radhakrishnan : George Allen & Unain, London, 1923.

Indian Realism by Jadunath Sinha: Trench Trubner & Co., Broadway House, London, 1938.

Introduction to Indian Philosophy by J. Sinha : Laxmi Narayan Agarwal, Agra, 1949.

Introduction to Pūrvamīmāṁsā of Pashupatinath Shastri : Chowkhamba Orientalia, Varanasi, 1923.

Jaiminisūtras of Jaimini : Anandashtram Sanskrit Granthamala—97, Pune.

Kiraṇāvavi of Udayana : Ed. Jitendra S. Jetly, Gaekwad Oriental Series 154, Baroda, 1971.

Kusumāñjaliprakaśa of Vardhamāna : Kashi Sanskrit Series—30, Benares, 1957.

Mānameyodaya of Narayaṇa : Ed. C.K. Raja, The Adyar Library, Madras, 1975.

Mīmāṁsā : The Vākyaśāstra of Ancient India by G.V. Devasthali, Bookseller's Publishing Co. Bombay, 1959.

Nayaviveka of Bhavanātha : Ed. S. Subrahmanya Shastri, Rashtriya Sanskrit Samsthan, New Delhi, 1977.

Nīlakaṇṭhaprakāśikā on *Tackadīpikā* of Nilakaṇṭha : The Kashi Sanskrit Series—187, Varanasi, 1969.

Nyāyabhāṣya of Vātsyāyana : Ed. Gangaratha Jha, Oriental Book Agency, Pune—1939.

Nyāyamañjari of Jayantabhaṭṭa : Ed. K.S. Varadacharya, Oriental Research Institute, Mysore, 1969.

Nyāyaśikhamaṇi (Comm.) of Rāmakṛṣṇādhvarin : Ed. N.S. Ramanuja Tatacharya, Kendriya Sanskrit Vidyapeeth, Tirupati, 1973.

Nyāyasiddhāntamañjasī of Janakinatha Bhattacharya : Ed. Gaurinath Shastri, Calcutta, 1885.

Nyāyasiddhāntamuktāvali of Viśvanatha : The Kashi Sanskrit Series-212, Benares, 1972.

Nyāyasūtras of Gautama : Ed. Ganganath Jha, Pune, 1939.

Outlines of Indian Philosoyhy by M. Hiriyanna : George Allen & Unwin, London, 1932.

Prakaraṇapañcikā of Śālikanatha Mishra : Ed. A Subrahmanya Shastri, B.H.U., Varaṇasi—1961.

Prābhākara School of Pūrvamīmānsā by Ganganath Jha : Motilal Banarsidass, Delhi, 1978.

Pūrvamīmāṁsā in its Sources by Ganganath Jha : Banares Hindu University, Varanasi, 1964.

Rahasya of Mathurānātha (on *TC*): Ed. Kamakhyanath Tarkavāgīśa, Bibliotheca Indica, Reprinted. Delhi, 1974.

Rāmarudriyan (on *Tarkasanprahadīpikā* of Rāmarudrabhaṭṭācharya : Kashi Sanskrit Series—187, Varanasi, 1969.

Śābarabhāṣya of Śabara : Anandashram Sanskrit Granthamala—97, Pune.

Saptapadārthī of Shivaditya Mishra : Theosophical Publishing House, Adyar, Madras, 1932.

Śāstradīpikā of Pārthasārathi Miśra : Chowkhamba Sanskrit Series No. 188, Varanasi.

Ślokavārtika of Kumārila Bhaṭṭa : Ed. S.K. Ramanath Shastri, University of Madras, 1971.

Tantrarahasya of Rāmānuja : Ed. R.S. Shastri, Oriental Institute, Baroda, 1956.

Tantravārtika of Kumārila : Anandashtram Sanskrit Granthamala—97, Pune.

Tarkāmṛta of Jagadīśa : The Asiatic Society of Bengal, Calcutta, 1974.

Tarkasaṅgrahadīpikā of Annambhaṭṭa : Ed. Satkari Sharma Vangiya, Chowkhamba Sanskrit Series No. 187, Varanasi, 1969.

Tattvacintāmaṇi of Gaṅgeśa : Ed. N.S. Ramanuja Tatacharya, Kendriya Sanskrit Vidyapeeth, Tirupati. 1973.

The Essentials of Indian Philosophy of M. Hiriyanna : George Allen & Unwin, London, 1949.

The Theories of Error in Indian Philosophy of Bijayanand Kar, Ajanta Publications, Delhi, 1978.

Vaiśeṣika-Upaskāra of Śaṅkara Miśra : Ed. Haridas Shastri Granthamala, Vaiśesika Vibhāga-3, No. 1, 1923.

Vyutpattivāda of Gadādhara : Chowkhamba Sanskrit Series Office, Varanasi, 1933.

JOURNALS

Arthavādādhikaraṇa of Murāri : *JORM* Vol. II, parts 3-4, 1928, pp. 270-78.

Ekādaśādyādhikanaṇa of Murāri : *ABORI* Vol. X. part 3-4, 1929, pp. 238-43.

Mantrādhikaraṇa of Murāri : *JORM*, Vol. V, part 3, 1931, pp. 1-5.

"*Murārch Tṛtīyaḥ Panthāḥ*" : by Umesh Mishra, Proceedings, fifth Indian Oriental Conference, Vol. II, 1930, pp 167-994.

Smṛtyadhikaraṇa of Murāri : *JORM*, Vol. V, part 3, 1931, pp. 6-8.

Index

T

U

V

W

Y

अनुक्रमणिका